LANGUAGE AND STATECRAFT IN EARLY MODERN VENICE

Although historians typically describe the state as emerging through a wide variety of processes and structures such as armies, bureaucracies, and administrative organizations, this book demonstrates that a crucial but unrecognized component of statebuilding was the management of public speech: controlling foul language. Ideas about language were deeply embedded in Venetian political culture. Instead of studying the history of language through literary, printed texts, Horodowich examines the speech of everyday people on the streets of Renaissance Venice by looking at their actual words as recorded in archival documents. By weaving together a variety of historical sources, including literature, statutes, laws, chronicles, trial testimony, and punitive sentences, Horodowich shows that the Venetian state constructed a normative language – a language based not only on grammatical correctness, but on standards of politeness, civility, and piety – to protect and reinforce its civic identity.

Elizabeth Horodowich is an assistant professor of history at New Mexico State University. She earned her BA from Oberlin College in 1992 and her PhD in European history from the University of Michigan in 2000. Her articles have been published in journals such as *Past and Present*, *Renaissance Studies*, and *The Sixteenth Century Journal* and she is the recipient of grants and fellowships from the National Endowment for the Humanities, the American Philosophical Society, the American Historical Association, and the Gladys Krieble Delmas Foundation. She is currently working on her second book, *A Brief History of Venice*.

Language and Statecraft in Early Modern Venice

Elizabeth Horodowich
New Mexico State University

CAMBRIDGE
UNIVERSITY PRESS

CAMBRIDGE UNIVERSITY PRESS
Cambridge, New York, Melbourne, Madrid, Cape Town, Singapore, São Paulo, Delhi

Cambridge University Press
32 Avenue of the Americas, New York, NY 10013–2473, USA

www.cambridge.org
Information on this title: www.cambridge.org/9780521894968

First published 2008

Printed in the United States of America

A catalog record for this publication is available from the British Library.

Library of Congress Cataloging in Publication Data

Horodowich, Elizabeth, 1970–
Language and statecraft in early modern Venice / Elizabeth Horodowich.
    p.   cm.
Includes bibliographical references and index.
ISBN 978-0-521-89496-8 (hardback)
1. Venice (Italy) – Civilization – 16th century.   2. Language policy – Italy – Venice –
History – 16th century.   3. Italian language – Italy – Venice – Political aspects.   4. Venice
(Italy) – Social life and customs – 16th century.   I. Title.
DG675.6.H59   2008
945′.703–dc22   2008005718

ISBN 978-0-521-89496-8 hardback

Contents

List of Figures

Acknowledgments

In the course of researching and writing this book – which by now has taken up most of my adult life – I have had the great fortune of getting to know many people who have enriched both my work and my life with their intelligence, personalities, and friendship. Meeting the people listed here has been the absolutely best part of writing this book. I offer them my thanks and appreciation for their various contributions to this work.

This book began as a dissertation thesis under Diane Owen Hughes. At the University of Michigan, I am most grateful to Kathleen Canning, Helmut Puff, and Patricia Simons for their unfailing support as mentors and friends. In Venice itself, I have gotten to know the lagoon city, its history, and its archives as a part of a community of scholars whose ideas have helped mold this book. I thank David D'Andrea, Filippo De Vivo, James Grubb, Holly Hurlburt, Frederick Ilchman, Eugene J. Johnson, Cynthia Klestinec, Benjamin Kohl, Steve Ortega, Dennis Romano, James Shaw, and Jonathan Walker for their suggestions, references, and friendship. I owe a huge debt to Linda Carroll, whose truly impressive knowledge of Venetian and skills in translation have saved me many a time. I am also grateful to Laura McGough, who has been by my side since the beginning and read an entire draft of the final manuscript. The staffs of both the *Archivio di Stato di Venezia* and the *Biblioteca Nazionale Marciana* patiently assisted the production of my manuscript over the course of many years, including many frigid Januaries and many sweltering summers. In addition, this book would not have been possible without my good friends in Venice. For well over a decade, Tamara Andruzkiewicz, Melissa Conn, Kate Davies, Maurizio Fabbio, Johanna

Fassl, Paolo Granzotto, JoAnn Titmarsh, and Suzanna Voltarel have all made Venice my second home.

Several individuals have generously shared their time and ideas with me as I worked on this book; I am grateful to Elizabeth Cohen, Tom Cohen, Trevor Dean, Valeria Finucci, John Martin, and Edward Muir for reading and commenting on parts of my manuscript. The support of several institutions also played a crucial role in the production of this book. I would like to thank the American Philosophical Society, the Gladys Krieble Delmas Foundation, the National Endowment for the Humanities, and the New Mexico State University College of Arts and Sciences for grants that enabled much of the book's research and writing. Many of my ideas about speech and gender percolated during a National Endowment for the Humanities Summer Institute "A Literature of Their Own? Women Writing – Venice, London, Paris – 1550–1750," directed by Albert Rabil in the summer of 2001. Conversations with Laura Gowing and Virginia Cox, in particular, helped shape chapters 4 and 5.

Chapter 2 is a revised version of an article first published as "Civic Identity and the Control of Blasphemy in Sixteenth-Century Venice," in *Past and Present* vol. 181 (2003), 3–34. Chapter 4 is also a revised version of the article "The Gossiping Tongue: Oral Networks, Public Life, and Political Culture in Early Modern Venice," first published in *Renaissance Studies* vol. 19 (2005), 22–45. I thank both Oxford University Press and Blackwell Publishing for permission to republish these essays here.

Making the unlikely move from the canals of Venice to the scorched earth of the Chihuahuan Desert, I have found myself among a truly excellent group of colleagues in the history department at New Mexico State University. With their creativity and wit, each and every one of my fellow historians has influenced how I think about the craft of history. I count myself most grateful to have landed among them. In particular, I thank Ken Hammond, Margaret Malamud, and Marsha Weisiger, who have read significant portions of my manuscript, and I offer perhaps my most important thanks to William Eamon, who has long been both my harshest critic and biggest supporter. I am truly lucky to have crossed his path in the Venetian archives many years ago, since that fortuitous meeting dramatically shaped both my life and, in turn, this book. He has been a mentor in the highest sense of the word.

I thank my mother, Peggy, for the inspiration she has offered from the beginning, and my brother Karl for giving me a life full of lessons on the delights of foul language. It was he who first introduced me to this art, of which he is truly the master. I thank Louis – who came into this world while I was researching and writing these chapters – for embodying my hopes for the future. My husband, Steve, I must acknowledge, has not undergone any particular suffering for the production of this book; on the contrary, he has enjoyed many a gourmet meal and many a trip to Italy during its production. Nevertheless, my debt to him, for his unwavering support and encouragement, is immeasurable.

Introduction

Discussions about language are always signs of other political and social changes. In his "Note for an Introduction to the Study of Grammar," Antonio Gramsci remarked:

> Every time that the language question appears, in one mode or another, it signifies that a series of other problems are beginning to impose themselves: the formation and enlargement of the ruling class, the need to stabilize the most intimate and secure links between that ruling group and the popular national masses, that is, to reorganize cultural hegemony.[1]

Gramsci suggested that concerns about the use of language betray deeper political motives and are always reflections of other cultural and social anxieties such as worries about class, gender, and power.

Gramsci penned these words in the early 1930s from his prison cell in Turi, a village outside of Bari, where Italian fascists had incarcerated him for his radical Marxist beliefs. Although Gramsci was not a historian, he was uniquely qualified to consider the relationship between language, politics, and history. He had studied the development of Italian as a national language as a student, and his education directly influenced his most fundamental contributions as a philosopher: his ideas about ideology, hegemony, and power. Gramsci argued that an ideology is not simply a system of beliefs, but is a shared group of ideas that ultimately justifies and benefits the interests of dominant groups. Ideologies work

---

[1] Antonio Gramsci, *Quaderni del carcere*, ed. Valentino Gerratana, vol. 3 (Turin: Einaudi, 1977), 2346. Unless otherwise noted, all translations are the author's.

to legitimize the different types of power that different groups have or do not have. By hegemony, Gramsci meant the social infiltration of an entire system of values and attitudes that effectively supported the status quo in power relations. Hegemony occurs when the general population internalizes the culture and morality of the ruling elite to the degree that such values appear as the natural order of things. According to Gramsci, the growth of a unified, standard Italian language reflected the ideology and hegemony of the ruling classes of Italy. Constructing such a national language, he argued, was ultimately about something else: it directly represented the exercise of political power on the part of Italian elites.

In sixteenth-century Venice, a wide variety of individuals demonstrated an interest in or concerns about the words people spoke in public, ranging from official state magistrates to bread bakers and midwives. Such concerns manifested themselves in treatises, comedies, legal compendia, legislation, trials, proverbs, chronicles, and verbal exchanges on the street. The Venetian republic went so far as to create an official magistracy in 1537 – the *Esecutori Contro la Bestemmia* – for the specific purpose of monitoring and disciplining blasphemy in the lagoon city: an action that no other early modern state went so far as to take. The republic enacted numerous laws against verbal insults in the sixteenth century, hoping to prevent its inhabitants from insulting both each other and visitors to the city, including the Turks. Various state agencies demonstrated specific concerns about the public language of the underclasses and sought to prosecute the unruly tongues of servants in particular. Many expressed the idea that women talked too much, and Venetian writers furthermore paid a disproportionate amount of attention to the language of courtesans. Stepping back and observing this panoply of concerns about public talk raises the question: Why did Venetians pay so much attention to spoken language in the sixteenth century, and following Gramsci's musings, what deeper anxieties did these concerns betray?

Renaissance culture as a whole expressed a profound interest in language. To offer just a few examples, while classical and medieval writers had long weighed the sins and merits of the tongue, the Italian Renaissance witnessed an explosion of interest in this subject, producing a quantity and quality of discussion about social speech that had never been seen before. The Renaissance revival of classical antiquity focused obsessively on rhetoric, and the ideas of Aristotle, Quintillian, and Cicero on oratory became central to the new canon of humanist learning. Based on these authors, Renaissance writers argued that the functioning of society, attributable to the art of language, relied on the power of the tongue to establish a common good. The smooth running of the household and city-state depended largely upon civil conversation, and the Renaissance educational curriculum trained generations of politicians and bureaucrats-to-be in the arts of rhetoric and oratory. Additional interest in language emerged in the debate that preoccupied many of Italy's foremost thinkers during the Cinquecento – the *questione della lingua*. By the sixteenth century, Italian had begun to surpass Latin as the language most frequently used in written expression. This, in turn, prompted heated discussion about the use of the vernacular and the forging of a shared language. What language should Italians speak and how they should speak it? What were the various merits of and differences between spoken and written forms of language? Such were the questions Pietro Bembo and others attempted to answer as they argued about the standard forms for vernacular Italian, similar to the process of developing a standard language that Gramsci later considered in the nineteenth century.[2]

Both the Renaissance focus on rhetoric and debates surrounding the *questione della lingua* suggest that during the Cinquecento, language came to be seen as a social rather than simply intellectual phenomenon. Other developments reflect this shift as well. For instance, conduct books that considered the art of conversation and the most effective ways to speak in public became highly popular in the sixteenth century, instructing Italians and Europeans alike on the practices of eloquence and verbal self-presentation. In addition, Tridentine culture was also deeply concerned about language and verbal propriety as a part of its program for spiritual reform, encouraging a new Christian modesty that included directives about measured and controlled speech for churchmen and laypeople alike. The second session of the council in 1546, for instance, decreed that whether it be during the performance of sacred services or at the dinner table, there should be no "idle conversation."[3] Alongside the Council of Trent, the Holy Office in sixteenth-century Europe worked

---

[2] See Bruno Migliorini, *Storia della lingua italiana* (Florence: Sansoni, 1961), 321–42, and Maurizio Vitale, *La questione della lingua* (Palermo: Palumbo, 1978).

[3] Rev. H.J. Schroeder, *Canons and Decrees of the Council of Trent* (London: B. Herder, 1941), 13–14, 105–6, 142, 152.

to stamp out heretical blasphemy and aimed to delineate clearly the boundaries between acceptable and heretical statements, both printed and spoken. Early modern Italy proved to be so fascinated with and concerned about the tongue that printmakers such as Cesare Vecellio and Nicoletto da Modena went so far as to depict this unruly organ in their prints and engravings. The Italian Renaissance interest in language can be explained at least in part, we shall see, as a result of Italians' sense of disenfranchisement in an age of foreign invasions and humiliation. As the Hapsburgs in particular placed much of Italy under their control in the course of the sixteenth century, Italian discussions about language were in part a manifestation of their sense of humiliation. Italian elites hoped to shore up their status by proving the nobility of their behavior and language in particular.

Some of this general background explains how and why Venetians paid so much attention to public speech. The *questione della lingua*, for instance, was deeply embedded in Venetian culture. The Venetian press was the largest in sixteenth-century Europe, publishing between 15,000 to 17,500 editions in the sixteenth century alone, which represented half or more of all the books printed in Cinquecento, Italy. Based on these figures, the literary scholar Carlo Dionisotti has argued that in this period, "Italian literature developed on a generally northern and specifically Venetian basis."[4] Many of these Venetian publications considered the specific questions of grammar, dialect, rhetoric, and pronunciation, and Venetian authors contributed significantly to this discussion; Giovan Francesco Fortunio, Iacomo Gabriele, Giulio Camillo, and Giangiorgio Trissino – among the first and most influential writers on Italian grammar – all lived and worked in Venice and the Veneto.[5] Furthermore, two texts fundamental to the history of Italian were first published in sixteenth-century Venice: the Aldine publication of the work of Petrarch in 1501, edited by Pietro Bembo; and the 1525 Aldine publication of Bembo's

---

[4] Carlo Dionisotti, *Geografia e storia della letteratura italiana* (Turin: Einaudi, 1967), 170–71. See also Paul Grendler, *The Roman Inquisition and the Venetian Press, 1540–1605* (Princeton: Princeton University Press, 1977), xvii, 6, and Migliorini, *Storia della lingua italiana*, 295.

[5] Migliorini, *Storia della lingua italiana*, 328–32. On the Venetian contribution to the *questione della lingua*, see the articles by Mazzacurati, Aquilecchia, Floriani, and Cortelazzo in *Storia della cultura veneta: Dal primo quattrocento al Concilio di Trento*, vol. 3:2, ed. Girolamo Arnaldi and Manlio Pastore Stocchi (Vicenza: Neri Pozzi, 1980).

own *Prose della volgar lingua,* which became the standard manual for sixteenth-century vernacular forms. Language – both its production as well as debates about its spoken and written use – was clearly at the center of Venetian concerns and commercial life. These linguistic concerns in literary and print culture did not necessarily reflect the same anxieties that arose about oral language and public speech; nevertheless, the world of the Venetian presses turned up the volume of these debates and drew the attentions of the city to debates about language. In addition, Venetian and Italian debates about the *questione* illuminate connections between language and political control. As Antonio Gramsci explained, the *questione* "was a reaction by intellectuals against the breakup of the political unity that had existed in Italy under the name of the 'equilibrium of Italian states'... and represents the attempt, that we can say was largely successful, to preserve and strengthen a harmonious intellectual class."[6]

A fuller explanation of Venetian concerns about spoken language, however, demands a more careful exploration of political, cultural, and social life in lagoon city itself. Ultimately, Venetian concerns about speech in the sixteenth century were direct expressions of Venetian statecraft. Directives about public talk reflected the desire to articulate more clearly what the social, economic, and political boundaries of the state were and to patrol and strengthen those boundaries against the incursions of outsiders. That is to say, a crucial but largely unrecognized component of statebuilding, in Venice and perhaps in other states as well, was the management of public speech: controlling unruly verbal outbursts and teaching citizens the rules of proper verbal comportment.

Charles Tilly has defined states, the world's most powerful form of association for thousands of years, as "coercion-wielding organizations that are distinct from households and kinship groups and exercise clear priority in some respects over all other organizations within substantial territories."[7] Such a definition remains controversial in the way that it is limiting; states are both bigger and smaller, more and less, than this. There exist national states that are centralized and autonomous, but also supra-national states such as empires and city-states that are more

---

[6] Gramsci, *Quaderni del carcere,* 2350.
[7] Charles Tilly, *Coercion, Capital and European States, AD 990–1990* (Cambridge, MA: Basil Blackwell, 1990), 1.

expansive and diverse. There are nation-states whose inhabitants claim to share strong linguistic, religious, and symbolic ties, or modern welfare states that work to re-distribute and equalize income in the hopes of bettering their societies. Some of the issues that have tended to dominate the study of states have, for instance, tried to explain the variety of states that have developed, or by contrast, their general convergence into the nation-state model in the West. They have developed and then destroyed assumptions that all developing states follow one main path towards a nation-state.[8] The interest of this study, by contrast, is more modest, or rather, more focused; it by no means proposes to give any kind of complete account of statebuilding or enter into these larger debates that surround it. It aims instead to focus on one of the building blocks or mechanisms by which states form and function: language.

Historians have typically described state formation as the cause and result of a number of standard institutional activities such as organizing taxation and military conscription more efficiently, developing a more elaborate bureaucracy and unified judiciary system, wielding greater control over both civic policing and the food supply, and perhaps most importantly, waging war. Amidst these factors reflecting and encouraging the development of the state, several studies have pointed to language as an additional ingredient, though few have actually investigated this concept of them with any depth. For instance, Jacob Burckhardt argued that because Italy in the early modern period did not have a king or a divinely appointed ruler, its states constructed their legitimacy by other means, such as through behavior or language. In his discussion of "The State as a Work of Art," Burckhardt claimed that because the foundation of the Italian states remained illegitimate, "the nobility, though by birth a caste, were forced in social intercourse to stand upon their personal qualifications alone."[9] For this reason, "the demeanour of individuals and all

---

[8] In addition to Tilly, *Coercion, Capital and European States,* see Perry Anderson, *Lineages of the Absolutist State* (London: N.L.B., 1974); Thomas Ertman, *The Birth of the Leviathan: Building States and Regimes in Medieval and Early Modern Europe* (Cambridge: Cambridge University Press, 1997); William H. McNeill, *The Pursuit of Power: Technology, Armed Force, and Society Since A.D. 1000* (Chicago: The University of Chicago Press, 1982); Max Weber, *Economy and Society* (Berkeley: University of California Press, 1978).

[9] Jacob Burckhardt, *The Civilization of the Renaissance in Italy,* vol. 1 (New York: Harper and Row, 1958), 70. See also Richard A. Goldthwaite, *Wealth and the Demand for Art in Italy, 1000–1600* (Baltimore and London: The Johns Hopkins University Press, 1993), 202.

the higher forms of social intercourse became ends pursued with a delib-
erate and artistic purpose" (2:361). As a result, language in Italy became
"the basis of social intercourse" and "an object of respect" because "people of every origin . . . spent their time in conversation and the polished
interchange of jest and earnest" (2:371–76). In addition, scholars have
demonstrated how the linguistic academies that first appeared in Northern Italy in the mid-sixteenth century, such as the *Accademia Fiorentina*
or *Accademia della Crusca*, were both a cause and effect of the formation
of early modern states.[10] Pierre Bourdieu also posited that an "official
language is bound up with the state, both in its genesis and in its social
uses. It is in the process of state formation that the conditions are created
for the constitution of a unified linguistic market, dominated by the official language."[11] As one further example, James Scott has argued that of
the many tools that governments use to make a state "legible" – the use
of standard weights and measures, population registers, the construction
of a standard legal discourse, or the organization of transportation – the
construction of a shared, normative language "may be the most powerful, and it is the precondition of many other simplifications" that allow a
state to monitor its population and facilitate interventions for taxation,
conscription, public health, and political surveillance more effectively.[12]
All these ideas suggest, as Gramsci posited, that political domination is
reproduced and reinforced by linguistic domination.

The ideas of Bourdieu, Scott, or Gramsci may at first appear problematic when applied to the early modern period, but this is not irreparably
the case. Their arguments primarily concern the form of language –
grammar, spelling, punctuation, and vocabulary – more than its content. However, this study will demonstrate that a normative language,
especially as it was conceived of by early modern thinkers, is also content based, comprised of ideas about manners and propriety as much as
grammar or pronunciation. Considering the construction of a normative

---

[10] See Eric Cochrane, "The Renaissance Academies in their Italian and European Setting," in
The Fairest Flower: The Emergence of Linguistic National Consciousness in Renaissance Europe
(Florence: Presso l'accademia [della Crusca], 1985), 23.

[11] Pierre Bourdieu, *Language and Symbolic Power*, ed. John B. Thompson (Cambridge, MA:
Harvard University Press, 1991), 45.

[12] James C. Scott, *Seeing Like a State: How Certain Schemes to Improve the Human Condition
Have Failed* (New Haven and London: Yale Unviersity Press, 1998), 1–8, 72–3.

language more broadly in this way, such theories have much to say about Renaissance Venice. It remains difficult to prove any clear or specific connections between the disciplining of language and, for instance, the improvement of taxation or conscription in early modern Venice, as Scott would argue there should be. However, the Venetian republic on several occasions passed laws to discourage unruly language from disrupting trade, and the promotion of a language of civility worked to reduce a chaotic, disorderly society to something more closely resembling administrative order. Enforcing linguistic civility was crucial to the maintenance of civic peace and the prevention of rebellions – significant in that one of the most unique aspects of Venice's history was its notable lack of organized, civic violence. If Venice was peaceful and therefore a good place to do business, perhaps this had something to do with its maintenance of verbal order.

How do Italy and Venice fit into traditional narratives about the development of European states? Many of the factors leading to stronger states – the growth of bureaucracies and military conscription, for instance – began to occur simultaneously in many European states in the early modern world, which is why many historians point to the period between the fifteenth and seventeenth centuries as crucial in European state formation. Specifically, in this period, absolutism emerged to become the first international state system in the modern world.[13] During this time, the centralized monarchies of France, England, and Spain ruptured the pyramid style sovereignty of medieval social formation by centralizing and militarizing their power. Italy, by contrast, did not develop an absolutist state and was characterized more by localized urban and courtly cultures, as Burckhardt first pointed out.[14] Historians have traditionally tended to concur that Italian states developed some, but not most or all, of the institutions necessary to the absolutist state. For instance, Florence developed an institutionalized bureaucracy but not a standing army. Venetians managed to dominate their own hinterland and

---

[13] Anderson, *Lineages of the Absolutist State*, 11, 48; Tilly, *Coercion, Capital, and European States*, 81.

[14] Burckhardt, *The Civilization of the Renaissance*, vol. 2, 334–37. On state development in Italy, see Giorgio Chittolini and Anthony Molho, *Origini dello stato: Processi di formazione statale in Italia fra medioevo e età moderna* (Bologna: Mulino, 1994), and Lauro Martines, *Power and Imagination: City-States in Renaissance Italy* (New York: Alfred A. Knopf, 1979).

occupy an international maritime market, providing the capital necessary for statebuilding, and the early modern city similarly witnessed the creation and growth of numerous bureaucratic institutions to confront the burdens and responsibilities of the growing state.[15] However, Venice never adopted absolutist politics; until Napoleon invaded the city in 1797, the Venetian state represented a peculiar mix of republicanism and aristocracy in its politics. It was a republic in name, in that political decisions were made by voting in its Great Council, but the Great Council and other governing bodies such as the senate were all controlled by a hereditary caste of some 2,500 nobles whose membership had been officially closed in 1297.[16] Historians such as Anthony Molho have often insisted on seeing Italian city-states, including Venice, as "anti-modernist" or personalistic, built on patron-client tires rather than on a "rational" bureaucracy of impersonal citizens.[17]

Furthermore, the Venetian state ultimately failed to become a fully "modernized" state because of its relatively small size. Capitalism stagnated in Venice and Italy in general became overwhelmed by more enterprising Atlantic societies. Venice and other Italian states could not compete with the armies or commercial capital accumulated by their larger European neighbors. According to this narrative, Venice and Italy at large

---

[15] Gaetano Cozzi, *Religione, moralità e giustizia a Venezia: Vicende della magistratura degli esecutori contro la bestemmia* (Padua: Cooperativa Libraria Editrice degli Studenti dell'Università di Padova, 1967–68), 1. Cozzi has similarly argued that the growth of the authority of the Venetian Council of Ten eclipsed the forces of more egalitarian law of the *Avogaria di Comun* in the course of the fifteenth and sixteenth centuries, reflecting the enhanced powers of a centralizing state. See Gaetano Cozzi, "Authority and Law in Renaissance Venice," in *Renaissance Venice*, ed. J.R. Hale (London: Kaber and Kaber, 1973), 293–345.

[16] On the Venetian constitution and government, see Gasparo Contarini, *De magistratibus et republica venetorum libri qinque* (Venice, 1551), 19–22, 63–65, and Andrea da Mosto, *L'Archivio di stato di Venezia: Indice generale, storico, descrittivo ed analitico*, vol. 1 (Rome, 1937–40), especially 21–38.

[17] See Anthony Molho, "Cosimo de Medici: *Pater Patriae or Padrino?*" *Stanford Italian Review* 1 (1979): 5–33, and "Patronage and the State in Early Modern Italy," in *Klientelsysteme im Europa der fruhen Neuzeit*, ed. Antoni Maczak (Munich: Verlag, 1988), 91–115. See also Gene Brucker, "Civic Traditions in Premodern Italy," *Journal of Interdisciplinary History* 29 (1999): 357–77, and Philip Gavitt, "Charity and State Building in Cinquecento Florence: Vincenzo Borghini as Administrator of the Ospedale degli Innocenti," *Journal of Modern History* 69 (1997): 230–70. These are all Florentine examples that argue, for example, that Florence's charitable institutions and bureaucracy did not beocme "modernized" or "rationalized" but rather enmeshed in patron-client relations. Venice had a similar system of patron-client relations that, as the argument goes, made the state more personalistic and the bureaucracy less "rationalized" than other states.

failed to become England, and therefore became backwards and deca-
dent. Such questions about modernization and the state have tended
to die down, in part because historians have come to view them as too
teleological and in part because more recent generations of historians do
not find Italy in the early modern and modern world to be at all deca-
dent. Nonetheless, this is the traditional portrait that historians have long
painted of both Italy as a whole and the Venetian state more specifically.

Although this is useful background, these narratives have limited
meaning, especially for this study. As Karl Appuhn has pointed out,
such accounts "equate a particular set of institutions with efficiency,
modernity, and power, thus excluding the possibility that other state
and institutional organizations might also be effective and modern."[18]
A close look at the relationship between speech and the state in Venice
affirms Appuhn's point, because it demonstrates that language – a force
not usually considered as contributing to state efficiency or power –
played an important role in Venetian statecraft. What I argue, however,
is essentially outside of the debates and narratives through which historians have traditionally described the state. How modern or anti-modern
the Venetian state was, how like or unlike other states, is not in question
here. Regardless of whether Venice successfully emulated the models of
state formation offered by other absolutist states or resisted such mod-
ernizing processes in favor of its own anti-modern model, what I aim
to demonstrate is that the construction of a normative language was a
tool of statecraft – until now largely overlooked – that enabled the Venetian state to directly affect the behavior of its citizens. Pulling together
a variety of government initiatives about language in Venice – usually
treated as disparate but here treated as a consistent program – advances
our understanding of the practices of Renaissance statecraft.

Language may play more of a role in the formation of some states than
others: perhaps more in republics than absolute monarchies, or maybe
the reverse. It may have played a greater role in the national states of the
nineteenth century that Gramsci studied than in the pre-modern forms
of states that preceded them. Although this study will draw comparisons

---

[18] Karl Appuhn, "Inventing Nature: Forests, Forestry, and State Power in Renaissance Venice,"
The Journal of Modern History 72 (2000): 863. See also Julius Kirshner, ed., *The Origins of the
State in Italy, 1300–1600* (Chicago: The University of Chicago Press, 1995).

between Venice and other cities and states from time to time and consider its commonalities with other parts of Italy and Europe when possible, it represents a case study and I attend primarily to the particularities of Venice. My analysis is not fundamentally comparative, and only further research will be able to illuminate the relative roles of language in different states. My goal here is to explore the link between language and the state and examine the place of language in political culture in one specific setting to allow us to better understand how the construction of states impinged on and affected people's daily lives. How did states tie everyday people and their sense of identity, including women, to a political center? How did they use rules about foul language and obscenity to do so? How were concerns about public speech connected to foreigners, immigration, and conceptions of "the other"? How did ideas about language and political culture cross-fertilize and influence one another? By considering a wide variety of sources that discuss both normative and deviant language, we can see how the disciplining of language functions as a means of defining a community, especially in a time of profound social change.

We shall see that many early modern rulers and states punished unruly language in the early modern period, but Venice appeared to do this more than other states. Was Venice unusual in creating so many institutions, magistracies, and laws to patrol speech? Though only additional research can prove or disprove whether Venice was exceptional in its prosecution of unruly language, I will argue that it was, in part, because of its penetrable urban space. Venice was, and is, a uniquely architecturally porous city. Elisabeth Crouzet-Pavan has described Venice as "a city without walls, without the ceremonial closure of doors, that could not sufficiently control the outside world."[19] Unlike its enclosed, mainland counterparts protected by castles, walls, and ramparts, Venice was an open city – an exposed island that anyone could enter from infinite points. Although the lagoon functioned as a type of wall and often protected the city militarily from the incursions of foreigners – a plaque in Venice's Naval History Museum describes the lagoon as "defended as by

---

[19] Elisabeth Crouzet-Pavan, "Potere politico e spazio sociale: Il controllo della notte a Venezia nei secoli XIII–XV," in *La notte: Ordine, sicurezza e disciplinamento in età moderna*, ed. Mario Sbriccoli (Florence: Ponte alle Grazie, 1991), 48, and *Venice Triumphant: The Horizons of a Myth* (Baltimore and London: The Johns Hopkins University Press, 2002), 10–11.

a wall of water" – it nevertheless left the city open to the movements of people.[20] It experienced a continual influx of people from around Europe and the Mediterranean and was home to large, permanent communities of foreigners. As a commercial hub and departure point for travel to and from the East, historians have long described Venice as the most cosmopolitan urban center in the early modern world.

The permeable nature of Venetian space uniquely permitted high levels of immigration, and the city experienced particularly dramatic demographic change during the sixteenth century. Thousands of immigrants poured into the city at this time, including a wave of immigration after Venice's devastating military defeat at Agnadello in 1509. Refugees, unassimilated and unfamiliar with Venetian mores, crowded the city and brought with them crime and civic unrest. Famine repeatedly struck the city and its surrounding mainland territories in this period, driving the poor and hungry into the urban center in search of sustenance. In addition, as Venice changed from a commercial to a manufacturing center in the course of the sixteenth century, it came to rely on an immigrant, itinerant, and often indigent labor force. The growing shipbuilding and textile industries brought more people and social problems to the city, including gambling and prostitution. This expanding foreign population resulting in part from such porous urban boundaries therefore demanded a type of social control different from other mainland cities. As a cosmopolitan, merchant city, the problems of controlling immigrants and foreigners presented themselves as more complex and pressing. At precisely this time, we shall see, public speech became a civic obsession. Through the lenses of a variety of archival and documentary sources, I argue that state magistracies used directives about language to define and enforce both Venetian identity and political culture.

Language is an active force used by individuals and groups to control others or to defend themselves against being controlled, to change society, or to prevent others from changing it. By creating a shared, normative language – that is, a language that is composed not only of rules of dialect, vocabulary, and grammar, but of conceptions of politeness, control, and

---

[20] This sixteenth-century decree by the *Savi Alle Acque* in the Venetian Museo Storico Navale states, "venetorum urbs divina disponente providentia in aquis fondata, aquarum ambitu circumsepta, aquis pro muro munitur."

religious values – Venice clearly represented what sociolinguists call a speech community: a community in which speakers share the linguistic constraints and options that govern social situations.[21] While based on this concept, my study considers the idea of the speech community and its shared/debated language beyond the more focused topics of grammar or Venetian dialect.[22] In the case of Venice, we shall see that ideas about public talk loomed large in Venetian political culture. The state used language broadly conceived – both the form and the content of speech – as a means of assimilating outsiders to Venetian ways, of protecting the economic and political interests of the state, and essentially of defining what it meant to be "Venetian."

Any study of the tongue naturally has something to contribute to the history of the body. Historians have argued that the sixteenth century witnessed the "'piecing out' of the body . . . be it by punitive dismemberment, pictorial isolation, poetic emblazoning, mythic *spargamos*, satirical biting, scientific categorizing, or medical anatomizing."[23] Among these disembodied organs and members, the tongue consistently emerged as a site of tremendous fascination, repulsion, possibility, and anxiety in a multiplicity of discourses in early modern Italy, especially in the world of medicine. There were extensive early modern debates about the physical origins of speech, most of which were rooted in antique thought on the workings of the body. Galen had located the source of speech in the head and brain. Aristotelian thought had instead asserted that the first principle of the voice was the heart, the heart being the efficient, and the voice the material cause of speech. Plato had similarly theorized in his *Timaeus* that certain small veins extended from the tongue to the heart, carrying pleasure and pain to that organ. Although medieval doctors

---

[21] On speech community, see *Directions in Sociolinguistics: The Ethnography of Communication*, ed. J.J. Gumperz and Dell Hymes (New York: Holt, Rinehart, and Winston, 1972), vi, 16. For the principal tenets of sociolinguistics, see Peter Burke, "Introduction," in *The Social History of Language*, ed. Peter Burke and Roy Porter (New York: Cambridge University Press, 1987), 1–20; Gumperz and Hymes, *Directions in Sociolinguistics*, 1–71; Dell H. Hymes, *Language in Culture and Society* (New York: Harper and Row, 1964); Suzanne Romaine, *Language in Society: An Introduction to Sociolinguistics* (Oxford: Oxford University Press, 1994).

[22] On the development and history of Venetian dialect, see Ronnie Ferguson, *A Linguistic History of Venice* (Florence: Leo S. Olschki, 2007).

[23] David Hillman and Carla Mazzio, "Introduction: Individual Parts," in *The Body in Parts: Fantasies of Corporeality in Early Modern Europe*, ed. David Hillman and Carla Mazzio (New York and London: Routledge, 1997), xi.

and philosophers tended to understand speech philosophically, as the product of the soul's action, Renaissance doctors began to return to the ideas of Galen, Aristotle, and Plato and view speech in more human and corporeal ways.[24] Well-known Venetian physicians such as Alessandro Benedetti and Niccolò Massa, as well as medical men like Gabriele Falloppia, Realdo Colombo, Juan Valverde, and Andreas Vesalius, all marveled at the complexity and strength of the muscles of the tongue and sought to explain the physical origins of speech.[25]

Scholarship on the history of the body has consistently described the early modern period in Europe as a time of increasing discipline and control over the body, following on the heels of the more fluid, porous body of the Middle Ages. Mikhail Bakhtin, for instance, charted the appearance of the early modern closed, classicizing body in which bodily regions were rearranged into a new hierarchy. The backside and the lower body became taboo, orifices had to be kept closed, yawning and any glimpse into the inside of the body was discouraged, and whatever protruded had to be drawn in or laced up.[26] The historian Barbara Duden has discussed "the strategic importance of the body and the symbolic value of its integrity ... when the power of the state was being established" in early modern Europe.[27] Duden cites a new consciousness of the body and regulation of corporeality that she locates in corporal punishment, new scientific dissection and medical insights, and new rituals surrounding a clean body. Last but not least, Michel Foucault also described an early modern movement from bodily "frankness" and "display" to physical and sexual confinement and concealment. Foucault

---

[24] Ynez Violé O'Neill, *Speech and Speech Disorders in Western Thought Before 1600* (Westport, CT: Greenwood Press, 1980), 37, 59.

[25] Alessandro Benedetti, *Historia corporis humani*, in L.R. Lind, *Studies in Pre-Vesalian Anatomy – Biography, Translations, Documents* (Philadelphia: The American Philosophical Society, 1975), 110–111; Niccolò Massa, *Liber introductorius anatomiae*, in Lind, *Studies in Pre-Vesalian Anatomy*, 225; Gabriele Falloppia, *Observationes*, vol. 2 (Modena: S.T.E.M. Mucchi, 1964), 171–175; Realdo Colombo, *De re anatomica* (Venice, 1569), 125–131; Giovan Valverde, *La anatomia del corpo unamo* (Venice, 1586), 40–44, 80–82; Andreas Vesalius, *On The Fabric of the Human Body – A Translation of De Humani Corporis Fabrica Libri Septem, Book II*, ed. and trans. William Frank Richardson and John Burd Carman (San Francisco: Norman Publishing, 1998), 196.

[26] Mikhail Bakhtin, *Rabelais and His World* (Cambridge: MIT Press, 1968).

[27] Barbara Duden, *The Woman Beneath the Skin: A Doctor's Patients in Eighteenth-Century Germany* (Cambridge: Harvard University Press, 1991), 10.

claimed that this process specifically impacted language and the tongue. "At the beginning of the seventeenth century," he claimed,

> words were said without undue reticence, and things were done without too much concealment.... But twilight soon fell upon this bright day, followed by the monotonous nights of the Victorian bourgeoisie. Sexuality was carefully confined.... [P]roper demeanor avoided contact with other bodies, and verbal decency sanitized one's speech.[28]

Along similar lines, the sociologist Norbert Elias famously argued in *The Civilizing Process* (1939) that "the thresholds of embarrassment and shame" were raised in the sixteenth century, resulting in new conceptions of manners, social differentiation, honor, and civility.[29] The body was increasingly subject to censure and containment in the early modern world, and actions such as spitting, sweating, gesturing, farting, and in particular, eating with one's hands became defined as shameful, resulting in a new inner discipline of the body. According to Elias, writers across early modern Europe in the time between the decline of the medieval social hierarchy and the stabilizing of the modern one focused intensively on manners and ritual behavior. Although this new bodily control first developed in courtly settings, it filtered down to the rest of society in the early modern period, especially as the state became more prominent in people's lives. Elias directly related the internal pacification of the body to state formation. He argued that as the state established an increasing monopoly over civic violence, this encouraged a greater restraint of the body. Such controls ultimately facilitated trade and economic growth, which in turn underwrote the economic and military authority of the centralizing state. For this reason, states systematically rewarded more restrained behavior.[30] Elias' argument ties the control over the body and

---

[28] Michel Foucault, *The History of Sexuality: Volume One, An Introduction* (New York: Vintage Books, 1990), 1.

[29] Norbert Elias, *The Civilizing Process: Volume 2, A History of Manners* (New York: Urizon Books, 1978), 70. For a description of a similar process in America, see also J. F. Kasson, *Rudeness and Civility: Manners in Nineteenth-Century Urban America* (New York: Hill and Wang, 1990).

[30] For critiques of Elias' argument, see Kevin Stagg, "The Body," in *Writing Early Modern History*, ed. Garthine Walker (London: Hodder Arnold, 2005), 208. See also Stephen Quilley and Steven Loyal, "Towards a 'Central Theory': The Scope and Relevance of the Sociology of Nobert Elias," in *The Sociology of Norbert Elias*, ed. Steven Loyal and Stephen Quilley (Cambridge: Cambridge University Press, 2004), 1–24.

its impulses to the rise of the early modern state and informs this study by raising the specific question of if and how the civilizing process existed or played itself out in urban settings like Venice.

Bakhtin, Foucault, Elias, and others have constructed a dynamic, compelling model of the body in the early modern period. Grounding these generalizing descriptions of the increased "discipline" of the body in specific historical evidence, however, raises another series of pressing questions: to what degree did this really happen? Did early modern individuals actually feel the need to control their bodies, and more specifically their tongues, in a new way? Were unruly tongues more systematically punished in the early modern world? If the early modern body was newly disciplined, exactly why and how did this occur? By now, many scholars have "rescued the body from the margins of critical attention;" however, this scholarship has remained primarily literary and art historical.[31] What do voices from the archives have to tell us about the discipline of the tongue and the body? Some of these questions are easier to answer than others, because ultimately, embodiment is not always so easy for early modern historians to explore. Many early modern sources such as literature, laws, and even trials to a great extent privilege the represented body rather than bodily experiences. Because bodies participate in all aspects of human activity, early modern studies of the history of the body often risk abstraction and generalization unless they either specifically address representation or are grounded in sources that allow for an exploration of physical experience.[32] For these reasons, this study does not focus on the history of the body per se; instead, it investigates connections between language, the state, and political culture, acknowledging that the body is of course always implicit in this relationship.

Grounded in these ideas, theories, and questions, this exploration of the verbal order of sixteenth-century Venice will reveal the links between

---

[31] Nina Taunton and Darryll Grantley, "Introduction," in *The Body in Late Medieval and Early Modern Culture*, ed. Darryll Grantley and Nina Taunton (Aldershot: Ashgate, 2000), 1. On literary and art historical studies of the body, see Florike Egmond and Robert Zwijnenberg, eds., *Bodily Extremities: Preoccupations with the Human Body in Early Modern European Culture* (Aldershot: Ashgate, 2003); E. Fudge, R. Gilbert, and S. Wiseman, eds., *At The Borders of the Human . . . Beasts, Bodies, and National Philosophy in the Early Modern Period* (London: Macmillan, 1999); L. Gent and N. Llewellyn, eds., *Renaissance Bodies: The Human Figure in English Culture, c. 1540–1660* (London: Reaktion Books, 1990).

[32] Stagg, "The Body," 206–7.

language and statecraft. I begin in chapter 1 by describing how literary texts in Italy at large developed an ideology of correct, mannered speech. I examine how writers such as Baldesar Castiglione, Giovanni Della Casa, and Stefano Guazzo described the art of conversation. In doing so, I hope to reveal some of the broadest parameters governing public speech, as well as how the discourse of verbal self-fashioning worked to inform Venetian ideas about talk. How can we explain the sheer quantity of writing dedicated to the topic of social speech in sixteenth-century Italy? Why did influential writers talk so much about talking, and why did their texts betray such anxiety about both class and gender? Here, I aim to remove this literature from the often hermeneutically sealed off world of literary studies to demonstrate instead how these textual discussions impacted ideas about language in urban society. I analyze the "language question" less as a debate among humanist elites and more as a social debate about speech and political control.

I then turn from the sphere of etiquette in literature to the sphere of law and its transgression by looking at the way that spoken language actually worked on the streets of the mobile city. Here, I shift the traditional focus of the study of language in courts – a topic that has been paramount because of the publication of Elias' works on courts and manners – to concentrate instead on urban speech. In chapters 2 and 3, I demonstrate the concrete links between language and statecraft by considering cases where the state disciplined forms of talk in the city. In chapter 2, I investigate the crime of blasphemy, using the archival records of the *Esecutori Contro la Bestemmia* to demonstrate how concerns about blasphemy reflected Venetian anxiety about both immigration and class. Similarly, in chapter 3, I consider how the prosecution of insults in the court of the *Avogaria di Comun* and other magistracies worked to clean up Venetian civic identity and protect the economic interests of the state by punishing those who insulted nobles, superiors, and the state itself.

In chapters 4 and 5, I broaden the scope of my argument to examine the role of speech in Venetian political culture at large. Here, I show the ways in which speech practices were woven into the workings of Venetian politics and political life. In this final section of the book, I go beyond showing how the state tried to control speech to examine Venetian attitudes and beliefs about the political nature of talk, including the ways they believed speech could both endanger and empower the state itself. In chapter 4, I turn to the practice of gossip. I consider trials from the *Sant'Uffizio* – the office of the Inquisition in Venice – to explore why it was that both individual Venetians and the state itself distrusted and discouraged gossip while simultaneously seeking to tap into the knowledge located in these verbal networks. Gossip was ambiguous, both destructive and constructive, and Venetians knew as much. They feared its powers, especially because they were commonly associated with women, but also sought to harness its knowledge in the service of state stability. Chapter 5 looks at the speech of courtesans. Renaissance writers paid more attention to the speech of courtesans than to the speech of any other single group or profession. By examining discussions about courtesans' language in the sixteenth-century lagoon in a variety of sources, we can see how, as with gossip, their language was both feared and admired. Venetians on the one hand were anxious that courtesans' sexualized speech could symbolically undermine the foundations of the state itself, while on the other hand, they also promoted and sought out their conversation as a type of diplomatic link between Venice and the rest of absolutist Europe.

Although each chapter will link discussion about forms of speech to the state and Venetian political culture, this is never meant to give the illusion that the Venetian state acted as a single will: a myth shattered some time ago by historians who demonstrated the variety of rifts that existed among Venetian elites, often resulting in their violent and disruptive behavior.[33] The Venetian state was far from harmonious, as members of this oligarchy struggled for preeminence within the city without ever ceding collective control to one person or family. Successive struggles over power produced a shifting hierarchy of councils and people who filled them from the doge to his advisors to the general assembly to all of the city's inhabitants, raising the question of what exactly the Venetian "state" was. Perhaps the best way to define the state in Venice is to say that it represented the interests of a variety of noble individuals at any one given time, understanding that these men often did not achieve consensus. Such a definition remains elusive in the way that it is constantly shifting, but it

---

[33] See Robert Finlay, *Politics in Renaissance Venice* (New Brunswick, NJ: Rutgers University Press, 1980); Donald Queller, *The Venetian Patriciate: Reality versus Myth* (Urbana and Chicago: University of Illinois Press, 1986).

is more accurate, productive, and useful than any definition of the state as a homogenous, monolithic, or stable political entity.

Some scholarship has already demonstrated how language functions as a cultural phenomenon worth studying in and of itself because it serves as an indicator of relationships in different historical settings. That is to say, while common sense might suggest that talking is simply a fundamentally human act – more or less the same in any given time or place – speech instead is culturally situated, much like other historical categories. Beginning in 1981, Peter Burke claimed that despite its importance, the social history of speech had been neglected. "What we need," he argued, "is a map of the whole linguistic terrain at different periods, both to situation our documents and to interpret change over time."[34] Many studies have responded to Burke's call by examining the meanings, uses, and political/social contexts of language and foul language in particular; the ways in which language reflects class and gender; language as resistance, sometimes in the form of "deep play"; the political usefulness of gossip and oral networks; and the fundamental relationship between language and power.[35] Although all of these studies have contributed to an understanding of particular aspects of and attitudes toward social speech, this book will go beyond them in several respects. Previous scholarship has often circled around the notion of speech, suggesting its importance and possibilities. Guido Ruggiero, for instance, suggested that "in [many] areas the sixteenth century in Italy saw a heightened emphasis on the

---

[34] Peter Burke, "Languages and Anti-languages in Early Modern Italy," *History Workshop* 11 (1981): 24.

[35] To cite a few key examples, see Sandy Bardsley, *Venomous Tongues: Speech and Gender in Late Medieval England* (Philadelphia: University of Pennsylvania Press, 2006); Peter Burke, *The Art of Conversation* (Cambridge: Polity Press, 1993); Peter Burke and Roy Porter, eds., *The Social History of Language*; Carla Casagrande, *I peccati della lingua: Disciplina ed etica della parola nella cultura medievale* (Rome: Istituto della Enciclopedia Italiana, 1987); Maureen Flynn, "Blasphemy and the Play of Anger in Sixteenth-Century Spain," *Past and Present* 149 (1995): 29–56; Laura Gowing, *Domestic Dangers: Women, Words, and Sex in Early Modern London* (Oxford: Clarendon Press, 1996); Jane Kamensky, *Governing the Tongue: The Politics of Speech in Early New England* (New York: Oxford University Press, 1997); Nancy Ries, *Russian Talk: Culture and Conversation During Perestroika* (Ithaca and London: Cornell University Press, 1997); David Sabean, *Power in the Blood: Popular Culture and Village Discourse in Early Modern Germany* (Cambridge: Cambridge University Press, 1984), 37–112; S.A. Smith, "The Social Meanings of Swearing: Workers and Bad Language in Late Imperial and Early Soviet Russia," *Past and Present* 160 (1998): 167–202; Chris Wickham, "Gossip and Resistance Among the Medieval Peasantry," *Past and Present* 160 (1998): 3–24.

significance of words."[36] I attempt to add complexity and nuance to his discussion by systematically considering the day-to-day workings of the spoken word on the streets of early modern Venice on both the macro- and microcosmic levels. I present a more textured picture of early modern orality, digging deep into one specific urban and republican context, juxtaposing a great variety of historical sources to show the centrality of spoken language and its control to the functioning of this state. Although many studies have considered language in the abstract – through literary sources or legislation against violent language – I compare prescriptive and legal texts and legislation with trial material to connect discourses about speech to the actual spoken words (or as close as we can come to them) of sixteenth-century Venetians.[37] Trials from the Holy Office and the State Lawyers reveal the foul language that Venetians hurled at one another and the state, allowing for a window onto actual verbal exchanges and battles. Venetian orations, sermons, or ambassadorial reports are therefore not considered here because they tend to reflect a more formulaic rather than spontaneous use of spoken language. In addition, what I discuss here are not the more dramatic crimes of speech such as treason that have tended to receive more scholarly attention. Instead, I focus on the words of everyday life and popular culture: the blasphemies, insults, curses, and gossip that Venetians flung at one another – and that the state often tried to control – as a part of their daily existence.

Venetian writers, state magistrates, and individuals at large expressed both a deep interest in disciplining the tongue and a profound anxiety about its powers. As Gramsci suggested they should be, Venetian efforts to control unruly speech were motivated by myriad concerns – increased immigration, economic losses, fear of divine punishment, republican respectability, aristocratic literary culture, Counter-Reformation modesty, the inertia of prior regulation, and the fear of the unleashed sexual power of speech, especially in women. In all of these discourses, the

---

[36] Guido Ruggiero, *Binding Passions: Tales of Magic, Marriage, and Power at the End of the Renaissance* (Oxford: Oxford University Press, 1993), 103.

[37] For studies that examine speech in history primarily through literary texts, see for instance, *Speaking the Medieval World*, ed. Jean E. Godsall-Myers (Leiden and Boston: Brill, 2003); G. Hughes, *Swearing: A Social History of Profanity, Oaths, and Foul Language in English* (Oxford: Blackwell, 1991); Lauro Martines, *Strong Words: Writing and Social Strain in the Italian Renaissance* (Baltimore and London: The Johns Hopkins University Press, 2001); A. Montague, *The Anatomy of Swearing* (Philadelphia: University of Pennsylvania Press, 1991).

tongue had the symbolic power to undermine the infrastructure of the state itself, prompting battles about its use. As Burckhardt tells us, we shall see that honor in Venice was measured by blood and by actions, but was also demonstrated in words. Spoken language revealed and measured nobility, evaluated neighbors, demarcated the good people from the bad and insiders from outsiders, and when well disciplined, served to protect and empower the state at large. In a highly verbal culture, Venetians expressed and reinforced both fear of and faith in the word at all levels of society. When we look closely at the practices of talk and listen carefully to the words Venetians uttered, they reveal a wealth of surprising beliefs, concerns, and anxieties that informed this culture.

1

Defining the Art of Conversation

No one time, place, or people introduced the world to the art of conversation, yet certain times and places appeared to celebrate eloquence more than others. The ancient Greeks, for instance, famously fostered an intellectual culture of dialogue, and the *symposium* was a key Hellenic social institution where men came together to drink, debate, and converse. Thousands of years later, members of the salons of eighteenth-century Paris debated ideas about citizenship, liberty, and natural rights, and the theatrical display of verbal wit was one of the main pastimes of both salon and courtly culture in pre-revolutionary France. Peter Burke has suggested, nevertheless, that a focus on conversation as an end in itself first began in Renaissance Italy.[1] Indeed, it is impossible to consider Renaissance culture without acknowledging the emphasis it placed on rhetoric and language. Ideas about speech and talking were central to conceptions of civil society across early modern Italy as a whole, so much so that Renaissance writers and political theorists such as Valla, Bruni, Macchiavelli, and Guicciardini famously stressed the importance of the active life: that is, of a life spent engaged in one's community as opposed to secluded behind a monastery's walls. Whereas medieval monastic culture had emphasized the dangers of garrulousness and verbosity, the early modern spirituality of the friars and Jesuits was decidedly verbal.[2] As part

---

[1] Burke, *The Art of Conversation*, 89.
[2] Lester K. Little, *Religious Poverty and the Profit Economy in Medieval Europe* (Ithaca: Cornell University Press, 1978), 198–99. See also Burke, "Notes for a Social History of Silence," in *The Art of Conversation*, 127; Daniel Lesnick, *Preaching in Medieval Florence* (Ithaca: Cornell University Press, 1978), 198–99. By contrast, Walter Ong has emphasized the extremely verbal nature of medieval manuscript culture, arguing that books were assimilated through oral

and parcel of the Renaissance revival of the ideas of classical antiquity, writers often pointed to Aristotle's beliefs that man was fundamentally a social creature and that it was the power of speech that differentiated man from beasts.[3] Renaissance people maintained that language had the capacity to bind individuals to a society and that spoken language was perhaps the most important component of this civilizing process. The formation and continuation of society depended largely on the tongue.

This belief that speech both reflected and created civility is made clear in what was one of the most popular literary genres of sixteenth-century Italy: conduct literature. Writers of books about manners and comportment offered their audiences advice on a wide range of social graces such as cleanliness, dress, dance, table manners, and in general, the presentation of the self in public and at court. They taught that how one dressed, ate, learned, and above all how one spoke formed one's public persona. Renaissance books of etiquette instructed Italians and Europeans alike on how to pick one's clothes, blow one's nose, and use cutlery at the table. They had much to say about social speech, and in some cases discussed the art of conversation more than any other topic. Examining what several of the most popular of these texts had to say about talk – Baldesar Castiglione's *Il libro del cortegiano* (1528), Giovanni Della Casa's *Galateo* (1558), and Stefano Guazzo's *La civil conversazione* (1574) – offers an introduction to sixteenth-century ideas about conversation. These three texts insistently focused their discursive energy on the topic of public speech, and in doing so, betrayed a variety of concerns about spoken language. They elaborated on a wide variety of issues relating to proper and improper talk, indicating that behavior was often judged as much by how one spoke as by how one acted.

---

utterance. See Walter Ong, "Orality, Literacy, and Medieval Textualization," in *New Literary History* 26 (1984): 1.

[3] "Speech is designed to indicate the advantageous and the harmful, and therefore also the right and the wrong...and it is partnership in these things that makes a household and a city-state," Aristotle, *The Politics*, trans. H. Rackham (London: Heinemann, 1932), 11. For early modern discussions of this idea, see Giovanni Bonifaccio, *L'arte de'cenni con la quale formandosi favella visibile, si tratta della muta eloquenza, che non e altro che un facondo silenzio* (Vicenza, 1616), 172; Giovambattista Giraldi Cinthio, *Discorsi* (Venice, 1554), 28; Stefano Guazzo, *La civil conversazione*, ed. Amedeo Quondam, vol. 1 (Modena: Panini, 1993), 17, 27, 82; Giovanni Pontano, *De sermone*, ed. Alessandra Mantovani (Rome: Carocci, 2002), 75; Francesco Sansovino, *L'edificio del corpo humano* (Venice, 1550), 12r-v.

These texts represented a peculiar and somewhat paradoxical genre. Though these writers may have aimed to present their prescriptions for the art of conversation with confidence and conviction, their discussions are rife with contradictions, indicating wider debates about social life and the control of the body. For instance, these writers were especially concerned and conflicted about the complex relationship between language and social class. These texts were one of the means by which Italian elites sought to legitimize their ranks; by defining and defending noble culture, they established the tenets of proper behavior in order to separate the civil from the un-civil. At the same time, however, these texts taught how one could become noble and suggested that ultimately, the definition of nobility came down to behavior and thus to one's speech. They argued that noble culture was separate and distinct from the world of commoners while paradoxically offering models of how to cross over this boundary. In addition, these texts expressed profound concerns and confusion about the ways that men and women should speak. They were at pains to argue that masculine and feminine speech were naturally different, yet regularly suggested that men speak in ways that were supposedly only appropriate to women.

These texts were by no means homogeneous; it would be wrong to think that comportment literature was evolving a single theory of talking. However, despite their varied or conflicting natures, Renaissance books of manners all gave primacy to the power of the spoken word – its capacity to persuade, its ability to impress, its effectiveness in intellectual arguments, and its potentially dangerous power to destroy reputations. A close look at their ideas about speech provides a useful background against which to study talk in Venice more specifically. They show us some of the ideas, anxieties, and desires that informed contemporary culture and its heightened attention to public talk. By exploring questions of class, gender, and speech in these texts, we can examine some of the fundamental ways that ideas about language both empowered and troubled this culture.

For a variety of reasons, an examination of Renaissance conduct literature may at first appear irrelevant in a study that purports to examine the relationship between language and statebuilding – and often language and popular culture – in the specific city of Venice. Venetians were not the most renowned authors of these texts, nor did they write the three to be examined here. In general, the contents of these texts offer limited insights in that they only reflect the ideas of noble men, primarily in the world of the courts. Moreover, as texts, they represent printed language rather than actual speech. Though these works were all conceived of in the dialogue format so popular in the early modern world, we cannot theorize that they in any way reflected real talk. These authors were not reporting but fabricating. However, some insight into this literature is central to understanding public speech and its control in Venice. These texts were wildly popular, offering incontestable evidence that they held much meaning for early modern society and reflected its *mentalité* and social structures at large. We shall see that these texts focused on how to talk, and while Venetian writers had much to say about questions of language and grammar, none of them considered speech per se with as much attention as these writers. Writers of conduct books wrote about the ways they saw people talking as well as the ways that they thought people should talk, so that while their narratives were invented, they were based on commonly held social expectations. Although unfortunately we cannot know for sure who read these texts, we can be certain that in a culture as literary as that of sixteenth-century Venice, many Venetians were familiar with this literature, in part because these texts were all at one time published there.

In addition, early modern Italy was perhaps the ideal example of what Walter Ong called a "residually oral" culture: a culture at once literate and speech centered. Many historians by now have argued for the interplay and cross-fertilization of oral and literary culture in the early modern world.[4] Such studies have traditionally emphasized how oral culture, such as popular songs or village gossip, influenced literature and print. In fact, in the first known collection of Venetian proverbs gathered after 1509 and first printed in 1535, no less than 35 proverbs instruct in the arts and dangers of speech, demonstrating how literary

---

[4] Walter J. Ong, *Presence of the Word: Some Prolegomena for Cultural and Religious History* (New Haven: Yale University Press, 1967), 12–13. On the cross-fertilization of oral and written culture, see Burke, *The Art of Conversation*, 118–20; J. Barry, "Literacy and Literature in *Popular Culture*," in *Popular Culture in England, 1500–1850*, ed. Tim Harris (New York: MacMillan, 1995), 69–94; Elizabeth S. Cohen and Thomas V. Cohen, "Camilla the Go-between: The Politics of Gender in a Roman Household (1559)," *Continuity and Change* 4 (1989): 53–77; *The Spoken Word: Oral Culture in Britain 1500–1800*, ed. Adam Fox and Daniel Woolf (Manchester and New York: Manchester University Press, 2002); Natalie Zemon Davis, "Printing and the People," in *Society and Culture in Early Modern France* (Stanford: Stanford University Press, 1975), 189–226.

culture drew on the spoken word for ideas about language.[5] However, if we are to take this body of scholarship seriously, we must also imagine that texts influenced oral culture as well. Though direct causality would be very difficult to prove, we shall see that the ways that individuals understood speech and its control in early modern Venice echoed many of the concerns expressed in conduct literature. As John Martin has argued, there is much persuasive evidence that "self-fashioning was an aspect of the lives of townspeople as well as those of courtiers."[6] Meaning, the verbal presentation of the self was of interest not only to aristocrats and courtiers but also to workers, artisans, and the ordinary men and women that populated early modern cities. Lastly, while literary scholars have studied comportment literature for generations with a focus on issues such as social performance, the world of the courts, or the relationship between art and life, these texts have not been considered with an eye to what they say about conversation and speech per se. If this literature has much to say about speech, and if Venetians were aware of such ideas to the degree that they even marginally seeped into their oral culture, the tenets presented in these texts form a useful springboard from which to begin exploring the practices of speech in the lagoon city. These texts, especially *Il libro del cortegiano*, became like second bibles for European gentlemen, and an appreciation of their ideas is necessary for an overall understanding of the relationship between power and language for a variety of social groups.

Texts about manners were by no means a new genre in the Renaissance. There existed many similarities between medieval monastic and courtly literature and Renaissance books of conduct.[7] Throughout the Middle Ages, Italian writers produced comportment books, often listing rules for proper speech, such as Rodolfo Ardente's *The Customs of the Tongue*

---

[5] *Le dieci tavole dei proverbi*, ed. Manlio Cortelazzo (Vicenza: Neri Pozza, 1995). See also Giovanni Antonio Cibotto, Proverbi del veneto (Florence: Giunti, 1995), ix.

[6] John Martin, "Inventing Sincerity, Refashioning Prudence: The Discovery of the Individual in Renaissance Europe," *The American Historical Review* 102 (1997): 1326. See also *La città e la corte: Buone e cattive maniere tra medioevo ed età moderna*, ed. Daniela Romagnoli and Elena Brambilla (Milan: Guerini, 1991), which also treats cities rather than courts as the site of the civilizing process.

[7] See Stephen Kolsky, "Making and Breaking the Rules: Castiglione's *Cortegiano*," *Renaissance Studies* 11 (1997): 358–380; Jonathan Nicholls, *The Matter of Courtesy: Medieval Courtesy Books and the Gawain Poet* (Woodbridge, Suffolk: D. S. Brewer, 1985), 1–74.

(1190), Albertano of Brescia's *The Arts of Speaking and Being Quiet* (1245), and Guglielmo Peraldo's *The Sins of the Tongue* (1250).[8] Though not aiming to teach manners per se, it is also interesting to note that medieval and early modern painters developed a range of techniques by which to visualize speech. For instance, they depicted a scroll emanating from a speaker's mouth, or inscribed a dialogue between Gabriel and the Virgin Mary on the surface of painted panels depicting the Annunciation.[9]

As we have seen, the theories of Elias and Burckhardt attempt to offer some explanation as to how and why early modern people became increasingly interested in establishing new standards of behavior that were different from or more nuanced than those of the Middle Ages. Namely, they argue that manners and comportment represented both a modicum of discipline and control for the state as well as a means of social and political legitimation. This was particularly true in Italy between 1494 and 1530 when Italy was humiliated by foreign invasions and virtually continuous warfare. Many of the great battles of these Italian wars such as that of Agnadello (1509), Marignano (1515), Pavia (1525), and the Sack of Rome (1527) demonstrated that foreigners were now in control of the peninsula. Such battles cruelly exposed the bankruptcy of the Italian upper classes. By 1540, Spain ruled Naples, Sicily, Milan, and Sardinia, as well as Tuscany and Genoa as dependent states, so that only Venice maintained its independence from foreign rule. In this historical and political context, more so than ever before, Italians longed for ways to render their culture's legitimacy. Although it is objectively difficult to measure a regime's "anxiety," especially in any quantitative way, many scholars have argued that a connection existed between the foreign invasions of Italy and these Italian concerns about culture.[10]

---

[8] See Bettina Lindorfer, "*Peccatum Linguae* and the Punishment of Speech Violations in the Middle Ages and Early Modern Times," in Godsall-Myers, *Speaking the Medieval World*, 26–7. See also Paolo da Certaldo, *Libro di buoni costumi*, ed. Alfredo Schiaffini (ca. 1320; Florence: Felice le Monnier, 1945), 64; Brunetto Latini, *L'ethica d'Aristotile* (ca. 1265; Lyon, 1568), 121–55; Bonvesin de la Riva, *Le cinquanta cortesie da tavola*, ed. Mario Cantella and Donatella Magrassi (ca. 1290; Milan: La Spiga, 1985), 30.

[9] See Louisa C. Matthew, "The Painter's Presence: Signatures in Venetian Renaissance Pictures," *Art Bulletin* 53 (1998): 617.

[10] "The Italian cultural elite felt an urgent need to remind the world of its existence precisely because it was the national elite of a nation which did not exist," Claudio Donati, *L'idea di nobiltà in Italia, secoli XIV–XVIII* (Rome: Laterza, 1988), 29. See also Virginia Cox, *The*

Conduct books became popular precisely at this time because they responded to this need to prove the worth of Italian civilization. They aimed to remedy Italians' pervasive sense of illegitimacy by providing unambiguous representations of nobility and civility. In the chaos of war and foreign invasion, books on behavior offered advice and models for order to help structure both the lives of individuals and societies. The quantity of this evidence is surely affected by the advent of printing; the sheer bulk of records that became available after the mid-fifteenth century may make this cultural interest in behavior appear greater than it was. Nevertheless, in a world where myriad topics were popular in print, comportment literature ranked extremely high in terms of contemporary popularity.[11] Furthermore, if Gramsci speculated that concerns about language were always fundamentally rooted in other anxieties, sixteenth-century thought on the art of conversation in conduct literature was a clear reflection of Italian worries about cultural crisis resulting from the Italian wars. It was no incidental coincidence that Giovanni Pontano began his book on the art of talk, *De sermone* (1509), by describing on the very first page the devastation recently wrought on Italian soil by French and Spanish troops.[12]

Against this background, many writers of Italian Renaissance books of manners considered the problem of how best to employ and govern the tongue. For instance, in his canonical 1435 treatise on the family, Leon Battista Alberti warned:

There is no worse poison, nothing as unhealthy as the words of a wicked tongue. No madness compares with the madness driving the spiteful talker.... One should avoid acquaintance or intimacy with evil speakers like the plague. These talkers and scoundrels come between a family and its friends and acquaintances.[13]

Renaissance Dialogue: Literary Dialogue in its Social and Political Contexts, Castiglione to Galileo (Cambridge and New York: Cambridge University Press, 1992), 25.

[11] See Rudolph M. Bell, *How to Do It: Guides to Good Living for Renaissance Italians* (Chicago and London: The University of Chicago Press, 1999), 1–16, 282–83. Bell discusses only comportment literature directed at sexuality, marriage, and family life, but his figures offer a good indication of the popularity of this literature as a whole.

[12] Pontano, *De sermone*, 71.

[13] Leon Batista Alberti, *The Family in Renaissance Florence*, trans. Renee Neu Watkins (Columbia, South Carolina: The University of South Carolina Press, 1969), 203.

Compiling epithets and rules for behavior in his 1565 *L'ore di ricreazione*, Lodovico Guicciardini praised silence on 13 counts and in 12 separate instances warned against the dangers of speaking when angry, when it is easy to say something regrettable. "In spoken language," he believed, "you can see the shape of the soul in the same way that you see the shape of the body reflected in a mirror. Socrates alluded to this idea when he received a friend's son to be evaluated, to whom Socrates said, 'Speak, so that I might know you.'"[14] If words indeed directly reflected or mirrored one's internal character, he argued, then speech needed to be considered carefully. In his 1573 book of advice for rearing children, the Tuscan Francesco Britti similarly recommended solemnity, silence, and the restraint of the mouth, especially at the table.

> Talking too much is a vice (in every setting) and one should always be silent.... Entertaining the table with moderation, with the body and head straight, neither raising the voice too much nor interrupting your companion (which has no place in any setting) nor speaking with a full mouth are courteous and praiseworthy acts.[15]

Writers continued to worry about the dangers a loose tongue could pose well into the seventeenth century. In his 1616 book on gestures, Giovanni Bonifaccio argued that having a mouth was a mixed blessing. The tongue, the best and worst member of the human body, the littlest but most powerful organ, both benefited and cursed its users. As nature typically helped us to cover our deficiencies, man was given the lips to conceal the "deformity" of the mouth. In fact, Bonifaccio mused whether humans might perhaps be better off without the tongue, communicating instead more safely through benign gestures – the subject of his text. In this way, "all the confusion resulting from speech and excessive talkativeness would be eliminated."[16]

---

[14] Lodovico Guicciardini, *L'ore di ricreazione*, ed. Anne-Marie van Passen (Rome: Bulzoni, 1990), 203.

[15] "Ch'il ragionar troppo e vitioso (come in ogni luoco) il tacer sempre.... Ch'il trattener la tavola con moderato ragionamento, co'l corpo, et capo dritto, ne levando pero troppo la voce, ne interrompendo il compagno (il che in nessun luoco ha luoco) ne parlando con la bocca piena, e atto cortegiano, et lodevole," Francesco Britti, *Ammaestramento de figliuoli* (Venice, 1573), 43.

[16] "Ouero come ella s'e compiacciuta di crear alcune genti la nell'ultima parte dell'Oriente senza lingua, a quali, come dice Plinio, pro sermone nutus, motusque membrorum est; cosi havesse fatto a tutti gli altri: perche a questo modo sarebbe del mondo levata ogni soverchia

These and numerous other Italian Renaissance manuals for behavior asserted the importance of verbal control.[17] Yet Baldesar Castiglione's *Il libro del cortegiano* offered a much more sweeping discussion of social graces and the art of conversation than had ever been published before. Castiglione (1478–1529) needs little introduction. He spent his life and career between the courts of Milan, Mantua, Rome, Madrid, and Urbino. As a courtier and scholar, he wrote on a great variety of topics, including poetry, humanistic scholarship, clothing, painting, courtly spectacle, and above all, questions of nobility and social interaction. Written between 1508 and 1516 and first published with the Aldine Press in Venice in 1528, *Il cortegiano* was an instant success. It underwent 62 reprintings in sixteenth- and seventeenth-century Italy, at least 48 of which were printed in Venice. By 1620, more than 50 editions had appeared in languages other than Italian, and European presses produced over 150 editions total by the eighteenth century, making it a Renaissance bestseller on par with Ariosto's *Orlando Furioso*.[18] The success of *Il cortegiano* was not so much due to its original content but to its innovative form.[19] Rather than simply

---

garrulità, e confusione de parlari, e gli huomini per esprimer i loro affetti, di questa nostra muta eloquenza giudiciosamente si servirebbono," Bonifaccio, *L'arte de cenni*, 227–29. See also 167, 172.

[17] See also Mario Equicola, *Novo corteggiano de vita cauta et morale* (c. 1530); Pelegro de' Grimaldi, *Discorsi ne'quali si ragiona di quanto far debbono i gentilhuomini ne'servigi de'lor signori per acquistarsi la gratia loro* (1543); Girolamo Muzio, *Il cavaliero* (1569) and *Il gentiluomo* (1571); Giovambattista Nenna, *Il nennio* (1542); Alessandro Piccolomini, *Istituzione morale di tutta la vita dell'uomo nato nobile* (1542); Annibale Romei, *Discorsi* (1585); Sperone Speroni, *I dialogi* (1542); Torquato Tasso, *Il forno* (1580), and *Il malpiglio overo de la corte* (1584).

[18] Peter Burke, "The Courtier Abroad: Or, the Uses of Italy," in *Die Renaissance im Blick der Nationen Europas*, ed. Georg Kauffman (Wiesbaden: Otto Harrassowitz, 1991), 1–14; Peter Burke, *The Fortunes of the Courtier* (Cambridge: Polity Press, 1995), 41. The literature on *Il cortegiano* is vast; see, for instance, Stephen Kolsky, *Courts and Courtiers in Renaissance Northern Italy* (Aldershot: Ashgate, 2003); John Larner, "Europe of the Courts," in *The Journal of Modern History* 55 (1983), 674–76; *La corte e il "Cortegiano,"* vol. 1: *La scena del testo*, ed. C. Ossola, and vol. 2: *Un modello europeo*, ed. A Prosperi (Rome: Bulzoni, 1980); *Castiglione: The Ideal and the Real in Renaissance Culture*, ed. David Rosand and Robert Hanning (New Haven: Yale University Press, 1983). For a summary of literary scholarship on *Il libro del cortegiano* as well as the *Galateo* and *La civil conversazione*, see *L'arte della conversazione nelle corti del Rinascimento*, ed. Floriana Calitti (Rome: Istituto Poligrafico, 2003), 1–182.

[19] The intellectual heritage of *Il cortegiano* is vast and complex. Castiglione borrowed much from Plato, Aristotle, Xenophon, and Cicero, as well as many of his own late medieval contemporaries, in particular Boccaccio, Leonardo Bruni, and Francesco da Barbaro, from whom he adopted his ideas about grace and restraint. On the sources for the *Il cortegiano*,

listing rules for behavior, *Il cortegiano* presented its teachings through conversations and speeches. It offered a comprehensive, narrative presentation of comportment, demonstrating *in situ* models for manners, etiquette, and conversation that included a wide variety of individuals and social situations. In addition, while other Latin texts such as Giovanni Pontano's *De sermone* had already paid much attention to talk and conversation, Castiglione's vernacular dialogue made his ideas accessible to many more readers. His text therefore offers a useful starting point for an examination of ideas about speech in Renaissance Italy.

Although wars ravaged the Italian peninsula in the early sixteenth century, or perhaps precisely because they did so, Castiglione turned his back on practical politics to examine the delicate complexities of courtly etiquette. In *Il cortegiano*, he furnished readers with a complete, polished portrait of manners and behavior by inventing a series of conversations that took place on four successive evenings in March of 1506 in the Ducal Palace of Urbino. Castiglione included such figures as Pietro Bembo, Bernardo Bibbiena, Federico Fregoso, Ludovico da Canossa, and Giuliano de'Medici in his dialogue, all of who were given the task "of depicting in words (*con parole*) a perfect courtier, setting forth all the conditions and particular qualities that are required of anyone who deserves this name" (1:12).[20] The text then followed the dialogue of some 32 characters as they pitted their verbal wit against one another in an attempt to define, through various topics, the ideal courtier.

By conceiving of his text as a dialogue, Castiglione emphasized the centrality of speech and verbal exchange to social graces in the basic structure of his text. His choice of the dialogue format was not surprising

---

see L. Valmaggi, "Per le fonti del *Cortegiano*," *Giornale storico della letteratura italiana* 14 (1889): 72–93.

[20] Quotations in Italian are from *Il libro del cortegiano*, ed. Carlo Cordié (Milan and Naples: Riccardo Ricciardi, 1960). English quotations are from the translation by Charles S. Singleton (New York: W.W. Norton, 2002). Material cited is identified by book and by chapter. It is important to note that the word *conversazione* in the sixteenth-century often implied interaction and behavior as much as it meant talking; *conversare* was both to associate and to converse, or to socialize through conversation. Language is action, and represents the means by which speakers interact and act upon each other. However, the social interaction indicated by this word in these texts almost always involved speech, and this consideration attempts to focus primarily on examples where *conversazione* clearly meant verbal interaction. Speech, conversation, and talk are also commonly indicated by other words such as *parole, parlare, ragionare or favellare*. I have tried to indicate these distinctions where appropriate.

because dialogic exchange was at the foundation of courtly social relations and entertainment; word games and verbal performance were among the most popular courtly pastimes.[21] In addition, the written dialogue was an extremely popular Renaissance genre, employed by writers such as Erasmus, More, Rabelais, Bracciolini, Bembo, Aretino, Tasso, and Galileo.[22] The format of the "documentary" dialogue – one that purports to be a transcription of a real conversation at a specific time and place – called attention to the act of communication itself and was particularly popular among humanists in Cinquecento Italy. Castiglione modeled much of his text after the specific example of Cicero's *De oratore*: a treatise, also composed in the form of a conversation, which argues for the importance of oratory and rhetoric to society and the state.[23] Written dialogues represented and celebrated the arts of conversation and language as practiced in Italian courts. They permitted writers to soften their address by filtering it through the more familiar and responsive medium of speech. Through the dialogue, speakers depicted eloquence through both prescription and example, presenting information while simultaneously representing the process by which that information is communicated. Dialogues instructed readers in the art of conversation through multiple, embedded layers of textuality, and offered models of speech through which members of courtly society could affirm their own social and cultural dignity.

---

[21] Donald Weinstein, "Fighting or Flyting? Verbal Dueling in Mid-Sixteenth-Century Italy," in *Crime, Society and the Law in Renaissance Italy*, ed. Trevor Dean and K.J.P. Lowe (Cambridge: Cambridge University Press, 1994), 204. On verbal competition, see also Burke, *The Art of Conversation*, 92.

[22] There is extensive literature on the Renaissance dialogue. See Peter Burke, "The Renaissance Dialogue," *Renaissance Studies* 4 (1989): 1–12; Cox, *The Renaissance Dialogue*; Raffaele Girardi, *La società del dialogo. Retorica e ideologia nella letteratura conviviale del Cinquecento* (Bari: Adriatica, 1989); *Printed Voices: The Renaissance Culture of Dialogue*, ed. Dorothea Heitsch and Jean-François Vallée (Toronto: The University of Toronto Press, 2004); David Marsh, *The Quattrocento Dialogue: Classical Tradition and Humanist Innovation* (Cambridge, MA: Harvard University Press, 1980); Jon Snyder, *Writing the Scene of Speaking: Theories of Dialogue in the Late Italian Renaissance* (Stanford: Stanford University Press, 1989).

[23] See Cox, *The Renaissance Dialogue*, 9–21; Wayne Rebhorn, *Courtly Performances: Masking and Festivity in Castiglione's Book of the Courtier* (Detroit: Wayne State University Press, 1978), 91–115, 154. As already suggested, though the dialogue format attempts to reflect reality, we can in no way assume that such dialogues represent actual transcriptions or "real" speech. This discussion therefore is not an attempt to analyze the form of the dialogue, but rather the content of these dialogues where they touched on the topic of speech.

The character Count Lodovico Canossa – a courtier at Urbino and a friend of Castiglione's who interpreted Castiglione's opinion throughout the dialogue – first began the dialogue's task of defining the perfect courtier. According to the count, the most important attributes of the ideal courtier were noble birth, skill in the profession of arms, and the possession of *sprezzatura*: Castiglione's famous term for nonchalance, or the art of making any and all actions seem easy. Avoiding any appearance of effort or affectation in all that the he did, the courtier should try always to appear to be graceful, "particularly in his speech (*massimamente nel parlare*)" (1:28). Such eloquence was embodied, for instance, by Cardinal Ippolito d'Este, a friend of Castiglione's who "in conversing with men and women of every station . . . shows a special sweetness and such gracious manners that no one who speaks with him or even sees him can do otherwise than feel an enduring affection for him" (1:14). Setting the tone for the entire text, Castiglione established talking as one of the principal means by which individuals both created social bonds and distinguished themselves socially. He pointed to conversation as among the first aspects of behavior that courtiers should attend to, suggesting the primacy of the act of speaking in the order of all behavior.

Canossa expounded upon the differences between writing and speaking as well as which writers offered the best models for imitation, namely Petrarch and Boccaccio. In this way, Castiglione gave the topic of the *questione della lingua* a prominent place in his text. Canossa's speech was soon interrupted, however, by Gaspare Pallavicino, who asserted:

> Certainly, this discussion about writing is well worth listening to; and yet it would be more to our purpose if you would teach us the manner the Courtier should observe in speaking, for I think he has greater need of that, because he has to use speech more often than writing. (1:31)

Castiglione understood that the spoken word was a powerful tool in social situations. The tongue, in fact, was often more powerful than the pen, especially at court. Canossa responded by outlining several general rules to follow in conversation. One should not blaspheme, speak badly of or around women, or sing to fill a lull in the conversation. Individuals should be silent if they had nothing significant to contribute. The courtier should never be an idle babbler, flatterer, or boaster. If self-praise was in order, courtiers must speak in such a way as "to seem always to avoid praising one's self, yet do so; but not in the manner of those boasters who open their mouths and let their words come out haphazardly" (1:18). Correct, mannered speech was polished, to the point, carefully considered, modest, and restrained.

Beyond these general prefatory remarks and introductory rules about talk, one of the most consistent of Castiglione's laws governing the art of conversation was that speech both revealed and determined social status. Like many sixteenth-century commentators on language and social order, Castiglione's characters repeatedly articulated the notion that people should speak in ways befitting their position.[24] They insisted that upper and lower class languages were naturally distinct and that speech patterns were directly linked to one's place in the social hierarchy. Pointing out the difference between the language of the fashionable, urban elite compared to the more dated and backwards language of country-dwellers, the speaker Bernardo Bibbiena commented that many Tuscan words "are no longer used in Florence [but] have remained with the peasants, and are rejected by the gentry as words that have been corrupted and spoiled by age" (1:31). Elites, who possessed knowledge of classical languages, established the standards for correct vocabulary and eloquence. They alone knew which specific words were fashionable and which were awkward or outdated. "Good usage in speech *(la bona consuetudine adunque del parlare),*" Canossa asserted, "springs from men who have talent (*ingegno*), and who through learning and experience have attained good judgment" (1:35). Bibbiena later related a telling story illustrating the links between speech and class. He described a peasant who was so well attired that "anyone not hearing him speak would have thought him a gallant cavalier." He danced and played music so well that no one knew he was a cowherd from Bergamo. This peasant was such a convincing courtier that when he finally did open his mouth and betray his "native Bergamasque dialect *(suo nativo parlare zaffi bergamasco),*" his audience thought he was merely performing an imitation. His listeners believed him to be acting, saying, "What a wonder to hear! How well he mimics the language!" Finally, the peasant aped a gentleman's speech, revealing to his audience

---

[24] See Adam Fox, *Oral and Literate Culture in England, 1500–1700* (Oxford: Oxford University Press, 2000), 100–11.

that he was, in fact, a peasant (2:85). Upon opening the mouth, class was revealed, and only an actor or magician could convincingly imitate the speech of someone from another class.

Eloquence involved not only an innate, class-based knowledge of vocabulary and pronunciation, but also an exacting physical control of the voice and body. The voice should be "not too thin or soft as a woman's, nor yet so stern and rough as to have a boorish quality, but sonorous, clear, gentle, and well-constituted, with distinct enunciation (*non troppo sottile o molle come di femina, né ancor tanto austere ed orrida che abbia del rustico, ma sonora, chiara, soave e ben composta, con la pronunzia espedita*)." Furthermore, appropriate gestures must always accompany one's speech. Such gestures should consist

> in certain movements of the entire body, not affected or violent, but tempered by a seemly expression of the face and a movement of the eyes such as to give grace and be consonant with the words, together with such gestures as shall signify as well as possible the intention and the feeling of the orator. (1:33)

The courtier knew how to monitor carefully his physical actions when talking, not allowing his voice to become too loud, his arms to flail, or his body to be moved by the emotion of his speech.

Following the precept of *sprezzatura*, speech was meant to be "natural" and unaffected, avoiding any semblance of effort or artificiality. The rules that applied to speaking were similar to those for writing, in that spoken language should gracefully balance both classical and contemporary usage. On the one hand, the speaker Federico Fregoso argued that Tuscan was clearly the most beautiful language and individuals should follow the models of Petrarch and Boccaccio when talking. However, language was also fluid, changing, and variable. People spoke in so many different ways that "there is [not] a noble city in Italy without its own manner of speech different from all the others (*che non abbia diversa maniera di parlar da tutte l'altre*)" (1:30). For this reason, one should not simply imitate ancient writers, medieval models, or contemporary fashion, because slavish imitation was ungraceful. Smooth conversation therefore imitated eloquent writers without employing outdated terminology. It

balanced tradition and innovation, classical models and "natural" contemporary and local expression without becoming artificial or pedantic.[25]
Castiglione described such *sprezzatura* in talk or graceful speech not only
through direct prescription, but also through the metaphors of nature he
used to describe language. When deciding which outdated words to eliminate from one's vocabulary, for example, the courtier should remember
that "just as the seasons of the year divest the earth of her flowers and
fruits, and then clothe her again with others, so time causes those first
words to fall, and usage brings others to life" (1:36).[26]

How could a courtier best learn all these skills? How could he learn to
converse in a way that was at once classicizing yet contemporary, both
planned yet appearing spontaneous and natural? How could individuals
strike a balance in their speech between imitation and innovation, nature
and artifice? Castiglione's interlocutors at once suggested that speakers
should look to the past without being antiquated, speak naturally without
straying from ideal models, control the body and words without seeming
too stiff, and speak easily and effortlessly without appearing uneducated.
Furthermore, following Ciceronean models of decorum, courtiers had
to consider a variety of other factors in both their speech and action,
including "the place where he [speaks], in whose presence, its timeliness,
the reason for doing it, his own age, his profession, the end at which
he aims, and the means by which he can reach it." As if performing a
balancing act, "our Courtier must be cautious in his every action and
see to it that prudence attends whatever he says or does (*ciò che dice o fa
sempre accompagni con prudenzia*)" (2:7). All told, the art of conversation
demanded numerous and often contradictory skills, which in the end,
Castiglione failed to resolve into any coherent scheme or single maxim.
"Good usage in speech," Canossa argued, was recognized "by virtue of a
certain natural judgment and not by any art or rule (*La bona consuetudine
adunque del parlare... nasca... per un certo giudicio naturale, e non per
arte o regula alcuna*)" (1:35).

The courtier simply needed to have good instincts, for "any attempt
reduce this matter [of all behavior, not just speech] to more precise rules
would be too difficult, and perhaps and superfluous" (2:6). Castiglione

[25] See Migliorini, *Storia della lingua italiana*, 314.
[26] See also 1:34–35.

at once laid down numerous rules governing the art of conversation and then refused to promote any rule-bound behavior. His vagueness suggested an exclusive understanding of eloquence that he ultimately refused to share, because elites would simply know what to say when they needed to. Yet Castiglione was unclear as to whether he intended for his text to be a definition of what nobility was or a guidebook to becoming noble. If individuals came from an elite background, they would have no need for such lessons in conversation or social graces, suggesting that those who read his text did so in order to learn noble behavior. However, interlocutors (in particular Canossa) also argued that nobility comes from birth (1:14); it could not be learned. The dialogue format allowed Castiglione to remain vague about how speech, class, and social advancement were related.

Castiglione further complicated his advice about the art of conversation with questions of gender. On the third night of dialogue, Castiglione assigned the characters Giuliano de'Medici and Cesare Gonzaga the task of describing the perfect court lady, and in turn, female speech. These interlocutors believed that the rules established for men's talk generally applied to women as well; like her male counterpart, the lady of the court should be able to decide instinctively on the right kind of conversation for the circumstances at hand. As Giuliano stated, "she will be able to entertain graciously every kind of man with agreeable and comely conversation (*sappia gentilmente intertenere ogni sorte d'omo con ragionamenti grati ed onesti*) suited to the time and place and to the station of the person with whom she speaks" (3:5). Like men, women should also know "how in her talk to choose those things that are suited to the kind of person with whom she is speaking, and be careful lest, unintentionally, she might sometimes utter words that could offend him (*elegger quelle che sono a proposito della condizion di colui con cui parla, e sia cauta in non dir talor non volendo parole che lo offendano*)" (3:6). The court lady should appear neither too withdrawn nor too vivacious in her speech; neither too serious nor too playful. Like the courtier, she should be reserved without appearing unsociable and speak naturally while following classical models for eloquence. Furthermore, she was instructed not to "utter unseemly words or enter into any immodest and unbridled familiarity (*dir parole disoneste, né usar una certa domestichezza intemperata*)," or "to gossip and eagerly listen to evil spoken of other women (*il dire ed ascoltare volentieri chi dice male d'altre donne*):" a vice that Giuliano de'Medici claimed to see women embrace with particular glee (3:5).

Women's speech, however, proved to be more complex than men's. According to Pallavicino – the infamous, misogynist curmudgeon of the dialogue – while men were honest, women tended toward deception. Pallavicino claimed to find himself "blushing with shame far more often at words uttered by women than by men (*sonomi trovato ad arossirmi di vergogna per parole dettemi da donne molto più spesso che da omini*) . . . because more often than not, those who seem to be the best are in fact quite the contrary" (2:69). Women, for instance, frequently lied and claimed that they were madly in love with a man only to enjoy his affections and the thrill of his pursuit. The character Unico Aretino concurred by describing the deception of a certain woman who,

> with an angel's eyes and a serpent's heart, never speaks as she thinks (*mai non accorda la lingua con l'animo*), and with a deceitful, feigned compassion attends to nothing but dissecting hearts. Nor is there in sandy Libya a snake so venomous, so avid of human blood, as this false one; who not only with the sweetness of her voice and her honeyed words (*la qual non solamente con la dolcezza della voce e meliflue parola*), but also with her eyes, her smiles, her looks, and in all her ways, is a veritable Siren. (1:9)

Women's voices, like those of Homer's temptresses, represented feminine duplicity and in turn caused the downfall of others. Women's application of makeup and the other "artificial tricks" they used to increase their beauty further reflected their deceptive nature (1:40). Because their conversation and appearance were "arranged" and not to be trusted, the characters Canossa and Pallavicino criticized women for their dishonesty, dissimulation, and deceptiveness. With these examples, Castiglione negatively coded deception or insincere speech as feminine, while speaking clearly and honestly, by contrast, represented masculine behavior. Deceit was not fitting for a man of honor. "I would have our courtier," stated the character Federico Fregoso, "take care not to acquire the name of liar or boaster (*né di bugiardo né di vano*). . . . Therefore, in all he says (*ne'suoi ragionamenti*), let him be always careful not to exceed the limits of verisimilitude, and not to tell too often those truths that have the appearance of falsehoods (*hanno faccia di menzogna*)" (2:41). Castiglione assertively declared the categories of masculine and feminine speech to be separate and distinct.

Yet, the great paradox of Castiglione's ideas about talk was that courtiers needed to employ femininely coded ways of speaking in order to succeed in the world of the court. On the one hand, he argued that courtiers should never speak in a feminine way (1:19). In fact, by imitating the practices of women, "the Italian name is reduced to opprobrium" (4:4). On the other hand, Canossa stated that the courtier should arrange and shape words "to his purpose like so much wax (*come cera formandole ad arbitrio suo*), [so] he can give them such a disposition and an order such as to cause them to reveal at a glance their dignity and splendor" (1:33). In effect, Castiglione instructed courtiers to employ words just as women used make-up – as an artificial front or disguise for the public. In fact, by advising the courtier to be at once natural and restrained, imitative and innovative, masculine and feminine in his spoken language, Castiglione by definition complicated the courtier's relationship to sincerity.[27]

Perhaps the clearest instructions for the art of conversation that the reader can extract from the text come from the ideas of the diplomat Federico Fregoso, the primary speaker of book two. Fregoso explicitly recommended the primacy of action over words, of not praising oneself unnecessarily, and of practicing "a certain studied dissimulation" (translation mine: *Però il parlar poco, il far assai e'l non laudar se stesso delle opere laudevoli, dissimulandole di bon modo*) in one's conversation (2:7). Although different speakers presented different ideas, the overall thrust of Castiglione's dialogue was that conversation was an art in which the speaker never said anything spontaneously or without careful consideration. Aside from rare moments alone with the prince himself (2:18), the courtier could almost never say what he thought, wanted, or believed because his speech remained circumscribed by a plethora of rules, the

---

[27] On the courtier as a masker or actor who consciously shaped his public self-image, see Martin, "Inventing Sincerity", and Rebhorn, *Courtly Performances*, 23–52. On the theme of "*dissimulazione onesta*" or "honest dissimulation" in the Renaissance, see Rosario Villari, *Elogio della dissimulazione: La lotta political nel Seicento* (Rome: Laterza, 1987), and Perez Zagorin, *Ways of Lying: Dissimulation, Persecution, and Conformity in Early Modern Europe* (Cambridge, MA: Harvard University Press, 1990).

vagaries of his audience, and the circumstances of his surroundings. In effect, the courtier must always perform and deceive; he must by definition speak like a woman.

Many scholars by now have noted how Castiglione had women talk themselves out of his dialogue altogether.[28] Although women's frequent silence in early modern literature is rather to be expected, this feminine silence in *Il cortegiano* is somewhat surprising because courtly women enjoyed different advantages over their female republican counterparts. Courts famously represented sites of feminine spectacle and display. They tended to offer women a position as arbiters in taste and courtly politics – a voice that was traditionally denied to republican women. Life at court, particularly during Castiglione's years at Urbino, was largely shaped by the personality of Elisabetta Gonzaga, and Castiglione himself stated that courts were places where women actively participated in the art of conversation.

> [N]o court, however great, can have adornment or splendor or gaiety in it without ladies, neither can any courtier be graceful or pleasing or brave, or do any gallant deed of chivalry unless he is moved by the society and by the love and charm of ladies: even discussion about the courtier is always imperfect unless ladies take part in it and add their part of that grace by which they make courtiership perfect and adorned. (3:3)[29]

Women in *Il cortegiano*, however, had little of substance to say and were denied this role as courtly conversationalists. Castiglione titled women the directors and centers of the conversation, but then subtly placed all the conversation in the mouths of men. Negatively coded as they may be, the feminine conversational roles that would usually be assigned to women – deception, dissimulation, and insincerity – were instead played by men,

---

[28] On the silenced female voice in *Il cortegiano*, see Valeria Finucci, *The Lady Vanishes: Subjectivity and Representation in Castiglione and Ariosto* (Stanford: Stanford University Press, 1992), 27–73; G.S. Battisti, "La donna, le donne nel Cortegiano," in *La corte e il 'Cortegiano'*, vol. 1, 221; Joan Kelly, "Did Women Have a Renaissance?" in *Women, History and Theory: The Essays of Joan Kelly* (Chicago: The University of Chicago Press, 1984), 30–47.

[29] Stefano Guazzo concurred. "E nel vero se voi considerate la forma delle feste, de'giuochi e de'conviti, voi direte che tutte queste raunanze e questi spettacoli sarebbono freddi e insipidi senza l'intervenimento delle donne," Guazzo, *La civil conversazione*, 166.

pushing women to the margins and silencing them to an existence as mere courtly ornaments.

Castiglione was clearly torn between various and contradictory ideas about speech.[30] At best, Castiglione's courtier was a resilient and flexible figure. He was able to bend and respond to the circumstances at hand, deciding in what proportions to mix the various ingredients of civil conversation to best fit the moment. At worst, conversationalists were more like nervous tightrope artists constantly at risk of falling, or as the poet Calmeta more ominously put it in the dialogue itself, "like caged birds" (translation mine, 2:22).

Some 20 years after the first publication of *Il cortegiano*, Giovanni Della Casa (1503–1556) composed his *Galateo*: a book of manners in many ways derived from *Il cortegiano* and betraying many of the same concerns, ambiguities, and contradictions that Castiglione had a generation before. Both of these texts are unclear or ambivalent about class mobility, and both focus on speech as a principally masculine phenomenon or masculine virtue. However, while Castiglione's text addressed a wide range of topics such as the *questione della lingua* and Neoplatonic philosophy, Della Casa's work followed Erasmus' *De civilitate* (1530) and more singularly and specifically considered manners alone. It was much more practical than theoretical. Unlike Castiglione's dialogue, Della Casa's text represented the advice of an old man (*vecchio idiota*) to a youth (supposedly Della Casa's nephew Annibale Rucellai) in the form of 30 short chapters, each focusing on a different topic about manners. Almost every chapter of Della Casa's touched at least tangentially on speech, and 10 out of his 30 chapters considered the subject specifically. While Castiglione's text was a resolutely literary one, Della Casa's was much more of a guidebook that outlined the fundamentals of good manners by offering practical advice outside of any sort of narrative context.

Born in Mugello near Florence, Della Casa studied law and the fundamentals of a humanist education in Bologna. He eventually decided,

---

[30] On the contradictory nature of the texts of Castiglione, Della Casa, and Guazzo, especially in terms of language, rhetoric, and politics, see Frank Whigham, *Ambition and Privilege: The Social Tropes of Elizabethan Courtesy Theory* (Berkeley: University of California Press, 1984), especially 88–136. Whigham focuses principally on Elizabethan courtesy treatises, but was one of the first to address the many contradictions inherent in this literature. I am grateful to Douglas Biow for this citation.

however, to pursue an ecclesiastical career and between 1530 and 1544 he lived and worked in Rome in the service of Cardinal Farnese. As a cleric in the years of the pontificate of Paul III, Della Casa worked in the climate of the Counter-Reformation and the first session of the Council of Trent (1545–48).[31] Both he and his text were emblematic of the age immediately following that of Castiglione and Bembo – an age that increasingly produced not only courtiers but also bureaucrats and *segretarii*. For this reason, Della Casa did not discuss the perfect courtier – the man who sought the praise and favors of his prince – but rather, the honorable gentleman and respected citizen. Though Della Casa was Tuscan by birth, he was well-connected to Venetian life. He eventually became the papal nunzio to Venice in 1544 and was the person responsible for establishing the office of the Inquisition in there in 1547. As a result, he lived in Venice for several years, enjoying a *palazzo* on the Grand Canal and a villa on Murano. He composed his *Galateo* in the early 1550s in the Badia di Nervesa sul Montello in the March of Treviso; it was first published in Venice by Nicolò Bevilacqua after his death in 1558.[32] Like *Il cortegiano*, the *Galateo* was instantly and hugely successful both in Italy and abroad. It was published no less than 38 times before the end of the sixteenth century, translated into all major European languages by the beginning of the seventeenth century, and published a total of 187 times between 1558 until 1971.[33] This work became so canonical that the word *Galateo* by definition eventually came to mean a normative code of behavior that defined relationships in civil society.[34]

---

[31] Roberto Fedi, "La Fondazione dei modelli: Bembo, Castiglione, Della Casa," in *Storia della letteratura italiana, Vol. 4, Il primo Cinquecento* (Rome: Salerno Editrice, 1996), 563. On the life of Della Casa, see Lanfranco Caretti, *Antichi e moderni: Studi di letteratura italiana* (Turin: Einaudi, 1976), 135–50.

[32] Eisenbichler and Bartlett, "Introduction," in Giovanni Della Casa, *Galateo*, trans. Konrad Eisenbichler and Kenneth R. Bartlett (Toronto: Centre for Reformation and Renaissance Studies, 1986), xi–xiii; Giorgio Patrizi, "*Galateo* di Giovanni Della Casa," in *Letteratura italiana: Le opere, Vol. II, Dal Cinquecento al Settecento* (Turin: Einaudi, 1993), 454; Giuseppe Toffanin, *Storia letteraria d'Italia*, 7th ed. (Milan: Casa Editrice Dr. Francesco Vallardi, 1965), 247–49.

[33] Antonio Santosuosso, *Vita di Giovanni Della Casa* (Rome: Bulzoni, 1979), 140.

[34] The title was inspired by the name of Galeazzo Florimonte, bishop of Sessa, who encouraged Della Casa to compose a manual of manners. See Nuccio Ordine, "Grandi modelli, rovesciamenti dei codici, precettistica del quotidiano," in *Manuale di letteratura italiana: Storia per generi e problemi*, ed. Franco Brioschi and Costanzodi Girolamo (Turin: Bollati Boringhieri, 1994), 520; Toffanin, *Storia letteraria*, 250.

Like Castiglione, Della Casa offered a list of general advice regarding the art of conversation. Speech should avoid a wide variety of gaffes; for instance, one should not fall asleep or get up and pace around the room in the middle of a conversation (6).[35] Good conversationalists knew to stay away from certain topics, such as arcane or blasphemous subject matter, depressing ideas, or boring stories about one's family (11). Speakers should be neither too vain nor too humble, but instead "should rather subtract something from one's merits than add something to them with words" (13). Della Casa advised his readers not to offer too much advice and thereby appear superior to others, nor to insult, mock others or laugh at them if jokes were not made in a friendly context. He gave advice about how best to tell a story (21) or how to pick the best word for any given situation (22). He believed people should always use accessible language and chose polite expressions over any obscene or indecent words (*fuggir di dire le parole meno che oneste*). Because Della Casa's advice about conversation was wide-ranging, he offered numerous concrete examples to clarify his ideas. For instance, one should say "her heart's desire" rather than "paramour," or use the expression "she satisfied him with her person" rather than another more crude expression denoting sexual intercourse. Speech should be clear and simple, avoiding any expressions that potentially had double meanings, such as "to do yourself behind" (translation mine: *farsi indietro*=sodomize) or "figs" (*fiche*=female genitalia) (22).

Amidst this miscellany of precepts and advice, several arguments about conversation emerge. Like Castiglione, Della Casa was conflicted about social mobility. Chapters 14 through 17, for example, addressed the topic of "ceremonies" or various forms of greetings and salutations, including the use of the formal and informal forms of address, *voi* and *tu*. He argued that one must always respect the age and social status of others when addressing them, and it was clearly not fitting "for the lower and middle classes to use those [formalities] that aristocrats affect among themselves." (16) Similarly, puns (*bisticcichi*) were nothing but "cheap, low-class witticisms" (*vili modi e plebei*) to be avoided at all cost

---

[35] Quotations in Italian are from *Galateo*, ed. Giuseppe Prezzolini (Milan: Rizzoli, 1985). English quotations are from the translation by Eisenbichler and Bartlett. Material cited is identified by chapter number.

(20). Like Castiglione, Della Casa posited that nobles were born with an innate sense of eloquence, enabling them to speak both more frequently and on a broader range of topics than the lower classes. For instance, because nobles possessed a better knowledge of style, they could occasionally speak on topics that were otherwise sure to be uninteresting, such as one's nighttime dreams; many such topics were not suitable for "unlearned men and for the common folk" to undertake in their conversation because they would make them boring to hear (12). Yet at the same time, he stated to his readers that he wanted them "to become accustomed not to the base speech of the dregs of the populace like the washer-woman and the street-hawker (*favellar sì bassamente come la feccia del popolo minuto, e come la lavandaia e la trecca*), but to that of gentlemen instead." In doing so, he claimed, "people will eagerly and pleasantly listen to you when you speak and you will maintain the degree and dignity proper to a well brought up and well-mannered gentleman" (23). Speech again paradoxically appeared both to determine one's place in the social hierarchy and allow one to change it.

For Della Casa, eloquence entailed an even more precise and strict discipline of the body and voice than it did for Castiglione. The voice "should be neither hoarse nor shrill (*La voce non vuole essere né roca né aspera*). One should not shriek, nor squeak like a pulley-wheel because of laughter or some other reason" (23). Moreover, a good conversationalist always maintained control over physical movements, avoiding trembling, shaking, stretching, contorting the face, leaning the head down, making the eyes bulge, twisting the mouth, spraying spittle onto themselves or others, or moving the hands and body "as if they want to shoo away flies" (30). Della Casa's narrator regularly emphasized the importance of not performing physically disgusting acts in the presence of others; for instance, one should not touch the genitals, undress, or blow his nose and then look into the contents of the handkerchief. Amongst these egregious acts, many involved the orifice of the mouth. Gentlemen should be as quiet and inconspicuous as possible when coughing or sneezing, and should yawn as little as possible and refrain from speaking or making noise when doing so. When involved in a conversation, one "should not get so close to the man that he breathes on his face, for you will find that many men do not like to smell someone else's breath" (5). When not speaking, the mouth should always remain closed, and one should not show the tongue (*non istà bene . . . mostrar la lingua*) (30).

Della Casa described conversation pragmatically like a social contract or a commercial exchange in that speakers invested in a conversation and received something in return: a concept that will prove informative in the Venetian context. Conversation demanded responsibilities such as reciprocity, attentiveness, and responsivity on the part of all its participants. Its goal was not the enjoyment of the speaker but the production of enjoyment for others and the group as a whole. When talking, the speaker must always observe the response of listeners to judge how his words were received. In turn, listeners must pay attention and at least appear interested. A good conversationalist knew how to be fundamentally agreeable; he did not say things like "that's not what happened" or "on the contrary, it was as I say" but instead allowed everyone to express themselves equally and "abide[d] by the opinion of the majority" (18). Della Casa stressed that not unlike in a commercial transaction, both speakers and listeners, like buyers and sellers, needed to make a deal and strike a balance between talking and listening. "Just as speaking too much is a nuisance, so keeping too silent is irritating, for to keep quiet where others are engaged in conversation seems to show an unwillingness to pay one's share of the bill (*pare un non voler metter su la sua parte dello scotto*)" (24).[36]

Della Casa remained vague about whether this "agreement" on which conversation was based was reserved only for the upper classes or if anyone who dedicated himself to the art of conversation could enter in. It was clear, in any case, that women were excluded from this contract. Women remained conspicuously absent from Della Casa's text, and this absence was central to Della Casa's construction of conversation as a civil/c act permitted only to men as free individuals. He clearly specified at the outset of his text that skill in conversation was necessary "to whomever decides to live in cities and among men, rather than in desert wastes or hermit's cells" (1). Della Casa, like many other authors of books of manners, believed that speech was the glue of civil society. It represented not just a medical, philosophical, or cultural issue, but also a political one. Women were not only unable to control their physical

---

[36] On equality in early modern conversation, see Burke, *The Art of Conversation*, 100.

bodies and tongues, but they also were not politically recognized as free or rational individuals. Denied access to the realm of politics, women were unable to form contracts (aside from the contract of marriage), including the contract of civil conversation.[37] Della Casa only mentioned women at all in a handful of passages, and he did not explicitly state that women were not permitted to participate in conversation. We can read their absence, nevertheless, as a sign that Della Casa adhered to traditional, Aristotelian constructions of women that posited that because women's speech did not count as sincere or rational expression, men could justify excluding women from the sphere of political culture and action.[38] As Castiglione's male interlocutors played the feminine roles of liars, gossips, and dissimulators while women were silent, marginal spectators, Della Casa simply excluded women from conversation altogether and defined civil conversation as an act exclusive to men.

Castiglione and Della Casa argued that eloquence was one of the central components of good manners. However, the conduct manual that considered speech the most thoroughly of all in sixteenth-century Italy was Stefano Guazzo's *La civil conversazione*. Guazzo went so far as to describe the types of speech suited to every and all possible positions in the social hierarchy. Guazzo (1530–93), like Castiglione, was a courtier. Early on, he established himself in the service of the Dukes of Mantua and worked as the personal secretary to Ludovico Gonzaga up until the duke's death. Like *Il cortegiano* – the primary source and model for

---

[37] Valeria Finucci has similarly noted for *The Courtier* how "the patriarchal regime that includes women as dependents, theoretically equal to either male siblings, is replaced by a fraternal order that leaves women out, unnamed and hence insignificant." See Valeria Finucci, "In the Name of the Brother: Male Rivalry and Social Order in Baldassare Castiglione's *Il libro del cortegiano,*" *Exemplaria* 9 (1997): 116. On women and political contracts, see Carole Pateman, *The Sexual Contract* (Stanford: Stanford University Press, 1988), 39–76.

[38] The physical characteristics of women – cold and moist humors, menstruation, the womb – had psychological implications in early modern science. Aristotle's *Historia animalium,* perhaps the most celebrated of the *loci classici* in which these physical traits are recorded, was commonly cited in the Renaissance. "[Woman] is . . . more prone to despondency and less hopeful than man, more void of shame or self-respect, more false of speech, more deceptive, and of more retentive memory," cited in Ian Maclean, *The Renaissance Notion of Woman* (Cambridge: Cambridge University Press, 1980), 42. Several statements in Justinian's *Digest* and Tribonian's *Institutes* suggest that in Roman law, speechlessness was in fact a legal impediment. The ability to speak was considered a necessary condition requisite for full Roman citizenship. "These stringent limitations placed upon the deaf and the mute would seem to document a thesis that under Roman law the functions of reason and speech were undifferentiated," O'Neill. *Speech and Speech Disorders,* 84–5.

Guazzo's text – *La civil conversazione* is a dialogue that supposedly took place on four successive days in Casale, most probably in 1567. The text's premise was that Guglielmo Guazzo, an ailing courtier, was granted a leave from his service to his master, Ludovico Gonzaga. During his recuperation, the physician Annibale Magnocavalli came to lift his spirits with lively conversation. The first three books of the dialogue outlined the general rules governing conversation, and the fourth, the description of a banquet, showed how these rules could actually be applied. Guglielmo found these talks so helpful and enlightening that he related them to his brother Stefano who then codified them in his text. *La civil conversazione* was first published in Brescia in 1574; 34 Italian editions appeared in total, most before 1600, and these were followed by 14 Latin editions, 10 French, two Dutch, six English, one German, and one Spanish.[39]

After spending time in Italian and French courts, Guazzo appeared to reject their stifling atmosphere, as well as the roles of the courtier, the intellectual, and the bureaucrat/*segretario* in favor of the bourgeois-citizen. In his text, the arguments of a doctor win out over those of a courtier. Guazzo filled his text with various common proverbs, folk-sayings and examples of everyday behavior to familiarize the tone and character of his dialogue. The protagonists and *exempla* who peopled it were a broad cast of characters, and Casale could easily be any city. With this more down-to-earth rhetorical tone that assumed a universal audience, Guazzo demonstrated that conversation was not only about honor and etiquette but represented a practical social tool useful to courtiers and citizens alike.[40] Unlike Castiglione and Della Casa, Guazzo was clear that nobility did not come exclusively from birth but could be learned, in part through the art of speaking. Guazzo's text also differed significantly in tone from that of Castiglione and Della Casa in its post-Tridentine religious and moral imperatives. For instance, it condemned heretics and gamblers and praised various aspects of Catholic culture

---

[39] Donati, *L'idea di nobiltà*, 152, and John Leon Lievsay, *Stefano Guazzo and the English Renaissance* (Chapel Hill: The University of North Carolina Press, 1961), 12. Lievsay and Donati report different publication figures, but agree that Guazzo's text was widely published. For general discussions of Guazzo's text, see Michel Jeanneret, *A Feast of Words: Banquets and Table Talk in the Renaissance* (Chicago: The University of Chicago Press, 1991), 46–49, and *Stefano Guazzo e la 'Civil conversazione'*, ed. G. Patrizi (Rome: Bulzoni, 1990).

[40] See Girardi, *La società del dialogo*, 66.

such as confession and sacramental marriage. Neither Castiglione nor Della Casa addressed these themes, indicating the effect that the Catholic Reformation had on ideas about speech and social behavior in general.

Guazzo immediately established the importance of conversation when the doctor Annibale suggested that Guglielmo's illness was most likely a result of his solitary condition (*la solitudine per veleno e la conversazione per antidoto e fondamento della vita*).[41] Talking and interaction were not just social, cultural, or political practices but also physical and embodied ones. It was not incidental that the main protagonist of Guazzo's treatise was a doctor who cured the sick with talk; in early modern culture, silence represented a symptom of melancholia, and conversation, like music, had long been understood as melancholia's curative.[42] Solitude, the doctor believed, was the enemy of health, whereas sociability facilitated physical and mental well-being and represented the natural state of man. Conversation was not only a healthy act, but led to the perfection of man, and social interaction satisfied more of man's needs, the doctor claimed, than the physical elements of air, fire, and water.[43] After only a day of conversation, Guglielmo announced that his mind was clearer and that he felt physically improved (34). By the end of the third book, Guglielmo was cured of his illness and claimed that "conversation is the best medicine (*conversazione è la vera medicina*)" (263).

Linking talking to health, Guazzo's interlocutors often related speech to digestion, food, and the stomach. Conversation, like food, was physically internalized and life sustaining (85, 96).[44] Language could also have negative effects upon the body. For instance, some individuals "had a stinking mouth for the many secrets that [they] allowed to rot inside."[45]

---

[41] Guazzo, *La civil conversazione*, 16.

[42] See Giovanni Boccaccio, *The Decameron*, trans. G.H. McWilliam (London: Penguin Books, 1972), 45, and Angus Gowland, "The Problem of Early Modern Melancholy," *Past and Present* 191 (2006): 110.

[43] Guazzo, *La civil conversazione*, 16–27.

[44] Medieval texts such as Robert of Sorbonne's *De lingua* (1250) often described reading out loud as the "chewing" or "masticating" of the words of the text. "Vocalization helped the reader to absorb the full meaning, to 'eat' the words," Walter Ong, "Orality, Literacy, and Medieval Textualization," 1. See also Francesco Sansovino, *L'arte oratoria secondo i modi della lingua volgare* (Venice, 1546), "S'aggiugne a questo il movimento del corpo che è cibo de gli occhi, essendo che le parole son cibo de gli orecchi, per i quali duoi sensi tutte le cose passano alla nostra mente," 52v.

[45] Guazzo, *La civil conversazione*, 50.

Similarly, flatterers had mouths that "expired a poisonous breath that weakened the soul which lent it its ears" (53). Not surprisingly, Annibale associated unmannered conversation with disease (32, 37, 42), believing that talk had the power "not only to give life but to take it away" (153).[46] When Guglielmo asked the doctor how to protect against these "infections" associated with language, Annibale admonished that instead of listening to flatterers and slanderers, "you must close your ears like Ulysses against the Sirens and go away, as they say, wearing shoes among thorns" (37). Or, one should place "a shield around the head that covers the ears against their beastly and damaging voices" (61, 52). For Guazzo, speech was clearly a tangible, powerful, physical force.

After emphasizing this link between conversation and physical well-being, Annibale stressed that all people were situated at a specific social and cultural location that determined how they should behave and how they should speak. For every social and cultural position, the young and old (*giovani et vecchi*), princes and private people (*principi et privati*), the learned and the common (*dotti et idioti*), citizens and foreigners (*cittadini et forestieri*), the religious and the secular (*religiosi et secolari*), men and women (*uomini et donne*), there existed a corresponding mode of interacting and talking. Nobles, for instance, should aim to speak clearly and slowly, varying their tone of voice and using appropriate gestures to reinforce the natural beauty of their speech. Women should speak modestly and quietly. Older people should speak "with gravity and feeling, and furthermore of things that serve as an example and instruction in life" (122). Youths, for their lack of experience, should speak prudently and try to remain silent. As suggested by both Castiglione and Della Casa, social engagement and the speech it involved (*la favella*) should reflect one's age, gender, profession, rank, and geographical origins (102–3). Though there existed many different ways of speaking – confidently, modestly,

---

[46] See also Giulio Cesare Cabei, *Ornamenti della gentildonna vedova* (Venice, 1574), "ma se le persone con cui ha da conversare sono conosciute meno buone di quello, che ricerca la sua honestà, le lassi a tutti i modi come morbo contagioso, e procuri la conversatione delle buone," 52. Similarly, according to Agnolo Firenzuola, the body had the natural, physical mechanisms of phlegm and a complex ear cavity to protect itself against harmful speech. He argued that ears were constructed in such as way "acciochè per cotal difficultà pasando la voce più lentamente . . . al senso dell'audito.. ma quando pur qualcuna ve ne entrasse, vi ritrova na certa materia viscosa, che la ritiene, acciochè non passi al fondo," Firenzuola, *Delle bellezze delle donne* (Venice, 1622), 38.

humorously – one should never speak outside of one's assigned conversational position. For instance, non-nobles should not try "to attribute to themselves the title of nobility with words or clothing" (139). Similarly, "youths who try to speak (*parlare*) like their elders... deserve strong reprehension" (120). Most importantly, men and women should never try to speak like each other.

> [S]eeing a young girl representing the liberty and boldness of a man in her gestures, appearance and speech (*parlare*) is a monstrous and abominable thing.... For this reason, young girls should learn to show modesty in their glances, gestures, language (*lingua*) and behavior. (239)

Speech existed at the intersection of a variety of social categories, simultaneously representing and constructing an individual's age, class, nationality, status, and gender. Like Castiglione, Guazzo suggested following an Aristotelian just mean or speaking in a balanced way (*mezzanamente*) or along a "middle road" (*strada di mezzo*) in order to balance these many demands (58, 256). Though typically applied to art and architecture, Aristotelian congruence here referred to social exchange. Speech should be "proportional" or congruent (*convenevole*) not only with one's gender, rank, and status, but also with the location and circumstances of the conversation. The great diversity to be found in social rank and status meant, however, that Guazzo like Castiglione also found it impossible to suggest any singular rule capable of governing all social interaction (39, 80, 119).

Beyond these generalizing rules governing the relationship between speech and status, Guazzo's interlocutors established several additional and more unique dichotomies to illustrate how one should govern the tongue. First and foremost among these were rules regarding public (*publico, palese, in piazza*) and private (*privato*) speech – the two categories of talk that in fact organized Guazzo's entire text.[47] The first book of Guazzo's dialogue considered conversation in general, the second "public" conversation (between nobles and their equals, nobles and non-nobles, fellow citizens and foreigners), and the third, conversation within the home (between husband and wife, father and son, brothers,

---

[47] See Quondam, *La civil conversazione*, vol. 2, 72–73.

masters and servants). In private conversation, one could safely be honest. The dialogue between Annibale and Guglielmo itself took place in the "small and remote rooms" (*picciole e rimote stanze*) which Guazzo himself usually reserved for reading and meditation (14): a site where dialogue could be sincere, not unlike the prince's chambers in *Il cortegiano*. The public world, by contrast, represented an arena of conversational display and spectacle where one must proceed with caution because it was full of slanderers (*maldicenti*) and words traveled quickly though gossip and hearsay (47). "We must absolutely remember," Guglielmo remarked, "that things said in the ear are then published in the *piazze*. If it is a terrible thing to reveal others' secrets, the opposing virtue is to know how to be quiet and bridle the tongue (*tacere e frena la sua lingua*)" (50). As Annibale put it, reputations "depend on opinions everywhere, which are so strong that reason has no say against them" (43). Along these lines, respectable people should avoid the conversation of "public" people such as prostitutes and pimps (71). As an examination of the practices of talk in early modern Venice will show, public talk determined one's honor and *fama*, reflecting Guazzo's recommendation that maintaining one's good reputation demanded vigilance in public speech.

Guazzo also emphasized the distinction between masculine and feminine conversation, which he believed reflected the order of nature "more than any other type of interaction" (178). Similar to the ideas of Castiglione, feminine speech was naturally slippery and women were prone to lying and deception, not necessarily out of ill intent but because they were physically incapable of controlling their minds (185–205). Women typically said one thing while thinking or doing another, so that women's speech was rarely genuine. If words "have the power to appear what they are not, or appear more than what they are" (88), women were by nature more apt to take advantage of the possibilities of spoken language by practicing dishonesty, deception, and dissimulation. For this reason, Guazzo argued that women should speak cautiously, modestly, and infrequently; like most other writers in the sixteenth century, he advised them to remain silent (205). Masculine speech, by contrast, was by nature clear and honest; men both should and did strive for sincerity. A man's tongue represented "the mirror and portrait of his soul, and as we know a coin's truth or falsity from its sound, so we understand the interior quality of a man and his manners from the sound of his words" (86). Guazzo advised men to avoid all types of dishonest talk, relating any flattery or dissembling to "a wolf in sheep's clothing . . . a dove with the tail of a scorpion . . . a man who has honey in his mouth and a razor at his belt . . . a tarnished grave . . . a sweetened pill . . . [and] gilded copper" (95).[48] Sincerity was considered a masculine virtue, but not a feminine one.

Beyond his ideas about public/private, masculine/feminine, and sincere/insincere speech, Guazzo added a final category of talk – speech from the heart and the tongue – a final pervasive dichotomy in his text.[49] The heart and tongue, he believed, possessed different capacities for sincerity. Although the heart always told the truth, the tongue "is fallible and often hides the meaning of the heart (*la lingua è fallace e asconde bene spesso l'affetto del cuore*)."[50] Though the heart and the tongue were separate organs, they were physically linked, at least in men, so that the tongue had the capacity to communicate directly the heart's ideas (92, 104): an idea also espoused by medical men.[51] Guazzo argued that it was reprehensible to speak with the tongue alone. For instance, those who fasted only with the tongue and not equally with the heart (meaning, those who talked about fasting but never really did so) did not truly imitate Christ (24). Flattery was a despicable form of speech because usually those who give praise with the tongue do not do so equally with the heart. Most princes knew that "people . . . honor them with their lips, but their heart is far" (63, 149). Women's hearts naturally remained unconnected to their tongues, and "where the heart is missing, there is therefore more tongue," resulting in women's loquacity (169).

With all these themes devised to categorize types of talk, Guazzo's interlocutors may at times have appeared to establish clear rules for

---

[48] See also 27, 52, 58.

[49] On the use of this metaphor in medieval and Renaissance literature, see John L. Harrison, "The Convention of the 'Heart and Tongue' and the Meaning of *Measure for Measure*," *Shakespeare Quarterly* 5 (1954): 2–4; Martin, "Inventing Sincerity," 1333; Carla Mazzio, "Sins of the Tongue," in Hillman and Mazzio, *The Body in Parts*, 63.

[50] Guazzo, *La civil conversazione*, 302. See also 3.

[51] Following the ideas of Plato, the Venetian doctor Alessandro Benedetti asserted in his history of the human body (1502) that "a vein . . . passes from the tongue to the seat of the heart. This nerve is the moderator of the articulated voice." See Alessandro Benedetti, *Anatomice*, in Lind, *Studies in Pre-Vesalian Anatomy*, 110–11. See also Girolamo Ercolani, *Le eroine della solitudine* (Venice, 1655), "In molte infermità, formano i medici della qualità del male, giudicio dalla lingua; mercè, che conforme gli anatomici con il mezzo d'un nervo, vassi à congiungere con il cuore: così anco dalla lingua, si può senza errore pronosticare l'interno del Christiano. . . . La lingua è il coperchio del cuore," 116.

social speech. As in Castiglione's text, however, these directives were riven with paradoxes and inconsistencies, especially in the way Guazzo described gendered speech. Guazzo consistently emphasized, like Castiglione, that men and women had separate and distinct ways of speaking. The male voice should not be too faint, sick, or shrill like a woman's (89–90). Similarly, if women spoke too loudly, frequently, or aggressively, they risked becoming too masculine (239). However, as for Castiglione, "performance," deception, and femininely coded ways of speaking such as flattery were again useful and necessary for men. Because the art of conversation involved changing one's speech to suit specific audiences, Annibale contradicted himself as Castiglione's interlocutors did by arguing that dissimulation was often more useful than sincerity.

> To be able to converse gracefully (*per trovar luogo di grazia nel conversare*), we must rid ourselves of our own habits and appear to put on the clothes of others, imitating them as much as reason permits. And in sum, concerning the study of honesty, one must always be oneself, but concerning the diversity of people with whom one interacts (*si prattichèra*), one must be a different person and follow that ancient saying: the heart must be completely unlike and the countenance must be completely like the common man. (72–73)

Spoken language functioned like clothing – a changeable system of signs and signifiers which communicated rank, status, mood, purpose, and occasion, and allowed an individual either to imitate or distance himself from those around him. Annibale went so far as to compare male conversation to the feminine boudoir.

> Just as women look at themselves in the mirror for advice and help before displaying their ornaments, before speaking, we must turn to our interior mirrors and organize our words inside so that listeners cannot discern these words arise from the mouth or from the heart. (104)

Men should arrange their verbal countenances to partake in conversation just as women arranged their clothes, jewelry, and faces; by concealing the inner-self through verbal dissembling and performing, male speakers directly appropriated feminine talents. Guazzo and Castiglione both encouraged men to speak like women. As in the other texts considered here, men in Guazzo's text did all the talking. Although men appropriated feminine ways of speaking, these writers removed women from the realm of language and social action altogether. Through this feminine silence, these texts created an enlarged space in which male speech could proliferate. Because women were typically described as deceptive, superficial gossips, they were instructed not to speak at all so that men could take on the conversational privilege of speaking for both genders.[52]

The attention given to speech in all of these texts – the numerous categories, boundaries, rules, and prescriptions placed on and around civil conversation and the rich variety of vocabulary and examples employed to discuss it – provides a wealth of evidence of the degree to which this culture was concerned about the verbal presentation of the self. Behavior in the Renaissance, at least according to these elite reflections on it, was clearly judged as much by how one spoke as how one acted. Castiglione, Della Casa, and Guazzo and scores of other writers like them instructed their readers on how to speak in a way that was pleasing (*piacevole*), honorable (*onesta*), and elegant (*leggiadra*), with a tongue that was both ready (*pronta*) and sharp (*mordace*) but cautious (*cauto*) and employed with prudence (*prudenzia*), all of which comprised the art of conversation that separated the civil from the un-civil. Moreover, these competing discourses of sincerity and prudence, heart and tongue, or of speaking in "masculine" or "feminine" ways, reflected the complexity of the Renaissance self. This self was neither an essentialist self with an independent, ontological status nor a self that was an entirely unfree, historicized construct or empty site onto which larger political and historical forces were inscribed.[53] Rather, it was a mixture, with the tongue representing the mediating device that negotiated the multifaceted and complicated

---

[52] An emerging group of women writers in the sixteenth century expressed ideas about language, class, gender, social life, the control of the body, and sincerity that often confronted and contradicted the ideas presented in comportment literature written by men. Writers like Tullia d'Aragona (*Dialogo dell'infinità d'amore*, 1547), Moderata Fonte (*Il merito delle donne*, 1600), and Lucrezia Marinella (*La nobiltà et l'eccellenza delle donne*, 1600), for instance, challenged Castiglione's setting in which women were supposed to be part of a group but not speak. Moderata Fonte in particular strongly defended sincerity in women, in contrast to Castiglione and Guazzo. These writers and their texts do not focus as insistently on talk, speech and conversation as central topics, and for this reason are not considered in depth here. However, it is important to note that male writers of texts about manners did not necessarily have the last word on the topics of language, class, and gender.

[53] Martin, "Inventing Sincerity," 1340.

relationship between one's interior world and one's exterior persona. In effect, the tongue represented the site where the self was performed.

Literary discussions of speech and conversation born in the Italian courts echoed, reflected, and perhaps even directed Venetian initiatives aimed at controlling the tongue in an urban setting. Since the founding of the republic, we shall see, speech and its control had been "a crucial requirement for the preservation of [Venetian] rule and their state."[54] In the urban world, the tongue had long been a public, legislated object, and speech a regulated act. This became increasingly true in the early modern period, at the very same time that books of manners and comportment became popular. The discipline of the tongue in early modern Venice was not simply the result of the trickling down of literary ideas about bodily control such as these, as Elias might have us believe. Rather, an increased attention to public speech reflected the larger, complicated process of early modern statebuilding and was a reaction to specific political and social changes occurring in the sixteenth-century lagoon city. Nonetheless, there was much overlap between the advice about talk presented by writers of conduct literature and the ways that the Venetian state and its inhabitants perceived the acts of talking and conversation. The vitality of these textual debates about appropriate forms of speech clearly informed ideas about the social construction of the state. Namely, talk possessed a power on par with physical force and action. Speech may have had the power to bind civil society together, but it also possessed the dangerous capacity to tear it apart. As we shall see, this resulted in numerous and varied attempts to govern the unruly tongue in the urban world, especially when it spoke in blasphemies and insults.

---

[54] Guido Ruggiero, *Violence in Early Renaissance Venice* (New Brunswick, NJ: Rutgers University Press, 1980), 125.

2

Regulating Blasphemy

In the summer of 1519, the Venetian chronicler Marin Sanudo described how the Venetian state punished a priest for the crime of blasphemy. Civic magistrates placed him on a barge and drove him up the Grand Canal as criers announced his crime along the way. Once having arrived at the Rialto bridge in the city's commercial center, his tongue was placed in a vise. From there, he made a public procession to the Piazza San Marco, the civic heart of Venice, where magistrates placed him on a stage and crowned him with a hat painted with devils. As his tongue became black, he was then forced into a cage and hauled halfway up the campanile of San Marco where he hung for 10 days before he was finally brought down to be placed in prison for 10 years, where he was fed only bread and water.[1] Public punishments for blasphemy such as this one made such a powerful impression on those who observed them that they may have inspired the mysterious poem "The Lament of Father Augustino,"

[1] "In questa matina, justa la sententia fata per el reverendissimo Patriarcha nostro, contra quel pre... oficiava a San Cassan, qual biastemò... hor fu posto sopra una piata, cridando per Canal grando la sua colpa, poi per terra menato a l'hostaria di[l Bo] in Rialto, dove fu posto la lengua in giova, et conduto a San Marco, dove fo su uno soler posto, e con una corona dipenta con diavoli fu posto sopra uno soler, et stete fino hore 22 e con la lengua in giova, la qual era molto negra, *demun* fu posto in una cheba, e tirato al campaniel di San Marco dove starà per 10 zorni, *demun* sarà posto in una preson a San Marco ditta *Frescha zoja*, dove dia star per anni 10 serato a pan et aqua," Marin Sanudo, *I diarii di Marino Sanudo*, ed. Rinaldo Fulin and others, 58 vols. (Venice: Fratelli Visentini, 1879–1903), vol. 27, 322. For similar punishments for blasphemy, see vol. 8, 71; vol. 27, 241, 258, 342, 536; vol. 36, 261. The Venetian year began on 1 March, and in both the main text and the notes, all the days and years have retained their Venetian dating.

(1542) in which the voice of a priest punished for blasphemy in Venice bemoaned his fate. "It would have been better if I had been mute," he sighed, "because this punishment is worse than death." Describing his *cheba* or wooden cage, he grieved, "I am a parrot without wings. Hear my song, which will be like a gift, to have heard my cries. I want to give you a good piece of advice: do the right thing and avoid gambling: do not blaspheme the saints or God, because if you blaspheme in this place, you will undergo my fate."[2]

The Venetian state clearly took the crime of blasphemy seriously. In 1537, the Venetian Council of Ten – Venice's most powerful, central security council – decided to combat this crime by creating the magistracy of the *Esecutori Contro la Bestemmia*, "The Executors Against Blasphemy." It did so to confront what many perceived had become a nagging and persistent problem: insults against God – usually spoken – within Venetian territory. As we have seen, much literary attention was devoted to language and speech in sixteenth-century Italy, but the establishment of this magistracy, though commonly unknown, represented a watershed moment in the history of language in the West. The Venetian state formed the *Esecutori* expressly to discipline blasphemous outbursts in the lagoon city. Although many decrees against both blasphemy and insults had been passed before, both in Venice and elsewhere, the installation of this magistracy demonstrated a concise turn from the abstract to the concrete, or from theoretical or haphazard thinking about language and society to a more focused articulation of the relationship between the two. Whereas medieval thought had typically described blasphemy as a mere subset of heresy in general and often conflated the two, the creation of the *Esecutori* represents a moment when early modern blasphemy

---

[2] "Meglio seria ch'io fussi stato mutto. . . . Io son un papagal che non ha ali, udite il mio cantar, che'l vi sia un dono haver uditi questi canti tali. . . . Un buon consiglio dar vi voglio io; fate pur ben: e fuggite dal giuoco: non biastemmate i santi, manco Idio, perche se biastemmate in questo luoco, gionger potresti, e divenirmi equali," *Lamento di Padre Augustino che si duole della sua sorte che lo habbia fatto imperator senza imperio, e messagli la lingua in giova per biastemmar, e al fin l'hanno messo in chebba condannato a pane e acqua*, (n.p. [Venice?], 1542, Biblioteca Nazionale Marciana, Misc.2231.6), 58r–59r. On this poem, see also Pompeo Molmenti, "La corruzione dei costumi veneziani nel Rinascimento," *Archivio storico italiano* Tome 31 (1903), 298, n. 1.

became delineated and defined as a specific act, more verbal than intellectual. As seen through archival documents, blasphemy took on a detectable rhetorical form beyond more general ideas about unorthodox thought and behavior.

Turning from textual sources that more broadly reflect Northern Italian culture to localized archival sources from the Venetian republic is not an attempt to see how generic prescriptions about elite comportment played themselves out in the lives of everyday people in Venice. Books of comportment, as we have seen, were often products of the courts aimed at instructing elite audiences, whereas legislative, judicial, and criminal records reflect the crimes committed more often by the illiterate underclasses. Gondoliers, servants, tailors, and bread bakers most likely did not read books of comportment; nor do we even have any sure way of knowing if their patrician counterparts did either. Yet, examining these two sources side-by-side – elite, prescriptive literature and Venetian criminal records – illuminates that in the realms of both of these sources, disciplining the unmannered tongue was central to maintaining a series of boundaries defining both class and civic identity.

Blasphemy in Venice was not simply an unorthodox expression nor its prosecution simply an attempt to discipline heretical behavior. On a deeper level, it also revealed profound connections between language and civic identity. Individuals wielded these words in an attempt to change culture; the state, in turn, disciplined blasphemy to prevent them from doing so. Although legal and theoretical constructions of blasphemy have been studied at length, the actual practice of this crime of speech and the ways people on the street used such language have not. By examining particular instances of blasphemy in social networks of identity and difference and by compiling a map of the cultural sites where blasphemy embodied collective aspects of meaning, we can uncover the ways in which the Venetian state used language, in particular directives against blasphemy, as a means of assimilating outsiders to Venetian ways. In disciplining blasphemy, the republic of Venice used definitions of proper speech to socialize new recruits and foreigners into the community. At their core, discussion about blasphemy and ultimately acts of blasphemy themselves functioned as cultural battles focusing on what it meant to be "Venetian."

Blasphemy and its repression have a long history in the Christian and pre-Christian West, codified perhaps first in the Ten Commandments.[3] As a general definition, blasphemy means attributing false traits to God (God is impotent, God is cruel), denying God his supernatural powers (God is not the creator and director of all things and actions), and attributing Godly characteristics to non-divine beings (images can confer grace, witches can tell the future). In the thirteenth century, particularly in the thought of Thomas Aquinas, blasphemy became the object of more profound philosophical analysis, and between the thirteenth and fifteenth centuries, numerous Italian communes began to pass statutes to punish this crime.[4] For example, in Umbria fines were from 20 to 50 *denari* – roughly the penalty for a physical injury, which received a fine of 10 *denari* and a blood wound a fine of 25 *denari*.[5] Medieval Tuscan fines ranged from two to 50 *lire* or five to 40 *soldi* – a moderate penalty, considering that the crime of climbing over city walls received a fine of 100 *soldi*. In thirteenth-century Pisa, those who could not pay their fines were whipped.[6] In the Veneto, penalties ranged from three *lire* in thirteenth-century Chioggia to 100 *soldi* or four *lire* in fifteenth-century Riva del Garda and Rovereto, compared to a fine of five *lire* for a verbal insult and five to 10 *lire* for a physical injury. Those accused were merely

---

[3] See R. H. Helmholz, "Blasphemy," in Joseph R. Strayer (ed.), *Dictionary of the Middle Ages*, vol. 2 (New York: Schocken Books, 1982), 271–72, and Leonard W. Levy, *Treason Against God: A History of the Offense of Blasphemy* (New York: Shocken Books, 1981).

[4] On medieval theories of blasphemy (more than its practice) and especially the central contributions of Aquinas to these theories, see Edwin D. Craun, " 'Inordinata Locutio': Blasphemy in Pastoral Literature, 1200–1500," *Traditio* 39 (1983): 135–62, and Edwin D. Craun, *Lies, Slander, and Obscenity in Medieval English Literature: Pastoral Rhetoric and the Deviant Speaker* (Cambridge: Cambridge University Press, 1997); Corinne Leveleux, *La parole interdite: Le blasphème dans la France médiévale (XIIIe–XVIe siècles): Du péché au crime* (Paris: De Boccard, 2001).

[5] *Lo statuto comunale di Monte San Pietrangeli*, ed. Giuseppe Avarucci (Padua: Editrice Antenore, 1987), 89–90; *Lo statuto di Gualdo Cattaneo del 1483*, eds. Maria Grazia and Nico Ottaviani (Spoleto: Centro Italiano di Studi Sull'Alto Medioevo, 1991), 88.

[6] *Statuto et ordinato è . . . Torri in Val di Pesa, una comunità della campagna fiorentina nei suoi statuti quattrocenteschi*, ed. Marco Bicchierai (Scandicci: Centrolibri, 1995), 86; *Bucine e la Val d'Ambra nel Dugento: Gli ordini dei conti Guidi*, eds. Maria A. Ceppari, Erminio Jacona, and Patrizia Turrini (Siena: Biblioteca Comunale di Bucine, 1995), 65; *Statuto del comune di Arezzo 1327*, ed. Attilio Droandi (Arezzo: Alberti and C. Editori, 1992), 195; "Breve Pisani Communis 1286," in *Statuti inediti della città di Pisa dal XII al XIV secolo*, ed. F. Isonaini, vol. 1. (Florence, 1854), 385.

dunked in water if they could not pay their fines in the communes of Rovereto, Ala, Val di Ledro, and Lendinara.[7] Judging the actual value of money in these communes is difficult because of enormous currency fluctuations; what may have been a stiff fine when a statute was drawn up may not have been several years later or in another commune. Moreover, there is also little evidence to demonstrate whether these decrees were seriously enforced. Nevertheless, these statutes show that in medieval Italy, blasphemy was considered a minor offence meriting a relatively benign punishment.

Like its mainland counterparts, Venice also had legislated against blasphemy since the thirteenth century, employing different councils and magistracies at different times to oversee this problem, including the Council of Ten, the Great Council, the *Avogaria di Comun,* the *Signori di Notte,* and the *Quarantia Criminal.*[8] Other island communities in the lagoon had passed statutes against blasphemy throughout the course of the Middle Ages, punishing the crime with fines and prison sentences.[9] The fourteenth-century founding statutes of individual *scuole grandi* – Venetian confraternities – also contained provisions against blasphemy.[10] As on the *terraferma,* medieval Venetian punishments for blasphemy were relatively light. A deliberation from the *Signori di Notte* in 1261 contained the fine of three *lire* for blasphemy against God, the Virgin, and the saints,

---

[7] *Statuti e capitolari di Chioggia del 1272–1279,* ed. Gianni Penao Doria and Sergio Perini (Venice: Il Cardo, 1993), 95; *Statuti di Lendinara del 1321,* ed. Marco Pozza (Rome: Jouvence, 1984), 68; *Statuti di Riva del Garda nel 1451,* ed. Ermanno Orlando (Venice: Il Cardo, 1994), 144; *Statuti di Pordenone del 1438,* ed. Giorgio Oscuro and Marco Pozza (Rome: Jouvence, 1986), 87; *Statuti di Ala e di Avio del secolo XV,* ed. Bruno Andreolli, Stefania Manente, Ermanno Orlando, and Alessandra Princivalli (Rome: Jouvence, 1990), 119; *Statuti di Rovereto del 1425,* ed. Federica Parcianello (Venice: Il Cardo, 1991), 95; *Statuti della Val di Ledro del 1435,* ed. Silvano Groff (Rome: Jouvence, 1989), 93–94.

[8] See Renzo Derosas, "Moralità e giustizia a Venezia nel '500-'600: Gli esecutori contro la bestemmia," in *Stato, società e giustizia nella repubblica veneta,* ed. Gaetano Cozzi (Rome: Società Editoriale Jouvence, 1980), 433, and Roberta Viaro, *La magistratura degli esecutori contro la bestemmia nel XVI secolo* (Ph.D. diss., University of Padua, 1969–70), 15.

[9] Mazzorbo in 1316, Malamocco in 1351, Torcello in 1462, and Murano in 1502. See *Statuti della laguna veneta dei secoli XIV-XVI,* ed. Gherardo Ortalli, Monica Pasqualetto, and Alessandra Rizzi (Rome: Jouvence, 1989).

[10] Brian Pullan, *Rich and Poor in Renaissance Venice: The Social Institutions of a Catholic State to 1620* (Oxford: Oxford University Press, 1971), 50. "Volemo et ordinemo da qui avant non se possa ne debia recever nela nostra scola nesun homo o femina che sia biastemador publico," in Antonio Niero, "Statuto della confraternità di Santa Maria della Misericordia di Chirignago (Venezia)," *Rivista di storia della chiesa in Italia* 20 (1966): 396.

with the penalty of being dunked in water for those who could not pay.[11] Several additional statutes followed in 1269, 1270, and 1300 which added the punishment of placing those incapable of paying in a pillory "for as long as the *Signori di Notte* wanted."[12] The council of the *Cinque Anziani alla Pace* also legislated against blasphemy in 1485, declaring a fine of four months in prison and 50 *lire* for insulting God or the Virgin, three months in prison and 25 *lire* for insulting the saints, and one month in prison and 15 *lire* for insulting any relics.[13] By the start of the sixteenth century, however, the republic became increasingly troubled by blasphemy. Between 1500 and 1530, the Council of Ten intervened eight times in attempt to repress blasphemy.[14] In 1500, the Ten took full responsibility for overseeing blasphemy and in 1507 established the punishment of cutting out the tongue for extreme cases. It increased punishments for lesser acts of blasphemy in 1514 and 1517; beyond paying 500 *lire di piccoli* (a much increased fine), blasphemers were banned from Venice for five years.[15] In 1517, the Ten decided to return blasphemy cases to the *Avogaria di Comun* – the Venetian state lawyers – and in 1533 the Ten reserved the right to judge all denunciations for blasphemy and delegate these cases to either the *Avogaria* or the *Signori di Notte*, one of the principal branches of the Venetian police force. The Ten posted additional proclamations against blasphemy at San Marco and the Rialto in 1533, and in 1534 extended punishments for blasphemy to the entire Venetian empire.[16]

Because the regulation of blasphemy and speech in general occurred through the work of various magistracies and their courts such as these,

---

[11] "Fuit capta pars quod nulla persona audeat de cetero blasfemare Deum sanctam Mariam vel sanctos in penam trium librarum et qui solvere non poterint eicantur in aqua et quicumque accusaverit habeat medietatem et teneatur in credencia et illi de nocte teneantur dictos denarios exigere et si non solverint ducere eos ad palacium," *Le magistrature giudiziarie veneziane e i loro capitolari fino al 1300*, ed. Melchiorre Roberti, vol. 3 (Padua, 1906–11), 31–32. "Una strana e ignominiosa pena era in antico riservata ai bestemmiatori che non avessero pagata la multa: quella di esser tuffati nell'acqua," Pompeo Molmenti, *La storia di Venezia nella vita privata dalle origini alla caduta della repubblica*, vol. 3 (Trieste: Edizioni Lint, 1973), 484.

[12] "Faciant stare quantum volverint," Roberti, *Le magistrature*, vol. 3, 31–32.

[13] Archivio di Stato di Venezia (hereafter ASV), *Cinque Anziani alla Pace*, bu. 1, 20 January 1485, fos. 34–35.

[14] Derosas, "Moralità e giustizia," 433.

[15] Cozzi, *Religione, moralità, e giustizia*, 8.

[16] See Cozzi, "Authority and Law," 323; ASV, *Esecutori Contro la Bestemmia*, bu. 54, 30 December 1523, fo. 1r, and 7 January 1533, fos. 1v–2r.

a brief word about court procedure will prove useful in understanding how these disciplinary systems worked. What exactly did this domain look like that made the regulation of public language possible? Venetian courts were staffed and run by patrician officials (who typically worked as judges), notaries, and clerks. Among these groups, noble judges played a relatively small role in the parsing out of justice because, as a result of the electoral system, they served short terms of office and moved almost constantly between different courts. Patrician judges also rarely had any serious training in the law. All this meant that a knowledge of both the law and courtroom procedure lay largely in the hands of courtroom clerks and public lawyers. Public lawyers, for instance, often acted as prosecutors. Clerks registered denunciations that they were given by various policing magistracies, examined witnesses in the courtroom, interrogated defendants, and used this information to write up a trial or *processo*. Then, noble judges would hold a final hearing where they would consider the evidence, hear lawyers' arguments, and pronounce a final sentence. This system of course varied among different magistracies. Procedure at the court of the Holy Office, for instance, tended to involve much more inquisitorial procedure on the part of the Inquisitor and judges. In general, however, courtroom procedure, including the procedure governing the punishment of blasphemy, unfolded in this way.[17]

Despite this flurry of activity in all these courts dedicated to eradicating blasphemy, or perhaps because of the confusion surrounding the jurisdiction over this crime, the republic saw little result. Sanudo had recorded in March of 1510, for instance, that the practice of blasphemy among soldiers in the field had become so prevalent that it would perhaps be necessary "to do as the Turks do and cut blasphemers in half" in order to curtail this habit.[18] The Ten decided on 20 December 1537 to create the *Esecutori Contro la Bestemmia* – The Executors Against Blasphemy –

---

[17] See James Shaw, *The Justice of Venice: Authorities and Liberties in the Urban Economy, 1550–1700* (Oxford: Oxford University Press for the British Academy, 2006), 45–47. Shaw describes how the court of the *Giustizia Vecchia* worked, but argues that its functioning was fairly representative of many other courts in Venice. On courtroom procedure in the court of the Inquisition, as well as the limitations of courtroom documents for the study of history, see Chapter Four.

[18] "Si'l volesse proveder bisogneria far a la turchescha che come blastemano sono tajati per mezo," Sanudo, *I diarii*, vol. 10, 33.

voting to elect annually "three of the leading nobles of excellent conscience for one year"[19] to punish those who

> dared to blaspheme, or curse the name of God, our lord Jesus Christ, and
> his glorious mother the Virgin Mary, or in their contempt say general
> or particular vituperous or contemptible words against the name of the
> celestial court, either expressly or in any way, form of words, or style.[20]

Venetians believed blasphemy had become so prevalent that it was endangering the state; it had become serious enough in fact to merit its own
magistracy. Once created, the *Esecutori* were required to assign "the most
rigorous and severe punishments against anyone who dared to blaspheme, and also against those who publicly spoke base, scandalous, and
indecent words."[21] The *Esecutori* did not have legislative powers, but were
granted the fullest disciplinary measures, "as if the trials were heard by the
Council of Ten itself,"[22] testifying to the perceived gravity of this crime.
Although other early modern states passed edicts, laws, and proclamations regarding blasphemy, only Venice went so far as to create an actual
independent council designed – at least upon its creation – to eradicate
this specific offense.[23]

The punishments of the *Esecutori* typically entailed a fine of 400 *lire di
piccoli* – roughly a month's salary for an unskilled worker – and a year of
imprisonment and/or a five-year banishment from the city. Lesser crimes
often incurred a fine of 10 to 20 ducats.[24] Towns on the Venetian mainland

---

[19] ASV, *Esecutori*, bu. 54, 20 December 1537, fo. 3v.

[20] "Ardisca biastemar, ne maledir el nome di dio, et signor nostro m. Jesu christo, et la sua
gloriosa madre verzene maria, ne in vilipendio loro dir parole vituperose ne particolarmente
ne in genere sotto nome della corte celestial ne espressamente ne per alcun color, o forma di
parole per alcun modo, ouer inzegno," Ibid., 7 January 1533, fo. 2r.

[21] "Più rigorose e severe pene contro ognuno, che ardisse di proferire qualunque bestemmia, ed
anche contro quelli che pubblicamente proferissero parole turpi, scandalose, ed indecenti,"
Marco Ferro, *Dizionario del diritto comune e veneto*, vol. 1 (Venice, 1843), 270.

[22] "Come se fosse sta fatto per questo cons.o espediti li loro processi," ASV, *Esecutori*, bu. 54,
20 December 1537, fo. 3v.

[23] The *Esecutori* rapidly took on other functions; see n. 63 below.

[24] To offer an idea of the significance of this sum of money, Reinhold Mueller calculated
that in 1540 an un-skilled to semi-skilled worker earned an average wage of 18.67 *lire di
piccoli* a day, so a fine of 400 *lire di piccoli* represented approximately a month's salary.
Similarly, Brian Pullan estimated that between 1550 and 1560, builders at the Scuola of San
Rocco earned an average wage of 20–30 *soldi di piccoli* a day – slightly more than the wage
calculated by Mueller. According to Lane and Mueller, in 1516 one gold ducat equaled 124
soldi di piccoli. Gino Luzzato calculated that in 1562, one ducat equaled approximately 200

enacted similar punishments.[25] Those incapable of paying the required
fine, such as vagabonds or the impoverished, were often punished with
galley service. Not infrequently, greater crimes resulted in public humiliation and torture in the ceremonial space between the columns in the
piazzetta of San Marco – the religious, political, and ceremonial center
of the city. As Sanudo had described, punishment sometimes involved
squeezing the tongue in a vise while the accused stood on a raised plat-
form for several hours, wearing a miter and a sign indicating punishment
for blasphemy. After this public display, the accused were then either set
free or returned to prison until they could pay their assigned fine. In more
extreme cases, following this public humiliation, the accused's tongue
was cut out, and in rare cases of severe punishment, the right hand and
right eye were removed. For instance, the 1554 sentence of Lazaro de Antonio demanded that his tongue be cut out "so that everyone has a frightful
reason to abstain from such a similar, detestable sin as blasphemy."[26] The
punishment of the porter Zuan Maria Zeter between the columns of San
Marco offers another such example. In a spectacular display of sovereign
power, officers were ordered to place him

> on a visible platform high enough to be well-seen, crown him with an
> ignominious miter and place his tongue in a vise, with a sign on his
> chest saying "for blasphemy" . . . leave him this way for an hour, then
> cut his tongue across in such a way that he cannot ever speak again, and
> then cut his right hand so that it separates from his body and remove

lire di piccoli. Therefore, a fine of fewer ducats equaled a fine of more *lire di piccoli*. On
fourteenth- and fifteenth-century wages, see Reinhold C. Mueller, *Money and Banking in
Medieval and Renaissance Venice, Volume II: The Venetian Money Market, Banks, Panics and
the Public Debt, 1200–1500* (Baltimore: The Johns Hopkins University Press, 1997), 664; and
Brian Pullan, "Wage Earners and the Venetian Economy, 1550–1630," in *Crisis and Change in
the Sixteenth and Seventeenth Centuries*, ed. Brian Pullan (London: Methuen, 1968), 156–57.
On the sixteenth-century relationship between ducats and *lire di piccoli*, see Frederic C. Lane
and Reinhold C. Mueller, *Money and Banking in Medieval and Renaissance Venice, Volume I:
Coins and Moneys of Account* (Baltimore: The Johns Hopkins University Press, 1985), 617, and
Gino Luzzato, *Storia economica di Venezia dall'11 al 16 secolo* (Venice: Centro Internazionale
delle Arti e del Costume, 1995), 186.

[25] Following a case of blasphemy in 1586, the city of Treviso re-proclaimed the punishment
of 400 *lire di piccoli* and a five-year ban. See ASV, *Avogaria di Comun, Penale*, bu. 423, fasc.
"Gregorio Pulsato," 20r–24r.

[26] "Accio che ogn'uno ad essempio suo habbia timorosa causa de astenirse da simil detestando
peccato de biastema," ASV, *Esecutori*, bu. 61, regr. 1548–71, 5 July 1554, fo. 56r.

his right eye so that it comes out of his head, and then send him back to the usual place to be watched and medicated.[27]

This level of punishment was infrequent. Most people could expect a simple monetary fine, and extreme examples are balanced in the records of the *Esecutori* by frequent pardons that altered, reduced, or suspended an initial sentence. Nevertheless, impressing upon the public at large the magnitude of crimes of the tongue was a primary goal of the *Esecutori*, who made the punishment of the convicted blasphemer a highly visible and, as we can imagine, audible spectacle. Far removed from the thirteenth-century humiliation of being fined several *lire* or dunked in water, the creation of the *Esecutori* ushered in a period of great concern about blasphemy as the republic began systematically to bring cases to trial and punish them more severely. Although the relationship between language and honor will be discussed more at length in later chapters, it is important to note here the way that honor was clearly a key concern in the disciplining of speech. The state's reaction to public blasphemy, the creation of the *Esecutori*, and its visible prosecutions and punishments demonstrate the powerful way in which honor was primarily analyzed through public speech and in a public arena.

Establishing the boundaries defining acceptable language was so important that the *Esecutori* went so far as to erect visual reminders about verbal propriety. The magistracy placed plaques throughout the city to warn the Venetian public and its visitors of the potential punishments for blasphemy. Proclamations, both in stone and on paper, were both physically erected and verbally decreed; printed warnings were also most probably distributed by hand.[28] A handful of such proclamations

---

[27] "Far condur fra le due collone Zuan Maria Zeter ditto fachinetto . . . sopra un eminente soler alto di modo che possa ben esse visto, lo faciate incoronar dalla mitria ignominiosa, et metterli la lingua in giova, con il breve al petto che dica per biastemar . . . sara cosi un'hora, li farete tagliar detta lengua a traverso di modo che non possa piu parlar, et da poi li farete tagliar la man destra tal che messi separata dal busto et cavar l'ochio destro si che'l sii fuori della testa, et poi lo manderete al loco solito per governar et medicinarsi," Ibid., bu. 56, regr. 1561–82, 22 May 1563, fo. 11v.

[28] *Buste* 74 and 76 of the *Esecutori* contain the records of civic proclamations and surviving printed material, respectively. A typical proclamation, posted by the church of San Simeon Profetta, reads as follows. "Che non sia alcuna persona sia di che stato, grado ò condition, essser si voglia che ardisca à giuoca à dadi ne carte ne à qual si voglia altro giuoco nella corte vicina al magazen da vin alla Chiesa di San Simeon Profetta, ne in quella far strepiti tumultuar biastemmar dir parole dishoneste ne far altri rumori che disturbino e molestino

PARTI
PRESE
NELL'ECCELSO
Confeglio di Dieci.

1548. *adi* 19. *Ottobre, et altri diuerfi tempi*.

Sopra ogni forte di Biaftematori.

Stampate per Antonio Pinelli,
Stampator Ducale.

A S. Maria Formofa, in Cale del Mondo Nouo.

Figure 1. Frontispiece of printed proclamation from the Esecutori Contro la Bestemmia, *Esecutori Contro la Bestemmia* bu. 76. Copy made by the photo-reproduction section of the State Archive. Published with the permission of the Minister for Cultural Assets and Property, deed no. 50/2007.

have survived (Figures 1 and 2) and three stone inscriptions remain today in the *campi* of Santo Stefano, San Polo, and San Zaccaria (Figures 3 and 4).[29] We can picture how the entire urban fabric of Venice slowly became densely inscribed with visual reminders about spoken decorum as one by one, public sites prohibited blasphemy as a potentially dangerous verbal

---

li circonvicini . . . sotto pena alli transgressori et inobedienti di pagar lire cento cinquanta," ASV, *Esecutori*, bu. 74, 29 July 1586. Similar proclamations were announced and re-announced for approximately 60 other public sites before 1600.

[29] Another small, presumably privately made plaque of unknown date but probably from the seventeenth or eighteenth century, exists on the eastern side of *calle larga*, in Cannaregio, just north of the *Fondamenta della Misericordia*. On the existing plaques of the *Esecutori*, see Sabino Roppo, *Lapidario veneziano* (Venice: Editoria Universitaria, 1996), 68, 72.

V Piamente prouifto per quefto Confeglio del 1523. Adì 7. de Genaro che non
fia alcuna perfona in quefta Città, & de-
ftretto fia de che grado ftado, o conditiõ
che effer fi voglia,che ardifca Biaftemar,
ne maledir il Santiffimo nome di Dio,& Signor noftrõ
Miffer Giesù Chrifto,& la fua Gloriofa Madre Vergine Maria: ne in vilipendio loro dir parole vituperofe,
nè particularmête,nè in genere fotto nome della Corte Celeftial,nè efpreffamente,nè per alcun color, o for
made parole per alcun modo,cuer ingegno. Et poi del
1537. Adì 20. Decembre furono Creati tre Effecutori;a quali fu commeffa la fopradetta parte:& per la loro diligentia fi vede hormai quafi effer eftirpato cofi
deteftando peccato. Ilche è ftato,& è di grande honor
alla Republica noftra. E vero che li trifti, & fcelerati
huomini:quali non per amor della virtù, ma per timor
della pena fi attengòno dalle Biaftemme efpreffe, &
note ad ogn'vno hanno trouato noui modi de Biaftem
mar il Signor Dio con parole fcandolofe, & che cedo-
no in vilipendio di fua Maeftà come è, che alcuni non
poffendo dir a defpetto,dicono al confpetto,& al con-
fpettazzo de Dio te romperò i brazzi:te cauerò el cor:
parola che è indubitata Biaftemma: oltra che la è cau-
fa (fi come da predetti Effecutori ne è ftato efpofto)
che molti quali dicono al defpetto fi coprono:con dir
che hanno ditto al confpetto, & anco a' Teftimonij
hanno campo di metter in dubio il Giudice dicendo
non poffo giurar,che l'habbi più ditto al defpetto,che
al côfpetto: & cofi molti futterfugono la meritata pena. Al che effendo necefsario prouedera laude della
Maieftà Diuina: & per dignità della Rep. noftra.
L'Anderà parte che tutti quelli,che de cetero vferã-
A 2   no

Figure 2. Printed proclamation from the Esecutori Contro la Bestemmia, *Esecutori Contro la Bestemmia* bu. 76. Copy made by the photo-reproduction section of the State Archive. Published with the permission of the Minister for Cultural Assets and Property, deed no. 50/2007.

manifestation of popular life. In this way, social discipline was not only legislated against but visualized in a systematic fashion.

In tandem with the workings of the *Esecutori*, Venetian legal theory – in many ways separate and distinct from the rest of peninsular, Roman legal practice – also began to define blasphemy with increasing precision in the early modern period. These *giuriste* or legal specialists such as Marc'Antonio Tiraboscho, a clerk at the *Esecutori*, outlined a theory and practice for prosecuting this crime that both reflected and constructed the workings of the *Esecutori*.[30] Legal writers detailed how blasphemers

[30] For standard definitions of blasphemy, dating between the seventeenth and nineteenth centuries, see Ferro, *Dizionario*, vol. 1, 268; Benedetto Pasqualigo, *Della giurisprudenza criminale teorica e pratica* (Venice, 1731), 364–65; Lorenzo Priori, *Prattica criminale secondo*

Figure 3. Plaque prohibiting blasphemy and scandalous behavior, Campo Santo Stefano, 1633, repr. from *Sette lapidi con iscrizione nel centro storico veneziano*, ed. Orietta Monaco (Centro Formazione Maestranze Edili ed Affini di Venezia e Provincia). By permission of Italia Nostra, Venice.

could be denounced, how many witnesses were required, and how blasphemy should be punished. No blasphemy could be completely excused, but a proven lack of intent could lessen punishment, because "really blasphemy is when one considers the significance of the words."[31] All legal texts distinguished between blasphemy committed intelligently and

il rito delle leggi della serenissima republica di Venetia (Venice, 1622), 123; Marc'Antonio Tiraboscho, *Ristretto di prattica criminale che serve per la formatione de processi ad offesa* (Venice, 1636), 6–7. Although several of these *giuriste* lived much after the sixteenth century – Marco Ferro died in 1784 – their texts were designed as historical compilations and reflected the history and tradition of these legal ideas regarding both blasphemy as well as insults and hearsay, as discussed in subsequent chapters.

[31] "Veramente la bestemmia e quando si considera la significatione delle parole," Priori, *Prattica criminale*, 123.

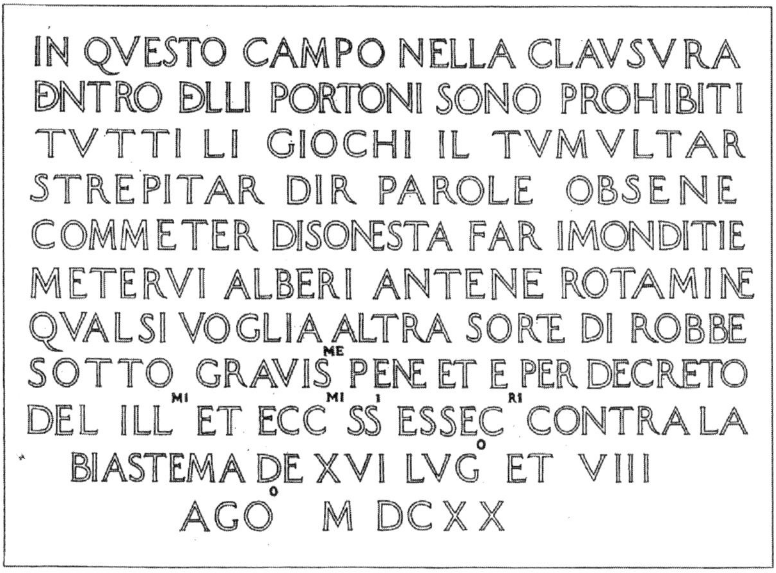

IN QVESTO CAMPO NELLA CLAVSVRA
ĐNTRO ĐLLI PORTONI SONO PROHIBITI
TVTTI LI GIOCHI IL TVMVLTAR
STREPITAR DIR PAROLE OBSENE
COMMETER DISONESTA FAR IMONDITIE
METERVI ALBERI ANTENE ROTAMIŊE
QVALSI VOGLIA ALTRA SORTE DI ROBBE
SOTTO GRAVIS PENE ET E PER DECRETO
DEL ILL ET ECC SS ESSEC CONTRA LA
BIASTEMA DE XVI LVG ET VIII
AGO M DCXX

Figure 4. Plaque prohibiting blasphemy and scandalous behavior, Campo San Zaccaria, 1620, repr. from *Sette lapidi con iscrizione nel centro storico veneziano,* ed. Orietta Monaco (Centro Formazione Maestranze Edili ed Affini di Venezia e Provincia). By permission of Italia Nostra, Venice.

consciously as opposed to words spoken irrationally, and the seriousness of the offence depended on the quality and intelligence of the person involved.[32] Paolo Sarpi agreed that "you cannot judge blasphemy without knowing the suspect."[33] Heretical blasphemy involving conscious intent fell under the jurisdiction of the Inquisition, while unintentional,

[32] "L'intenzione e la qualità delle persone; se un idiota, a cagion d'esempio, che non ha una chiara idea della distinzione delle Divine Persone, giurasse per il Corpo, o Sangue di Dio, cio non si chiamerebbe bestemmia, ma sarebbe soggetto soltanto a pena straordinaria, per la irriverenzza; ma non così pero se si trattasse di persona intelligente," Ferro, *Dizionario,* vol. 1, 268–69. "Quando uno biastemmasse in collera, o per ubbriachezza, sarebbe punibile con minor rigore ad arbitrio del Giudice . . . se un villano, ovvero altra persona ignorante dicesse al suo padrone, dio non puo far . . . ella veramente sarebbe biastemma, ma meritarebbe una qualche iscusa per l'ignoranza," Antonio Barbaro, *Pratica criminale del nobil homo sier Antonio Barbaro* (Venice, 1739), 202.

[33] "Non si potesse giudicar la Bestemmia senza conoscer il sospetto," Paolo Sarpi, *Discorso dell'origine forma, leggi, ed uso dell'ufficio dell'inquisitione nella città, e dominio di Venetia del P. Paolo dell'ordine de'servi* (Venice, 1638), 85. On the question of intent, see also Flynn, "Blasphemy and the Play of Anger," 42–43.

casual blasphemy – an unconsidered outburst – was the responsibility of civic magistracies and eventually the *Esecutori*.[34]

Unfortunately, legal theorists failed to demonstrate exactly how to distinguish between intelligent and less intelligent people, between casual cursing and well-developed, anti-Catholic doctrines. In the end, such decisions were left to individual Venetian judges. In any case, whether there was clearly established intent or not, blasphemy was unanimously considered a *delitto pubblico* – a crime not only against God but against public well being, as suggested by spectacular public punishments.[35] According to all legal writers, blasphemy was "one of the most monstrous and grave crimes that one can commit, and laws to punish delinquents [are] always more rigorous."[36] It was "the most bestial sin offending God."[37] Theoretical legal compendia are by no means perfect indicators of how blasphemy was practically defined and punished in sixteenth-century Venice, especially because Venetian judges were famous for flouting not only the conventions of Roman law, but also Venetian statutes and legal precedent itself, basing their decisions instead on their own individual reactions to individual cases.[38] Some of these legal texts written later may indicate generic Venetian definitions of blasphemy rather than its precise sixteenth-century meanings. Nevertheless, these texts demonstrate how Venetian legal culture began to pay close attention to

---

[34] "Nelle Bestemmie ereticali però la cognizione e il giudizio sono devoluti al Tribunale del Santo Officio, o Sacra Inquisitione, che questa Serenissima Repubblica quanto pia altrettanto saggia ammettè nello Stato fino al tempo del Pontefice Niccolo IV," Z.G. Grecchi, *Le formalità del processo criminale nel dominio veneto* (Padua, 1790), quoted in Gianni Buganza, "Il teste e la testimonianza tra magistratura secolare e magistratura ecclesiastica," *Atti dell'istituto veneto di scienze, lettere ed arti* 145 (1986–87), 261–2. "Nella pratica quotidiana la distinzione avveniva nel senso che al Sant'Uffizio finivano color cui poteva addebitarsi una vera e propria incredulità, oltre a chi accompagnava le consuete bestemmie con opinioni religiosamente eterodosse: davanti agli Esecutori comparivano solitamente dei violenti, o intemperanti, per cui tutto si concludeva nell'esclamazione o nel gesto ingiuriose verso Dio o la Vergine," Cozzi *Religione, moralità e giustizia*, 12.

[35] "Tanto e più grave, et scelerata, quando che vien fatta publicamente, et palesemente, con scandolo delle persone," Priori, *Prattica criminale*, 123. See also Ferro, *Dizionario*, vol. 1, 269.

[36] "Uno de'più enormi e gravi delitti che si possano commettere, furono sempremai rigorose le leggi nel punirne i delinquenti," Ferro, *Dizionario*, vol. 1, 269.

[37] "Più bestiale peccato, quale si commette in offesa immediate di Dio," Barbaro, *Pratica criminale*, 201.

[38] See Buganza, "Il teste," 269–70, and Shaw, *The Justice of Venice*, 11–18.

blasphemy in the early modern period, as the crime became both more distinct and disturbing at this time.

Despite the investment of more manpower to address this problem – both on the street and with the pen – blasphemy nevertheless proved difficult to control. Clever individuals constantly found new ways of insulting God that skirted old rules while the gaze of the *Esecutori* became evermore thorough over time, thereby generating new legislation during the course of the sixteenth century. For example, in 1553, the *Esecutori* specifically legislated against those who blasphemed in boats and galleys.[39] As Venetian fortunes were made and broken on the seas, it was especially important to protect against divine wrath in this particular setting. Maritime blasphemy was therefore not only heretical but also treasonous, potentially depriving the state of both the profits of trade and possible maritime victories. A decree from the Council of Ten, in 1571, sought to limit drinking and gaming in *osterie*, because "people speak with no respect for any quality of person; they blaspheme, gamble, display themselves, and finally perform every type of bad behavior."[40] Laws against blasphemy in the city and district of Venice were re-issued in 1548, 1555, 1568, 1569, and 1596, testifying to the persistence of the crime and the continued importance of prosecuting it. After a disturbing incident on 26 November 1593 in which a group of young men had paraded around the city insulting various saints, the Doge himself "wept copiously and [fell] to his knees with all his family," promising to continue to take the most severe action possible against this crime.[41] Blasphemy continued to be perceived as such a worrisome issue that, in 1575, the well-known Venetian print-maker Cesare Vecellio supplicated the Senate to protect the publishing

---

[39] ASV, *Esecutori*, 28 March 1553, fo. 6r. On maritime blasphemy, see Alain Cabantous, "Le blaspheme en milieu maritime a l'époque moderne," in *Injures et blasphèmes*, ed. Jean Delumeau (Paris: Imago, 1989), 83–98. For several examples of blasphemy on the high seas in the case of Venice, see ASV, *Avogaria di Comun, Penale*, bu. 37, fasc. 4, "Giana da Candia per ingiuria," 3 August 1600; and fasc. 52, "Antonio da Zante per ferimento," 1 January 1598.

[40] "Si parla senza rispetto d'ogni qualità di persone, biastemano, giuocano, luxuriano, et finalmente fanno ogni sorte di mancamento," ASV, *Consiglio dei Dieci, Comuni*, regr. 30, 31 July 1571, cited in Derosas, "Moralità e giustizia," 449.

[41] ASV, *Collegio*, series *Esposizioni Roma*, trans. Brian Pullan, cited in *Venice: A Documentary History*, ed. David Chambers and Brian Pullan (Oxford: Oxford University Press, 1992), 128.

privilege of his copper print "In Detestation of Blasphemy."[42] Vecellio described his print – the figures of Christ and saints, against whom blasphemies are uttered – as "useful to the Christian population."[43] Unlike many other sixteenth-century Venetian artists such as Titian or Veronese who painted classical, mythological subjects, Vecellio was an astute reporter of everyday events, suggesting that he personally witnessed blasphemy and was disturbed by it. This copper engraving does not appear to exist any longer or perhaps Vecellio never produced it. Nevertheless, Vecellio knew that there would be a market for his print, suggesting that blasphemy remained as concerning as ever through the last part of the sixteenth century.

Unfortunately for the historian, there remains little archival material from the workings of the *Esecutori* in this period. A brief sketch will serve as an outline. Between 1550 and 1570, as a sampling, the *Esecutori* punished 218 individuals for blasphemy and verbal crimes.[44] These sentences are brief, sparsely detailed, and typically do not offer any precise information about the location or nature of the crime. Additionally, no actual trial material from this period has survived. Occasionally, language indicates that the crime was particularly heinous, stating that the accused had used "vituperous words" or "horrendous blasphemy." Often

---

[42] "Che per autorita di questo Consilio si concesse a Cesare Vecellio, che altri, che egli, o chi harra causa da lui, non possa per lo spacio di anni quendeci stampar, o far stampar nel Dominio nostro, over altrove stampata in esso vender la figura per lui fatta in stampa di Rame in detestatione della Biastema, et come nella Supplicatione sua hora letta si contiene, sotto pena di ducati 300 da esser divisa in un terzo all'accusator, uno al Magistrato, che fara l'essecutione, et l'altro alla casa nostra dell'Arsenal. Dovendo osservar quanto e disposto per le leggi nostre in materia di stampe," ASV, *Senato Terra*, regr. 51, 28 September 1575, fo. 12r. This citation was given to me by professor E.J. Johnson.

[43] "Havendo io Cesare Vecellio Humillissimo servitor di vostra Serrenita con molta faticha e spesa di mia inventione fatta un stampa in figura et fattala intagliare diligentissimamente cosa la qual e devota et santa et utile al populo cristiano contro la biastemia del nome del Signor Dio nela qual si contiene a torno detta figura in breve parolle molti exempli cavati dalla sacra scrittura et molti altri santi contra che quelli i quali biastemano: la qual figura sta in questo modo cavata da queste sante parolle le quali gli sono atorno IN NOMINE IESU OMNE GENU FLECTATUR CELESTIUM TERRESTRIUM ET INFERNORUM. Prima indetta figura su il cielo con IL NOME DI IESU in mezo atorno corri di Angioli che adorano poi su la terra con la circoncisione del Signor con gli prencipi del mondo che ingenochi l'adorano di sotto uno inferno pieno di demoni che stanno con grandissima riverentia al detto Santo nome: la qual figura ha poi in quattro cantoni Proffeti con detti che laudano detto nome: questa e catolica," ASV, *Senato Terra*, filza 67, July–October 1575.

[44] This sample reflects the register of sentences from bu. 61, regr. 1548–71.

sentences state that blasphemers spoke *al cospetto di dio, al cospetazzo di dio*, or *al dispetto di dio*, representing the equivalent of renouncing God, doubting his omnipotence, or disregarding his power. This notable lack of description in sentencing indicates in part the systematic and efficient functioning of this magistracy, which transcribed its business quickly and succinctly; it was expensive and time-consuming to record unnecessary details. The absence of specific language also stems from the reality that words were always more evanescent than deeds, offering less lasting or tangible elements that could function as evidence.[45] However, the fact that specific words or language were never transcribed nevertheless remains remarkable. The exact content of spoken blasphemy was systematically avoided, and there exists little to no evidence of the specific crime for which this council was expressly created. Because these sentences offer so little information about the crimes they record, there is no easy way to categorize these cases. There exists no set of conditions such as the specific words used or the place they were spoken that make them easy to organize quantitatively into any chart, graph, or list.

Existing archival material seems to circle around an undefined, dangerously unmentionable center (a lacuna around which the historian is forced to circle as well), indicating the disturbing, supernatural power of blasphemous words. This language had already endangered civic piety once in its spoken incarnation. Its absence from written documents suggests that there was no need to incur additional risks or permit these words to live on by transcribing them for posterity. Despite the fact that no trials remain from the *Esecutori* in the sixteenth century, its sentences reveal a surprising amount of information about blasphemy and its repression in the sixteenth-century lagoon. Read along with related descriptions and extant cases of foul language from other courts in this period, the perceived meanings of blasphemy and the symbolic nature of its control come into focus. But first, the more pressing question: why was the republic suddenly much more troubled by this crime in the first half of the sixteenth century than ever before?

---

[45] The fleeting nature of words made false accusations of blasphemy common, motivated by vendettas or accusers in search of lucre and profit. For examples, see ASV, *Avogaria di Comun, Penale*, bu. 393, fasc. 13 "Candido Barbaro per bestemmie," 1660, no date given; *Consilio di Dieci, Parti Comuni*, filza 124, 26 August 1575, "Francesco Rompiasio."

The forces of the Counter-Reformation shook the early modern world as a whole and encouraged more attention to blasphemy across all of Europe. As we can recall, Stefano Guazzo's *La civil conversazione* was clearly influenced by the culture of the Counter-Reformation. When listing human vices, he began with the abuse of blasphemy, lamenting the horrors of this crime "which by now [is] spoken so much that there are few men who do not confirm and seal their speech with these ungodly and detestable voices," illuminating how the new culture of Catholic reform impressed itself upon social behavior.[46] Echoing Guazzo's worries, both civic and ecclesiastical legislation in France, Germany, Flanders, Spain, and England explicitly and frequently punished this crime and enforcement began to produce actual cases in court.[47] In Italy, Cosimo I published a strict ban on blasphemy in Florence in 1542, requiring all cities in the Grand Duchy to enact extra provisions to extinguish immoral vices which provoked divine wrath, the worst of which was blasphemy.[48]

---

[46] Guazzo, *La civil conversazione*, 42.

[47] See Elisabeth Belmas, "La monté des blasphèmes a l'âge moderne: Du moyen âge au XVIIe siècle," in Delumeau, *Injures et blasphèmes*, 13–33, and A. Cabantous, *Histoire du blasphème en occident : Fin XVIe-milieu XIXe siécle* (Paris: Editions Albin Michel, 1998), ch. 2–3. Louis XII of France introduced a strict ordinance against blasphemy in 1510, declaring that blasphemy was to be punishable with monetary fines, exposure to public insult and injury while being held in a pillory, or slitting the lips and cutting out the tongue. This law was reconfirmed by Francis I in 1514, and by successive leaders in 1524, 1534, 1535, and 1546; see Cozzi, *Religione, moralità e giustizia*, 6–7, and Derosas, "Moralità e giustizia," 436. In Germany, the repression of blasphemy was supervised by the *Reichspolizeiordnung* from 1530, and Flanders produced an edict issuing severe punishments against blasphemers in 1517. For blasphemy trials in the German context, see F. Loetz, *Mit Gott handeln: Von den Zuercher Gotteslaesterern der Fruehen Neuzeit zu einer Kulturgeschichte des Religioesen* (Goettingen: Vandenhoeck, 2002). The kingdom of Valencia in Spain became particularly concerned with blasphemy in the 1560s as both the Inquisition and local governments focused on public morality; see Stephen Haliczer, *Inquisition and Society in the Kingdom of Valencia, 1478–1834* (Berkeley: University of California Press, 1990), 296. On Spain, see also Flynn, "Blasphemy and the Play of Anger," 32. Swearing was also viewed more negatively in Elizabethan and Stuart England, where statutes against blasphemy were issued in 1533 and 1547. In 1648 both heresy and blasphemy were declared crimes meriting capital punishment; see David Nash, *Blasphemy in Modern Britain: 1789 to the Present* (Aldershot: Ashgate, 1999), 26–7; G.D. Nokes, *A History of the Crime of Blasphemy* (London: Sweet and Maxwell, 1928), 6–7, 12–15; Paolo Prodi, *Il sacramento del potere* (Bologna: Mulino, 1992), 384–85.

[48] "Molto necessario a ciascheduno Stato oltre qualunque altra provisione ordinar per le sue città e Dominio che li vitii al tutto si spenghino, quelli massime che sogliono provocare a ire el sommo e onnipotente Dio.... Peccato che più offende sua Maiestà che li altri, dal quale procedono nel mondo turbolentie e inopinati flagelli," *Legislazione toscana raccolta e illustrata da Lorenzo Cantini* (Florence, 1800), 210, cited in Derosas, "Moralità e giustizia," 436–37.

In 1559, the senate of Milan issued an edict against blasphemy, as did pope Pius V for the papal states in 1564, which stated that the crime was punishable by public beating, exile, galley work, and the piercing of the tongue.[49] As we have seen, Venice similarly sought to re-define and enforce the boundaries between heretical and non-heretical language. In addition, because Venice was close to the lands where the Reformation flourished, and because of its trade relationship with German merchants, the city was particularly exposed to Protestantism and the ideas of Martin Luther made themselves felt forcefully and early in Venice.[50] The sixteenth-century papacy was particularly worried about the infiltration of Reformation ideas in the lagoon, and this resulted in the arrival of the Holy Office in Venice in 1547 to confront the growth of heresy. As the most conspicuous sign of the effects of the Counter-Reformation on the city, the Inquisition came to weed out a range of heretical crimes associated with Protestantism, including blasphemy.[51]

Increased concern for blasphemy also resulted from new political and economic pressures facing the Venetian state. Venice – once a great mainland and Mediterranean empire – suffered substantial territorial losses both on the *terraferma* and sea throughout the first half of the sixteenth century. In response to the Turkish capture of Modone in 1500 – a Peloponnesian island regularly used by the Venetian fleet and considered one of the strategic "eyes" of the republic – the chronicler Sanudo

---

[49] Peter Burke, *The Historical Anthropology of Early Modern Italy: Essays on Perception and Cummunication* (Cambridge: Cambridge University Press, 1987), 102; Flynn, "Blasphemy and the Play of Anger," 30.

[50] On the Protestant Reformation in Italy and Venice, see Dermot Fenlon, *Heresy and Obedience in Tridentine Italy* (Cambridge, MA: Harvard University Press, 1972); Elizabeth Gleason, *Gasparo Contarini: Venice, Rome, and Reform* (Berkeley: University of California Press, 1993); John Martin, *Venice's Hidden Enemies: Italian Heretics in a Renaissance City* (Berkeley: University of California Press, 1993).

[51] According to jurists, heretical blasphemy involved premeditated, intentional, heretical thought and fell under the jurisdiction of the church and the office of the Inquisition. This study is more concerned with everyday, unruly verbal outbursts that fell instead under civic jurisdiction and the discipline of the *Esecutori*. As legal compendia have shown, there often existed a fine line between the two, but trials for heretical blasphemy (and not casual blasphemy) abound in the records of the *Sant'Uffizio*. For a few typical cases of heretical blasphemy and their language as distinct from non-heretical blasphemy, see for instance the trial of brother Francesco de Calcagno, ASV, *Sant'Uffizio*, bu. 8, 7 February 1550, who said that "the host and the chalice are all bullshit," or the case of Domenico Longino (bu. 33, 14 November 1573) who sang a song about the pope buggering a cardinal.

reported that the Council of Ten immediately reacted "with many pro-visions" to correct Venetian immorality and the particular problem of blasphemy.[52] Venice lost the majority of its mainland territories following the battle of Agnadello in 1509. Its colony on Corfu was lost to Ottoman forces in 1537 – immediately preceding the creation of the *Esecutori*. Although most of the mainland territory was recovered, the trauma of such losses endured. Sanudo recorded the words of a letter written by an anonymous "servant of God," demanding that the state react more forcefully to the Turkish threat. He proclaimed, "arm yourselves with true patience and take steps against the injustices, blasphemies, the oppression of the poor and ecclesiastical property, sacrilege and filthy lasciviousness that you practice without fear in your city."[53] Venice also suffered repeated bouts of plague at the turn of the sixteenth century. Sanudo related the words of a traveling friar in December of 1497 who asserted:

> If we would like to address the causes that induce the plague, these are the horrendous sins the people practice: blaspheming God and the saints, the schools of sodomy, the infinite contracts of usury that are undertaken at the Rialto, and everywhere the selling of justice, acting in favor of the rich and against the poor.[54]

City authorities targeted immoral living as the cause of the republic's downturned fortunes, reflected in increasingly severe attitudes towards luxury expenditure, prostitution, sodomy, lascivious behavior, and blas-phemy.[55] Blasphemy was a crime that disrupted civic tranquility; it was

---

[52] Sanudo, *I diarii*, vol. 3, 688.

[53] "Armatevi di vera patientia e provedete a le iniustitie, blasfemie, oppressione di poveri e beni ecclesiastici, sacrilegii et sporcata luxuria che se fa in la terra vostra senza timor," Ibid., 626.

[54] "Se voria remediar a le cause che induce la peste, ch'è li peccati orendi che si fa: e biastemar Dio e santi; le scole di le sodomie; li infiniti contrati usurarii si fa a Rialto; e per tutto el vender di la justicia et far in favor dil richo et contra il povero," Ibid., vol. 1, 836. See also vol. 22, 97–98.

[55] "The view that moral corruption was the decisive reason for the decline of Venetian power was expressed not only by private citizens but was an officially held and recognized thesis," Felix Gilbert, "Venice in the Crisis of the League of Cambrai," in Hale, *Renaissance Venice*, 277. See also Cozzi, *Religione, moralità e giustizia*, 5–8, and Derosas, "Moralità e giustizia," 438. Even before the creation of the *Esecutori*, this perceived connection between public behavior and the fate of the city was evidenced in late-fifteenth century sumptuary legislation and by the re-instatement and empowerment of the *Provveditori Sopra le Pompe* in 1512, which

an offense resulting in numerous social consequences such as plague, famine, and economic loss, so that preserving social order necessarily entailed controlling such outbursts. The trying events of the beginning of the sixteenth century pushed the republic to eliminate the behaviors that stirred up divine wrath and incurred divine punishment, transforming the political fear of external enemies into a fear of internal corruption and vice.

Attention to blasphemy as a result of the Reformation and immoral behavior, however, was commonplace in the early modern period. Natural disasters in Florence in the middle of the sixteenth century similarly inspired laws against sodomy as people feared that earthquakes and lightning bolts were portents of divine ruin meriting reforms to correct civic behavior.[56] The forces of the Reformation and fear of divine punishment only partly explain Venetian anxieties about correct verbal behavior. Equally pressing were concerns about regularizing the numerous foreigners and immigrants present in the city. Generations of scholars have emphasized the multi-ethnic nature of Venetian culture. Already at the end of the fifteenth century, Philippe de Commynes observed that in Venice, "most of the people are foreigners." Girolamo Priuli similarly noted that "with the exception of the patricians and some *cittadini*, all the rest are foreigners and very few are Venetians."[57]

Adding to its already cosmopolitan base, sixteenth-century Venice underwent additional and substantial demographic change, including a wave of immigration after its military defeat at Agnadello in 1509. Refugees, unassimilated and unfamiliar with Venetian mores, crowded the city and brought with them crime and civic unrest.[58] The city and its

instituted a code restricting Venetian luxury expenditures on dress, housing, and festivities in the wake of Agnadello. See Giulio Bistort, *Il magistrato alle pompe della repubblica di Venezia* (Venice: Sodietà, 1912), 51.

[56] Michael Rocke, *Forbidden Friendships: Homosexuality and Male Culture in Renaissance Florence* (New York: Oxford University Press, 1996), 232–33.

[57] Philippe de Commynes, *Mémoires*, ed. Joseph Calmette (Paris: Societe D'Edition, 1965–81), vol. 3, 114; Girolamo Priuli, *I diarii di Girolamo Priuli [A.A. 1499–1512]*, ed. Roberto Cessi, *Rerum italicarum scriptores* 24, pt. 3, vol. 4 (Bologna, 1938), 101, both cited in *Venice Reconsidered: The History and Civilization of an Italian City State, 1297–1797*, ed. John Jeffires Martin and Dennis Romano (Baltimore: The Johns Hopkins University Press, 2000) 20–21.

[58] "The city . . . became more crowded than ever. Nobles and *popolari* had taken refuge there from cities occupied by the enemy and found much in its favour; little by little refugee peasants from the devastated countryside sought asylum there, confident that in Venice,

surrounding mainland territories were also repeatedly struck by famine in this period, driving the poor and hungry into the urban center in search of sustenance. In the spring of 1527, for instance, Sanudo noted that many foreigners had come to live in the city, driving up the prices of food. In the winter of 1527–28, Sanudo recorded

> a great horde of poor by day and by night, and many peasants are beginning to come here with their children, looking for food, because of the great famine outside. . . . And many have come from the provinces of Vicenza and Brescia – a shocking thing. You cannot hear mass without ten paupers coming to beg for alms, or open your purse to buy something without the poor asking for a farthing. Late in the evening, they go knocking at the doors, and crying through the streets, "I am dying of hunger!" Yet no public measures are taken against this.[59]

In addition, as Venice changed from a commercial to a manufacturing center in the course of the sixteenth century, it came to rely on an new immigrant labor force.[60] New forms of work found in the Arsenal and the textile industry were quickly expanding and replacing mercantile trade, thereby bringing more people and social problems to the city. Even in 1581, Francesco Sansovino continued to note that "peoples from the most distant parts of the world gather here to trade and to conduct

the place of fabled wealth and abundance, a roof and subsistence would not be wanting. . . . There were too many people amid too much confusion. The religious, and laymen who like Priuli were prompted by a concern for tradition, lamented the pleasure-seeking atmosphere of certain quarters of the city, the modish disregard for civil and religious duties, the adoption of French fashions by men and women, and the spread of blasphemy. . . . Some measures had to be taken to cope with this delinquency," Cozzi, "Authority and Law," 311. "Veramente conchorevanno et giongevano a Venettia tante vilane cum li putti loro in brazo et cum la sua roba et li polami sui et robe da vivere, che hera zertamente quasi incredibile potere pensare il numero grande di questi contadini capitavanno continuamente a Venetia," Girolamo Priuli, *I diarii*, vol. 4, 315–23. On the relationship between poverty, immigration, and crime, see Piero Camporesi, *Il pane selvaggio* (Bologna: Mulino, 1980), 63–72.

[59] Sanudo, *I diarii*, vol. 44, 599; vol. 45, 356; vol. 46, 550, 612, cited in Pullan, *Rich and Poor*, 243–44.

[60] On economic and social change in the sixteenth century, see Martin, *Venice's Hidden Enemies*, 152–59.

business."[61] Writers like Commynes, Priuli, Sanudo, and Sansovino may have exaggerated, but not by much.

The permeable nature of Venetian civic space uniquely permitted such levels of immigration. Unlike other Italian cities, Venice had no gates to close to prevent the comings and goings of people. In addition, because of its strategic position between the Mediterranean sea and trans-alpine passes, it was both a commercial hub and departure point for travel to and from the East, making it a bustling stage for the movements of travelers and traders. Venice experienced a continual influx of people from around Europe and the Mediterranean – merchants, pilgrims, crusaders, travelers, sailors, day laborers, servants, and slaves. It was home to large, permanent communities of Albanians, Greeks, Armenians, French, and Germans, and was perhaps the most cosmopolitan city in early modern Europe. As Thomas Coryat praised it in his 1611 travel account, Venice was so diverse that the Piazza San Marco in fact represented and reflected the world at large.

> Here you may both see all manner of fashions of attire, and heare all the languages of Christendome, besides those that are spoken by the barbarous Ethnickes...a man may very properly call it rather Orbis than Urbis forum, that is, a market place of the world, not of the citie.[62]

Venetian space and its resulting polyglot population therefore demanded different mechanisms for social regulation. Shifting social conditions, immigration, and waves of foreigners arriving in the city loomed large among the driving forces behind the enforcement of a stricter code of civic language.

The creation and work of the *Esecutori* were motivated by these factors. In effect, as new numbers of people entered the city, the state sought to define civic identity clearly through the enforcement of proper language

---

[61] Franceesco Sansovino, *Venetia città nobilissima et singolare, con aggiunta da Giustiniano Martinioni* (1663; reprint, Venice: Filippi, 1968), vol. 1, 4. On foreigners in Venice, see Brunehilde Imhaus, *Le minoranze orientali a venezia, 1300–1510* (Rome: Il Veltro, 1997), and Giorgio Fedalto, "Stranieri a Venezia e a Padova," in *Storia della cultura veneta*, vol. 3:1, ed. Arnaldi and Stocchi, 499–503. The population statistics presented by Daniele Beltrami similarly demonstrate massive immigration; see Chapter 5, n. 25.

[62] Thomas Coryat, *Coryat's Crudities*, vol. 1 (Glasgow: James Maclehose and Sons, 1905), 314.

for immigrants and newcomers. In the course of the sixteenth century, the *Esecutori* were assigned several additional responsibilities – among those, in 1539, jurisdiction over gambling, and in 1583, the registration of foreigners present in the city. Both of these tasks were intrinsically connected to perceptions and prosecution of blasphemy.[63] The *Esecutori* were neither the first nor the last to establish a connection between gambling and blasphemy, which had been clearly recognized in the Middle Ages. The sermons of San Bernardino of Siena, well known to Renaissance Italians, had regularly emphasized these related vices.[64] However, the assignment of overseeing this crime to the *Esecutori* confirmed the fact that gambling and blasphemy were perceived as crimes of foreigners, who were in fact over-represented in gambling prosecutions.[65] The work of registering and monitoring foreigners in the city was also neither incidental nor unrelated to the work of patrolling blasphemy. Eighty-two of the 218 names listed in the sentences of the *Esecutori* sampled in this period are of foreign origin: meaning, they were either recent immigrants or came from families that were originally foreign. This list includes names such as Beltrame da Pui Francese, Tognetto Greicho, Mathio Napolitan, or Nicola da Bologna, with a large number of names indicating origins in nearby Friuli in particular. Although it is impossible to know how long a foreigner had lived in the city, the high number of non-Venetian names in the *Esecutori*'s sentences for blasphemy suggests that this magistracy aimed to instruct foreigners in the correct use of public language. The *Esecutori* later decreed in 1628 that

> foreigners, and those of alien jurisdiction with most pernicious effects . . . can wound to the quick the interests of our government, with the introduction of fraud, of continual gambling, and likewise

---

[63] In addition, in 1541 the council was assigned the responsibility of overseeing sacred sites, in 1543 printing and the illegal sales of unauthorized texts, in 1553 prostitution, in 1571 the minor crimes of nobles, in 1577 clandestine marriages and false promises of marriage, and in 1578 additional jurisdiction over prostitutes. As chaotic and fragmentary as these tasks might seem, this was no random grouping. The *Esecutori* sought to eliminate all public behavior that was immodest and impious, as well as behavior that threatened to produce civic agitation.

[64] See San Bernardino da Siena, *Prediche vulgari sul campo di Siena, 1427*, ed. Carlo Delcorno, vol. 1 (Milan: Rusconi, 1989), 182, 429–31, 732.

[65] See Jonathan Walker "Gambling and Venetian Noblemen, c. 1500–1700," *Past and Present* 162 (1999): 38, 42, 46. On the implicit connection between foreigners and crime, see Imhaus, *Le minoranze*, 333–73.

the most grave losses, the deviation and ruin of youth and families, incredible disturbances of houses, of property, of good manners.[66]

Although this passage does not discuss language per se, it nonetheless points to the concrete connections this magistracy made between foreigners and deleterious effects of their indecent behavior in the city.

In addition, historians have noted how sixteenth-century attitudes toward the poor became progressively more negative, reversing more traditional medieval attitudes of benevolence. The destitute, who once represented the image of Christ, became increasingly perceived as disgusting, degenerate vagabonds who needed to be eliminated from the sixteenth-century city.[67] Of the 218 total cases in this sampling, only four nobles were punished for spoken blasphemy. Of the 214 non-nobles punished, many were servants, gondoliers, clothing-manufacturers, hatmakers, fruit-sellers, mirror-makers, printers, bread-bakers, porters, and tailors – jobs often taken on by foreigners. Admittedly, the absence of nobles in sentencing is not surprising. Nobles were often able to flout the law, and various courts often did not force nobles to even answer charges or testify. Nobles simply blasphemed and got away with it as their status often placed them beyond the reach of justice.[68] In addition, because the Venetian noble class was closed and numerically restricted, nobles naturally represented a smaller proportion of the Venetian population in general.[69] The sentences of the *Esecutori* nevertheless suggest additional speculative connections between foreigners, the poor, and blasphemy. Although many who came to Venice found employment, immigrants and foreigners often arrived with no prospects for work. Blasphemy was typically understood to be intrinsically connected to

---

[66] ASV, *Esecutori*, December 1628, cited in Walker, "Gambling," 37; see also 46–47.

[67] On changing attitudes towards the poor in sixteenth-century Venice and Europe, see Peter Burke, *Popular Culture in Early Modern Europe* (New York: Harper and Row, 1978), 207–43; *Il libro dei vagabondi*, ed. Piero Camporesi (Turin: Einaudi, 1973), xiv, xcvii–xcix; Pullan, *Rich and Poor*, 186, 221, 361–71.

[68] Shaw, *The Justice of Venice*, 103. By contrast, Alain Cabantous suggests that if nobles were under-represented in blasphemy cases, it was because they were better able to control their tongues and they knew not to blaspheme in public. See Cabantous, *Histoire du blasphème*, 104–5.

[69] Stanley Chojnacki, "Social Identity in Renaissance Venice: The Second Serrata," *Renaissance Studies* 8 (1994): 341–58.

other immoral, deviant behavior associated with the impoverished.[70] Put simply, the tasks assigned the *Esecutori* made clear the perceived nexus conflating foreigners, joblessness, prostitution, gambling, violence, and blasphemy.[71]

Defining the boundary between mannered and unmannered speech was therefore a means by which the Venetian state sought to define itself and its residents in a moment of intense demographic change. As one historian of Venice has noted, "the mother tongue constitutes, for a minority, the biggest obstacle to assimilation; nevertheless language is also one of the principal means of integration."[72] The open lagoon city could not stop immigration with walls or physical checkpoints, but it could erect symbolic barriers defining inclusion and exclusion such as those requiring proper speech. Citizenship, broadly defined, entailed instruction in and obedience to specific codes of verbal decorum. In this way, Venice enforced the boundaries around the sociolinguistic concept of a "speech community." It demonstrated through legal and disciplinary means that Venetians shared a common language, composed not only of dialect, vocabulary, and grammar, but of conceptions of politeness, ritual, and religious values.[73] The Venetian state imposed correct forms of language to define community identity, as "a fully competent member of a speech community . . . needs to know how, when and where to speak."[74] The *Esecutori* aimed to teach what sociolinguists call "communicative competence" – referring to the social knowledge needed to communicate effectively in culturally significant settings, or the ability to decide what types of verbal messages were appropriate in the Venetian

---

[70] To vagabonds were attributed "delitti enormi e scandalosi, in modo che l'esercizio di mendicare in Roma dirsi poteva una scuola di furto, d'impurità, di bestemmia, di sfrenatezza e d'ogni sorta di abbominazione," *La mendicità proveduta, nella città di Roma coll'ospizio publico* (Rome, 1693), 24, cited in Camporesi, *Il pane selvaggio*, 229; "Il peggio è che tra questa spaventosa moltitudine di veri poveri, ve n'era un'altra maggiore, e da far più paura assai, de'finti, degli scipoerati, e de'vagabondi, che fattosi un mestiere della guidoneria, tutte le lor manifatture consistevano in ladronecci, in disonestà, in bestemmie, in impietà e in ogni sorta d'abbominazione," *Il mendicare abolito nella città di Montalbano da un pubblico uffizio di carità* (Florence, 1693), 19–20, cited in Camporesi, *Il pane selvaggio*, 229–30. See also Derosas, "Moralità e giustizia," 450–51.

[71] See Cozzi, *Religione, moralità, e giustizia*, 35, and Derosas, "Moralità e giustizia," 456–57.

[72] Imhaus, *Le minoranze*, 401.

[73] On speech community, see Gumperz and Hymes, *Directions in Sociolinguistics*, vi, 16.

[74] Lesley Milroy, *Language and Social Networks* (Baltimore: The Johns Hopkins University Press, 1980), 108.

context.[75] A certain social knowledge – the ability to control unruly verbal outbursts and practice mannered speech – was deemed necessary for membership in the Venetian community. Anxiety about blasphemy was, in part, anxiety about outsiders, foreigners, and the "other" entering the lagoon in large numbers.

Such an understanding of blasphemy fits into a longstanding European tendency to associate language and difference. Such connections predated Christianity, as the Greeks first called foreigners barbarians or "babblers" to distinguish Greek speakers from those who spoke other languages or vulgarized dialects of Greek. The biblical *locus classicus* of blasphemy is in Leviticus 24:10–23. Here, a foreigner to Jewish rules (the son of an Israelite and an Egyptian) commits blasphemy by cursing God. As a result, Moses removes the offender to outside the camp, where he has him stoned to death, stating that "aliens as well as citizens, when they blaspheme the Name, shall be put to death." This biblical example, like Venetian cases, links language and the treatment of outsiders or "others," as blasphemy represented a language that pushed the boundaries of amicable co-existence between those within a community and those entering and trying to integrate from outside.[76] Before the conversion of the Roman Empire to Christianity, church leaders similarly used blasphemy as means of marking the un-Christian behavior of Jews, pagans, and heretics and of drawing a firm distinction between church members and outsiders.[77] To a certain degree historically, and particularly in sixteenth-century Venice, blasphemy represented a discourse for constructing alterity. It was a rhetoric with which those at the center could confer a marginal status onto others. It allowed groups to define identity and difference within the Christian community, and learning to manage the expression of blasphemy functioned as a rite of passage for entrance into the boundaries of community life. Indeed, we have already seen how writers of conduct literature emphasized that speech should naturally reflect one's geographical origins so that in a general sense,

---

[75] On communicative competence, see Gumperz and Hymes, *Directions in Sociolinguistics*, vii; Romaine, *Language in Society*, 24.

[76] On blasphemy in Leviticus, see David Lawton, *Blasphemy* (Philadelphia: University of Pennsylvania Press, 1993), 42.

[77] See Leveleux, *La parole interdite*, and Clive Unsworth, "Blasphemy, Cultural Divergence and Legal Relativism," *The Modern Law Review* 58 (1995): 670.

they too acknowledged the links between language, comportment, and community.

Additional instruction in verbal decorum included the respect of the noble class as representative of the state. In the overall period between 1550 and 1590, 30 cases before the *Esecutori* involved one person insulting another. Seven of these 30 were cases of damaging words against a churchman – cases which clearly fell under the stated jurisdiction of the *Esecutori*. However, 23 of these cases involved one individual verbally insulting another, with no clear indication of blasphemy or impiety. Of these 23 cases, 20 were trials initiated by nobles against the insults of commoners. Two typical sentences ran as follows. "Menega the washerwoman ... having spoke injurious words to a son of the nobleman sir Daniel Condulmer, against the honor and reputation of this nobleman at his house, is condemned to be confined to the women's prison for one month." "Agustin Zambon, hat maker, who usually keeps shop at the bridge of San Maritio, for having used unsuitable words against the nobleman Andrea Marcello ... is confined to prison for six months."[78] Only two cases involved non-nobles accusing nobles, and one case exists of a non-noble accusing a non-noble.

The fact that the *Esecutori* dealt with 20 instances of commoners insulting nobles is puzzling. If these outbursts had involved blasphemous insults, they would be comprehensible; however, the wording of these sentences contains no indication of blasphemy – only aggressive language. Though these 20 cases represent only 10 percent of all trials in this sampling, run-of-the-mill verbal insults in no way fell under the jurisdiction of the *Esecutori*. This suggests that some nobles used the office of the *Esecutori* to seek out and punish verbal assaults against the nobility.[79] Trials and sentencing worked to restore the honor undermined

---

[78] "Menega lavandara ... haver detto parole ingiurose ad un fiol del nobel homo ser Daniel Condulmer et contra l'honor et fama di detto nobel homo a casa sua, l'hanno condennata a star nella pregione delle donne per mese uno," ASV, *Esecutori*, bu. 56, regr. 1561–82, 14 November 1563, fo. 122v; "Agustin Zambon capeller solito tener bottega al ponte de s. maritio haver usato parole non convenienti contra il nobel homo Andrea Marcello ... star mesi sei in preggion," Ibid., bu. 57, regr. 1582–97, 20 September 1585, fo. 46v.

[79] Guido Ruggiero found a similar pattern of insults against the state, superiors, and nobles in the Trecento. He noted a greater number of prosecutions against the verbal aggression of nobles that does not appear to be the case in the sixteenth-century trials of either the *Esecutori*, or as we shall see, the *Avogaria di Comun*. See Ruggiero, *Violence*, 66–67, 77–79, 96–98, 125–37.

by unruly language, whether it was blasphemous or not. As we have seen, prescriptive literature, legislative materials, and archival documents at large consistently refer to blasphemy as a crime of honor. That is to say, it was not simply a spiritual or civic crime, but a crime symbolically offending the honor of God, Mary, and the saints, the honor of the state, or in this case, the honor of nobles as its representatives. The fact that this magistracy let alone heard and further prosecuted these cases suggests that insulting nobles functioned as a form of blasphemy, as the Venetian order located in class hierarchy reflected divine will. Blasphemy was cast as aggressive language up the social scale, including God and his more immediate representatives, the Venetian nobility. As we shall see, the prosecution of blasphemy that insulted nobles closely conformed to the way that other state magistracies such as the *Avogaria di Comun* punished insults against the patricians and their sense of honor.

Historians have long demonstrated the myriad and powerful connections between gender and the Venetian state. Was blasphemy gendered? In other words, if prosecuting blasphemy functioned as a means of state-building, did men and women practice blasphemy differently, or was the control of gendered speech implicit in state formation as well? Though both the historians Derosas and Cozzi note the significant presence of women in blasphemy trials in the seventeenth-century, this did not seem to be the case earlier. Between 1550 and 1570, 26 women were charged with blasphemy – approximately 12 percent of the cases surveyed in this period – one of whom had her tongue removed. In her book *The Nobility and Excellence of Women and the Defects and Shortcomings of Men* (1600), Lucrezia Marinella asserted that

> as blasphemy is wicked and foul, women remain far from it and the contempt for God and the saints, as they are most religious and most devout, which is something that has no need of proof. But the typical man, hardly fearful of divine justice or His power, often bursts out in horrendous and wicked blasphemy.[80]

---

[80] "Scelerati, e iniqui che sono, dalle donne sono lontane le bestemmie, e il disprezzo di Dio e de'Santi, come quelle, che sono religiosissime, e devotissime; cosa che non ha bisogno di prova; ma il buon maschio poco timoroso della divina giustitia, e della sua potenza prorompe spesso in bestemmie horrende, e inique," Lucrezia Marinella, *Le nobilità et eccellenze delle donne, et i diffetti e mancamenti degli huomini* (Venice, 1600), 79r.

Marinella cited numerous examples of blaspheming men from antiquity, mythology, and the Bible, noting the complete absence of female
examples. Men, she claimed, would not be taken seriously if they did not
blaspheme and were always looking for new turns of phrase by which to
outdo one another.[81] Marinella's ideas cannot be taken seriously because
she discussed blasphemy as it suited the purpose of her book: to praise
the female sex and criticize men. Nevertheless, she provides a feminine
interpretation of the phenomenon of male blasphemy, which she argued
was a means of displaying virility.

In addition, blasphemy regularly punctuated the speech of the characters of the Paduan playwright Angelo Beolco, also known as Ruzante,
whose works were performed in Venice and the Veneto in the first quarter
of the sixteenth century. Here too, blasphemy appeared to function as a
masculine weapon. An illegitimate child of the authoritarian patriarch
of a minor noble family, Ruzante used his plays to express his identi-
fication with "the peasants' exclusion from governing institutions and
the blocking of their access to wealth."[82] In the period between 1517
and 1536, Ruzante's plays "presented peasant concerns to an audience
of Venetian nobles who governed them."[83] Though his works remain
composed, theatrical texts, his plays were popular and widely attended;
we can safely assume that, to a great degree, his language reflected both
contemporary and popular usage as well as perceptions of it. His play
Bilora, for instance, influenced by Lucian's *Tyrannicide* that had been
translated into Italian and published in Venice in 1516, presents a case
of blasphemy. In this story, the peasant Bilora schemes to recover his
wife who has been stolen by a Venetian merchant named Andronico.
In a central scene, Bilora convinces his friend Pitaro to go and speak to
Andronico on his behalf. If Andronico resists, Bilora says, "tell him that I

---

[81] "Veniva trattato da un'huomo di poco conto un gentilhuomo di Bologna savio e discreto, il
    quale essendo andato alla corte di un Principe, e pratticando con gli altri cortigiani, quando
    bisognava, che affermasse alcuna cosa con giuramento, diceva al corpo della gallina, per la
    qual cosa da'gli altri di corte veniva reputato un buffone, e un'huomo di poca levatura, e
    bisognò alla fine che ancor egli cominciasse à trovar Christo e i Santi, per non essere tenuto
    un'huomo da niente," Ibid.

[82] Linda L. Carroll, "A Nontheistic Paradise in Renaissance Padua," *The Sixteenth Century
    Journal* 24 (1993): 881.

[83] Linda L. Carroll, "Ruzante's Early Adaptations from More and Erasmus," *Italica* 66 (1989):
    29.

am a big, bad thug and that I blaspheme, and tell him that I was a soldier: do not forget, see!"[84] Blaspheming against the Madonna and God, Bilora states: "If he gives her to me, it is better, and if not, by the blood of the Virgin Mary, I will pull the thorn out of his ass."[85] When Pitaro returns, unsuccessful, from his meeting with Andronico, Bilora exclaims:

> By the blood of God-be-with-you, you really must know how to talk! You did not yell or say that I have been banished, you did not blaspheme, nothing! My God, blood of a she-wolf, what kind of pox are you? If you had blasphemed, if you had said that I was banished, I am certain that he would have given her back to me.[86]

In the following scene, giving up on his friend's help, Bilora contemplates how he will single-handedly force Andronico to return his wife.

> He will be afraid if I speak to him like a Spanish soldier, and its seems like there are more than eight of them. I had better practice a bit how I will do this. Let's see now, I will pull out the knife. Let me see if it gleams. Pox, it is not shiny. He will not be afraid. Let us say, pardon my language, that he is this twat and I am myself, Bilora, who knows how to thrust when he wants [thrusting a knife into and out of a jug, imitating both injury and rape]. So I will start to blaspheme and pull out all the Christ-have-mercies that there are in Padua, as well as the Blessed-Mothers and Lord-Be-With-Yous. . . . Cunt that generated you, you old damned impotent Jew. May this violate you! I'm sure going to get rid of that itch in your ass. [to himself:] Ok, thrust now, come on, and then I'll grab his clothes and take them for myself, and I'll leave him here splattered on the ground like a big cow plop.[87]

---

[84] "Dighe pur ch'a son sbraoso e biastemè, e dighe ch'a soon stò soldò, no ve'l desmenteghè vi," Ruzante, *Bilora, in Teatro Italiano: le origini e il rinascimento*, ed. Silvio D'Amico (Milan: Nuova Accademia, 1955), 491.

[85] "Se'l me la dà, Dio con ben; se anca no, al sangue della Verghene Malgatera, che ghe parerò el verin dal culo," Ibid., 492.

[86] "Mo al sangue de Domenesteche! a saì ben dire. A no gh'aí criò, dito che a supia sbandizò, e sì n'aì biastemò, nè niente, vu! Miedio, sangue del mal dela lova, da che cànchero sìvu? S'aessè biastemò, e se aessè dito ch'a' giera sbandizò, a tegno fremamèn che'l me l'arae dò," Ibid., 498.

[87] "L'harà paura se a fago a sto muò. E po faelerò da soldò spagnaruolo che i sonerà pì d'oto. L'è miegio che proa un pò a che muò farè. Orbentena, a cavarè fuora la cortela. Làgme vere se la luse. Càncaro, la n'è tropo lusente. El n'harà tropo paura. E po a meto – verbo grazia – che questo cotale supie elo, e mi supie mi, Bilora, che sa ben menare quando el vuole. E sì a scomenzerè a biastemmare e a catare quanti Cristelèisone è in Pava, e la Madrebeata

Bilora comically rehearsed mixing blasphemy with physical threats, including a phallically thrusting knife, in the hopes of defeating his adversary. By showing Andronico that he was not afraid of even God's wrath – that he was, in fact, fearless – he would clearly prove that he was not afraid of Andronico, his male rival for his wife's affection.

Like Marinella and Ruzante, historians of blasphemy have tended to argue that blasphemy was primarily a manifestation "of male energy and virility," yet no plausible theory has been offered to explain this.[88] As the above figures prove, women did blaspheme, but either blasphemed less or entered the records of the *Esecutori* less, perhaps because they moved in a more narrow public sphere than men did and therefore were prosecuted less frequently, though women's public presence in Venice, we shall see, is much debated. In any case, it is unclear why women were prosecuted for blasphemy less than men, especially because as cases of insults and gossip will reveal, women were clearly adept and colorful speakers who transgressed the rules of spoken decorum on par with their male counterparts.

The *Esecutori* was but one of several magistracies that the Venetian Council of Ten created in the sixteenth century in order to articulate its powers and extend its control.[89] Its creation was part of a wider process of developing the necessary instruments that would guarantee the state the powers for repressive intervention – a process that occurred

---

e il Dominesteco. Pota chi te inzenderò, e de quel zodìo, vecio sgureguro maledeto, che tu puostu abavare. Com a saeràve mi po adesso te vuò cavare el reore del culo. E mena, e dài, tanto che l'harò amazò, e po a ghe cavarè la gonela e a ghe la torò mi, e sì a'l lagherè chialondena stravacò a muò un gran boazón," Ibid., 499–500. On blasphemy in sixteenth-century Venetian comedy, see also Burke, *Historical Anthropology,* 100.

[88] Belmas, "La monté des blasphèmes," 21; Cabantous, *Histoire du blasphème,* 103; Flynn, "Blasphemy and the Play of Anger," 53.

[89] For example, the state formed the *Cinque Savi alla Mercanzia* in 1515 to remedy the loss of trade that followed Venice's defeat at Agnadello, the *Provveditori Sopra i Monasteri* in 1521 to oversee ecclesiastical life, the *Provveditori agli Olii* in 1532 to regulate the buying and selling of oil, the *Inquisitori Contro la Propalazione dei Segreti* in 1539 to prevent the divulging of state secrets, the *Provveditori alle Beccarie* in 1545 to monitor meat sales, the *Provveditori alla Sanità* in 1556 to deal with disease and eventually prostitutes in the city, the *Provveditori Sopra gli Usurpi dei Beni Comunali* in 1574 to organize the material patrimony acquired with the conquest of the mainland, and the *Provveditori Sopra le Artiglierie* in 1588 to oversee the distribution of arms and munitions. Many additional magistracies were created beyond the examples cited here. See Giuseppe Maranini, *La costituzione di Venezia,* vol. 2 (Florence: La Nuova Italia, 1974), 180–91.

throughout early modern Europe. Seen in the light of the sixteenth-century European climate of discipline and control associated with the Counter-Reformation, Venetian concerns about blasphemy were neither new nor unique. Similar investigations into other early modern communities might yield similar insights into the process of modernization.[90] The particular social and demographic conditions challenging sixteenth-century Venice, linked to the punishment of public speech, suggest powerful connections between language and statebuilding. The evolution of the offence of blasphemy forms a clear part "of the genealogy of the legal constitution of the modern state."[91] The imposition of rules for normative speech – in this case the prosecution of blasphemy and unruly language – was a political act aimed at controlling and conditioning the *popolo*. It reflected an increasing desire to regulate language as a reflection of the city's attempt to define itself and its inhabitants in a period of demographic and social flux. Venetian legislation asserted that residing in the city necessarily meant sharing a common language: a language composed not only of grammatical norms, but of religious, moral, and political standards. Officials trained in the written word were pitted against the dangers of oral culture, and the control of language was employed as a means to define, shape, and discipline civic society.

As one scholar of blasphemy has pointed out, "the issue of blasphemy normally arises in a community that is divided, and it normally arises *because* the community is divided."[92] With its large immigrant population, Venice in the sixteenth century indeed represented such a site of cultural and civic division. As a result, Venetian magistrates used the power of law to construct a notion of a speech community that sought to override community differences. However, it is important to note that those who blasphemed, cursed, or hurled insults, in effect, sought to reverse these repressive linguistic discourses. They wielded weapons of language that had been framed by the state against the state itself. As

---

[90] "Other European princes continued to concentrate power in their own hands.... New financial, military, and ecclesiastical organs of government were created to confront the new burdens and responsibilities of the early modern world," Cozzi, *Religione, moralità e giustizia*, 1.

[91] Unsworth, "Blasphemy," 663.

[92] Lawton, *Blasphemy*, 118, emphasis mine.

we shall see in the next chapter, a look at insults reveals that disruptive individuals often unleashed their tongues with particular venom and dexterity. With an almost eerie yet unwitting echo, the magistracies that prosecuted the foul language of insults also targeted the lower classes, as did the *Esecutori*, revealing a widespread, systematic state program aimed at constructing a verbal order based on aristocratic norms and social stratification.

3

Insults

In 1526, four officers of the *Capi di Sestiere* – a police force that patrolled the city at night – were doing their nightly watch when they ran across a woman disguised as a man, together with her probable boyfriend. The officers began to argue with the couple and were preparing to arrest them when the noble Andrea Loredan came to the balcony of his house, directly over the altercation, and threw down a bucket of water, probably annoyed at having been woken up in the middle of the night by this disturbance. According to witnesses, the suspects broke away from the officers, who then began to shout "thief, fucking cuckold, dog," at Loredan, throwing rocks and launching arrows at Loredan's house. After being tried by the *Avogaria di Comun* – the city's State Lawyers – these men were deprived of their offices and subject to public humiliation between the two columns of San Marco; all of them, that is, except for the officer Andrea Querini, who because of his noble status, does not appear to have been prosecuted despite his participation in these verbal and physical assaults.[1]

A case like this one, amidst the seemingly endless documents of the Venetian archives, is in some ways entirely trivial. Famously organized to combat crime and violence, the various magistracies of the Venetian republic heard numerous cases like this on a daily basis, making this and similar examples so unimportant as to be practically negligible, especially compared to the traditionally more compelling cases of murder or treason. And yet, we shall see that this seemingly microscopic incident offers a window onto a significant and larger process that was unfolding

---

[1] ASV, *Avogaria di Comun, Penale*, bu. 254, fasc. 13 "Paolo Targer, Francesco da Venezia, Marino Cucchia, Bartolomeo Toscano, violenze, 1526."

in the lagoon city: the construction of a hierarchical code of civic language. Examining cases such as this one reveals that just as laws against blasphemy protected the state, so did the prosecution of insults. By piecing together evidence from a series of state magistracies and examining their work, it becomes clear that various groups representing the Venetian state aimed to silence insults up the social ladder – like these insults aimed at Andrea Loredan. In doing so, the state targeted the underclasses as among the main instigators of such verbal violence. The content and context of insults in sixteenth-century Venice were in many ways as predictable as they were in other early modern cities. Venice was not exceptional in the manner that its inhabitants lobbed insults about sexual honor or respectability at one another. The way that branches of the state protected verbal assaults against the interests of the state, and in particular against the noble class, however, suggests that as with blasphemy, the maintenance of a code of civil, civic language was crucial to promoting state stability and protecting its economy.

According to Peter Burke, language describing insults in sixteenth-century Italy was incredibly rich, referring to "*affronto, calumnia, parole contumeliose, diffamazione, detupazione, infamia, ingiuria, insolenza, maldicenza, mentita, vilipendio,* [and] *vituperazione.*"[2] The existence of so many distinctions points to both the complex and varied relationship between language and honor and a contemporary sensitivity to the language of vilification. In fact, opening the volumes of Sanudo's sixteenth-century chronicle of Venetian daily life and politics, the reader might think that the only language spoken or understood on the streets was that of insults and profanity. Sanudo's account is regularly peppered with examples of obscenity and foul language. For instance, on 9 July 1498, a certain Zorzi Zernovich was placed in prison for using "*parole bestial.*" On 14 June 1504, the scandalous words of an outspoken citizen were punished with the *strappado* – being dropped several times from a rope tied around the wrists. Several young noblemen insulted Marino Grimani at the Rialto on 9 February 1521, saying "'Idiot, take off those clothes, you are not worthy of wearing them since you never go to the Senate,' with other offensive words" (*parole obrobriose*). On 9 April 1524,

---

[2] Burke, "Insults and Blasphemy in Early Modern Europe," in *Historical Anthropology*, 96.

Francesco Contarini was retained for having said "*villania grandissima*" to the state lawyer Alvise Bon; he was punished with two months, imprisonment and deprived of public office for two years. An individual named Lodovico Zorzi was also tried for having said "fuck you" (*voio foter*) to Lodovico Foscarini in 1524.[3]

Like blasphemy, insults and concerns about them were of course not unique to Venice or new in the sixteenth century. The belief that hostile words could physically injure another individual had a long history. Both ritual cursing and everyday insults had been common throughout the Middle Ages.[4] Public insults had troubled Italian communes well before the early modern period, and many city-states published statutes against verbal injury.[5] To offer just a few examples, the 1325 statutes of Florence punished insults with a fine of 10 *lire*. The fourteenth-century statutes of Canale near Orvieto included a fine of 25 *lire* for those "who had evil tongues [and] spoke badly about the *signori* of the commune." Insults against other people in general were punished with a fine of five *soldi*. These were not incredibly high fines, where the fine for sodomy was 100 *lire* and the fine for climbing over the city walls was 100 *soldi*. The thirteenth-century fine for an insult in the commune of Bucine near Siena ranged from five to 10 *soldi* – equivalent to the fine of 10 *soldi* for an unarmed, physical assault.[6] Verbal injury in the Veneto was punished with three to six *lire* in fifteenth-century Riva del Garda and from 10 *lire* to 60 *soldi* in Val di Ledro near Trent – roughly the same punishment

[3] Sanudo, *I diarii*, vol. 1, 1006; vol. 29, 630; vol. 36, 193, 284. See also vol. 1, 1011, 1045; vol. 36, 361.

[4] Keith Thomas, *Religion and the Decline of Magic: Studies in Popular Beliefs in Sixteenth- and Seventeenth-century England* (London: Weidenfeld and Nicolson, 1971), 502–12.

[5] See A. Manfredini, *La diffamazione verbale nel diritto romano* (Milan: A. Giuffré, 1979); Annamaria Nada Patrone, *Il messaggio dell'ingiuria nel Piemonte del tardo medioevo* (Cavallermaggiore: Gribaudo, 1993), especially 7, 21–22, 31, 38.

[6] *Statuti della repubblica fiorentina*, ed. Romolo Caggese, vol. 2 (Florence: Olschki, 1949), 222; *Statuto di canale*, ed. Gina Scentoni (Spoleto: Centro Italiano di Studi sull'Alto Medioevo, 1994), 146–51; *Bucine e la Val d'Ambra nel Dugento*, ed. Ceppari, Jacona, and Turrini, 42, 47. For other examples, see *Statuto del comune di Arezzo*, ed. Droandi, 177–78; *Lo statuto di Gualdo Cattaneo del 1483*, ed. Ottaviani, 84; *Gli statuti criminali del comune di Mombaruzzo nell'anno 1322*, ed. Vittorio Ferraris (Turin: Edizioni dell'Orso, 1994), 44, 47. Richard Trexler has pointed out that a common medieval Latin word for military assault was *insultus*; late medieval Tuscan used *insultus* to characterize physical as well as verbal assault. See Richard C. Trexler, "Correre La Terra: Collective Insults in the Late Middle Ages," *Mélanges de l'école française de Rome, moyen âge temps modernes* 96 (1984), 847.

as that given for physical blows. The statutes of many Italian communes went so far as to penalize the use of specific words. For instance, in the early fourteenth century, the Venetian state instituted a monetary fine against those who used the insult *vermocane* or "ulcer." The 1438 statutes of Pordenone fined the insults of cuckold, son-of-a-whore, false, assassin, servant, and other words with three *lire* and five *soldi*. In the fifteenth century on the island of Torcello, injury against an official was fined five *lire di piccoli* and a month in prison; verbal insults in general were fined two *lire di piccoli*; calling someone a whore who was not publicly acknowledged as one was also fined two *lire di piccoli*. The fine for similar crimes on early sixteenth-century Murano was five *lire di piccoli*, which was roughly equivalent to the three to five *lire di piccoli* fine for physical blows.[7]

What was new in the early modern period, as with blasphemy, was the attention that Venetian jurists paid to verbal injury. Advocates concurred that insults were actions "without sense or justice, committed in various ways, mainly through words and deeds, but also through writing and gestures."[8] Indeed, it is important to emphasize that practical communication, in all times and places, is never just a matter of words, but of gestures and actions, just as the use of the word *conversare* by writers of conduct literature indicated interaction (and action) as well as conversation. Early modern writers of legal theory, however, considered words to be as powerful as physical actions themselves. Although physical injury could result in pain or the loss of any eye or limb, verbal insults resulted in the loss of reputation – damage equally as grave in the early modern world.[9] The advocate Marco Ferro argued that defamation

---

[7] See Trevor Dean, "Gender and Insult in an Italian City: Bologna in the Later Middle Ages," *Social History* 29 (2004): 224–25; *Statuti di Riva del Garda del 1451*, ed. Orlando, 144–45; *Statuti della Val di Ledro del 1435*, ed. Groff, 95, 100–1; *Statuti di Pordenone del 1438*, ed. Oscuro and Pozza, 92–93; *Statuti della laguna veneta*, ed. Ortalli, Pasqualetto, and Rizzi, 171, 191, 193, 271–72.

[8] "Ingiuria vuol dire quasi ragion iniqua, cioe una cosa, che manchi di ragione, et di giustitia, si commette in piu modi, cioe col fatto, et con le parole principalmente, man anco vi si puo aggionger con la scrittura, et co'l gesto," Priori, *Prattica criminale*, 195. For similar descriptions, see also Barbaro, *Pratica criminale*, 235; Tiraboscho, *Ristretto di prattica criminale*, 11.

[9] "E anco ingiuria, anzi e furto spirituale, quando che uno ingiustamente tuol la fama d'un'altro dolosamente," Priori, *Prattica criminale*, 196.

occurred when, either in the presence or absence of a person, a second person "states damaging words against him, when he gives him a damaging reproach, or when he threatens or damages his person, goods, or honor."[10] Jurist Benedetto Pasqualigo offered a particularly detailed definition of insults.

> Verbal insult is committed in many ways: accusing someone outside of court of having committed general or specific evil deeds, offending with words someone's dignity, defaming someone and soiling the good opinion held of someone by saying false things, by spreading scandalous, bitter, threatening, or cursing voices about someone's habits or past, present, or future interests . . . by deriding some natural defect, such as making fun of a bastard, someone cross-eyed, a hunchback, lame person, or leper, [or] by stirring up neighborhood children to make fun of someone.[11]

In a world where most news still traveled orally and an insult quickly reached the ears of many, jurists understood that damaging words had far-reaching consequences; once words were spoken, it was difficult to contain their effect, particularly on extended alliances of family and kinship. As Pasqualigo stated, "any spoken word that insults a person also offends those close to him and those connected by family. So an insult against the father injures the son, or the wife the husband, and a case could be started equally by anyone involved."[12] Venetian *giuriste* also agreed that insults against nobles and superiors were the most serious of all. Antonino

[10] "Le ingiurie verbali si commettono quando alla presenza di qualcheduno, o in di lui assenza si proferiscono parole ingiuriose contro il medesimo, quando gli si da qualche rimprovero oltraggioso, quando si fa ad esso qualche minaccia di danno nella persona, nei beni o nell'onore," Ferro, *Dizionario*, vol. 2, 107.

[11] "Comettesi delitto d'ingiuria col detto per molte guise, con l'imputarsi stragiudizialmente ad altri scelleratezza cosi in genere come in spezie con l'offendere di parole la dignità d'alcuno, infamarne la persona, e scemargli la buona opinione con dicerie benche false; col proferire voci scandalose, accerbe, minacciante, o imprecatorie contra le di lui costumanze ed interessi passati, presenti, e venturi . . . col mottegiarne qualche naturale difetto, vale a dire, con lo spacciarlo per bastardo, guercio, gobbo, zoppo, o lebbroso; con l'eccitare per le contrade gli ragazzi a farne schimazzo," Pasqualigo, *Della giurisprudenza criminale*, 275. See also Grecchi, *Le formalità del processo*, 268, and Priori, *Pratica criminale*, 197–98.

[12] "Taluna ingiuria inferitasi col detto ad una persona, offende stessamente l'altra d'affetto, e di stretta relazione congionta. Quindi con l'oltraggio del padre, ingiuriasi il figlio, e con quello della moglie il marito; e ne conviene allora la ragione della querela cosi agli uni, come agli altri," Pasqualigo, *Della giurisprudenza criminale*, 275. See also Ferro, *Dizionario*, vol. 2, 107.

Barbaro believed that "he who falsely accuses a noble person of a heinous crime commits a serious insult." Giambatista Grecchi concurred that an insult "directed to high people or public representatives... was an atrocious crime subject to the supreme authority of the excellent Council of Ten."[13] An insult, though perhaps aimed at one individual, was never so easily contained. Verbal injury had extensive repercussions, potentially damaging wider family networks, the noble class, or as we shall see, the state itself.

Considering insults, slander, and defamation in the early modern world at large, the archives of crime have revealed a range of regional patterns. For instance, in New France between 1658 and 1760, Peter Moogk argued that dishonesty was the biggest insult to men and a lack of chastity the insult most commonly flung at women, though among these cases, only one-tenth of the aggressors were women. Trevor Dean found that women were insulted through their sexuality and men through their honesty, courage, and worth in fifteenth-century Bologna. Daniel Lesnick found a similar pattern of insults (men being accused of dishonesty and women of a lack of chastity), but with a greater female participation (27.5% of the aggressors) in insult trials in medieval Todi, with the perceived seriousness of an insult having much to do with where verbal aggression took place. In seventeenth-century London, Laura Gowing noted the high number of defamation cases involving women and argued that slander offered women the possibility to assert their legal agency. In the case of sixteenth-century York, J.A. Sharpe found the most common insults to be about theft, disease, drunkenness, and sexual reputation – again with a high degree of female participation. For eighteenth-century Paris, David Garrioch saw most insults to be about dishonesty, fraud, and sexual reputation – though not about cuckoldry, which was a popular insult in other areas. The vast majority of the insults in the above studies were exchanged between people who knew each other, neighbors or colleagues, often (though not always) of similar rank and not usually in a position of dependence such as servants or subordinates. All these studies show the prevalence of concerns about personal and family honor,

---

[13] "L'accusator falso di persona nobile, o pure di delitto infame, commette grave ingiuria," Barbaro, *Pratica criminale*, 236; "Indirizzata ad alti personaggi, o a pubblici rappresentanti... diviene essa allora un delitto atroce soggetto alla suprema autorità dell'Eccelso consiglio di dieci," Grecchi, *Le formalità del processo*, 269.

often far from the Mediterranean.[14] As with blasphemy, honor, language, and the disciplining of speech were inherently connected. Early modern people and their communities perceived insults not simply as crimes disrupting civic peace but acts undermining personal and civic honor. Or rather, as we shall see, the maintenance of civic peace and prosperity depended intrinsically on the maintenance of the honor of the state and its citizens through defense against verbal injuries.

A similar systematic study of verbal injury in sixteenth-century Venice presents certain archival challenges. Guido Ruggiero has shown how Venetians were troubled by slander and public insults in the Middle Ages and often brought their adversaries to court, resulting in heavy fines and serious punishments.[15] However, although several different magistracies established statutes to punish insults against state officials during the Middle Ages, there does not appear to have been – or to exist any longer – any statute prohibiting insults against other people in general.[16] This was not unusual; victims of verbal abuse brought their complaints to various courts regardless of whether or not statutes existed, but it does make it more challenging to ascertain the exact penalty that early modern Venetians placed on insults and how these compared to penalties for

---

[14] Dean, "Gender and Insult," 217–31; David Garrioch, "Verbal Insults in Eighteenth-Century Paris," in *The Social History of Language,* ed. Burke and Porter, 104–19; Laura Gowing, "Language, Power, and the Law: Women's Slander Litigation in Early Modern London," in *Feminism and Renaissance Studies,* ed. Lorna Hutson (Oxford: Oxford University Press, 1999), 428–49; Martin Ingram, "Law, Litigants and the Construction of 'Honour': Slander Suits in Early Modern England," in *The Moral World of the Law,* ed. Peter Coss (Cambridge: Cambridge University Press, 2000), 134–60; Daniel R. Lesnick, "Insults and Threats in Medieval Todi," *Journal of Medieval History* 17 (1991): 71–89; Peter N. Moogk, "'Thieving Buggers' and 'Stupid Sluts': Insults and Popular Culture in New France," *William and Mary Quarterly* 36 (1979): 524–47; J.A. Sharpe, "Defamation and Sexual Slander in Early Modern England: The Church Courts at York," *Borthwick Papers* 58 (1980): 1–36. See also Peter Burke, "The Art of Insult in Early Modern Italy," *Culture and History* 2 (1987): 68–79; Burke, "Insults and Blasphemy in Early Modern Europe," in *Historical Anthropology,* 95–109.

[15] Ruggiero, *Violence,* 125–37.

[16] "Item si aliqua persona occasione huius offitii me vel aliquem sociorum meorum iniuriabitur in verbis vel aliter, perdere debeat libras c. hoc modo quod debeamus dicere iniuriam vel iniurias nobis dictas in maiori consilio et pars debeat ire circum de ipsis centum libris," Roberti, *Le magistrature,* vol. 3, 134, 150, 156; "Verba turpia et inhonesta contra personam et honorem ipsius domini ducis et honorem comunis;" "verba turpia et inhonesta contra statutum ducalis domini;" "verba turpia et inhonesta contra honorem dominationis nostri," *Le deliberazione del consiglio dei XL della repubblica di Venezia,* vol. 1–3, in *Deputazione di storia patria per le Venezie,* ed. A. Lombardo (Venice, 1957–67), reg. 22, 34, 76, 124–25, cited in Crouzet-Pavan, "Potere politico," 59.

other crimes.[17] Furthermore, there was no single magistracy or council that oversaw the task of patrolling verbal injuries in the early modern period. This responsibility appears to have been shouldered primarily by the *Signori di Notte al Criminal* in the fourteenth century and later given to the *Signori di Notte al Civil* in the sixteenth and seventeenth centuries.[18] Very little archival material exists from the *Signori di Notte al Criminal* or *Civil* from the sixteenth century, yet what does remain suggests considerable litigation pertaining to verbal injury. For example, Cattarina Faura was punished in 1544 with 15 days in prison for insults against a certain Giovanna. Domenego Bernardin endured four days in prison and one ducat for insults against Cecilia Veronese in 1545.[19] In addition, testimony from other courts in the sixteenth century clearly demonstrates that when individuals were verbally attacked, they took their complaints first to the *Signori di Notte.*[20]

We, therefore, cannot examine cases of insults from the magistracy that appears to have overseen this crime. As a result, unfortunately, we also cannot ascertain with any certainty whether the prosecution of insults or the severity of their punishment escalated, either quantitatively or qualitatively, in the early modern period. However, documents remain from one magistracy that offer an understanding of verbal injury – the *Avogaria di Comun* or the Venetian state lawyers. The *Avogaria* was founded in the twelfth century and included three men elected to oversee the regular and systematic application of laws passed. One was always present during sessions of the Council of Ten, and one during the meetings of the Great Council. They also operated as public accusers in a wide variety

---

[17] The city statutes of Bologna also had no stated penalties for insults, yet many cases were tried in the late Middle Ages. See Dean, "Gender and Insult," 218.

[18] These magistracies were assigned responsibility over a wide spectrum of crimes including crimes of blood, illegal arms, crimes against property and honor, improper behavior, injury, fraud, and generally violent or improper practices. Though the fourteenth-century statutes of the *Signori di Notte al Criminal* list punishments for blasphemy, they do not list any for verbal injury. Nevertheless, this magistracy clearly dealt with cases of insults, as verbal injury trials abound in the records of the *Criminal* in the fourteenth century and then in the records of the *Civil* starting around the mid-seventeenth century.

[19] ASV, *Signori di Notte al Criminal*, bu. 1, regr. 1564–1733, 2 April 1544, fo. 11r; 12 August 1545, fo. 13r.

[20] In a witchcraft trial, a witness declared, "Io non so, che questa Angela, o queste altre donne faccino strigarie, se non che gia un'anno in circa fui querelato da questa Angela Greca per alcune parole, che gli disse ingiuriose, che fu alli Sigori di Notte Civil," ASV, *Sant'Uffizio*, bu. 66, "Elisabetta Greca," 21 July 1590, fo. 6r–v. See also Ibid., "Antonio Venturon," 9 August 1590; bu. 64, "Girolama da Venezia," 23 June 1590.

of cases ranging from homicide and physical fights to theft, rape, and physical and verbal injury. Between 1500 and 1625, the *Avogaria* processed approximately 58 cases in which verbal injury was one of the primary accusations: not a high number of cases, but then again this crime was not among this magistracy's central responsibilities. Examining this limited set of data, including several cases that fall in the seventeenth century, may suggest a desire to hang large interpretations on relatively small numbers; however, where pre-modern phenomena are concerned, historians are often forced to work with imperfect or smaller pools of data. In addition, the theoretical underpinnings of microhistory work to validate the study of few cases or the single, unrepeated event as meaningful indicators of broader themes. Other scholars have drawn convincing conclusions about insults and public life in other early modern contexts based on a similarly small pool of examples.[21] The trials of the *Avogaria*, though few in number, allow us to conduct a general survey of insults in sixteenth-century Venice, revealing why, where, and how individual actors insulted one another, how people reacted to violent language, and how the state disciplined these unruly outbursts.

Insults in Venice tended to conform in some ways to patterns already established by studies in other places (See Appendix A). For instance, in cases before the *Avogaria*, insults against sexual honor figured prominently – the most popular epithet by far being *becco fotuo* or fuck-ing/fucked cuckold. *Becco* literally means goat, and this animal metaphor was popular in verbal abuse because goats allowed their mates to be mounted by other animals.[22] By flinging this insult, individuals ritually insulted male honor by placing men in a symbolically female position. In addition, insults such as whore, son-of-a-whore, bugger, procuress, and sodomite were also popular (*puttana, fatto e ditto, buzerar/buzerona, ruf-fiana, bardassa*). Sexual slurs featured prominently in 52 of these cases. This is not at all surprising, because as other scholars have demon-strated, "there was – and is – no more common metaphor to describe the strengths and weaknesses of opponents, after all, than the sex-ual."[23] Sexual insults "offend" individual honor in that husbands who were cuckolds or sodomites became feminized and lost their domestic

---

[21] See most importantly Dean, "Gender and Insult," and Elizabeth S. Cohen, "Honor and Gender in Early Modern Rome," *Journal of Interdisciplinary History* 4 (1992): 597–626.

[22] Burke, *Historical Anthropology*, 96–97.

[23] Trexler, "Correre La Terra," 871. See also Gowing, *Domestic Dangers*, 101.

power, as did women who were whores, because their houses became dishonest.

Although the relationship between speech and sexuality will be explored more fully later, it is important to mention here that sexual speech had metaphorical connotations specific to republican Venice, because controlling both speech and sexuality was intrinsically related to state stability. The same years in the middle of the sixteenth century that saw an increased attention to blasphemy and perhaps insults also witnessed the expansion of the powers of both the offices of the *Sanità* and the *Esecutori* to include patrolling prostitution in the city.[24] Though such patrolling was perhaps parallel more than overlapping, if we can suggest at least a symbolic, speculative relationship between the tongue and the penis, a Venetian desire to control the sexualized tongue would not be at all surprising. In republics, political legitimacy was based upon familial legitimacy and a disciplined sexuality was intrinsic to the maintenance of family, community, and republican order. In particular, we can see clear links between the state and sexuality in the way that the republic increasingly sought to regulate marriage in the fifteenth and sixteenth centuries.[25] Unruly sexuality and sexualized language referring to it were therefore not merely disruptive in Venice, but actually symbolically undermined the institutions of marriage and the family: the bedrock of the Venetian state. Again, although sexual insults were common across the early modern world, the desire to control the social body in Venice had a particular importance and further legitimated controlling the actions of the physical body, including sexual insults.

Insults challenging honesty and respectability (*furfante, mariol, furbo, ladro, traditor*) were also popular and featured prominently in 36 cases,

---

[24] The office of the *Sanità* was originally founded in 1478 to combat the plague, but then gained control over prostitution in 1539, demanding that foreign prostitutes leave, forbidding prostitutes from keeping young female servants and living near churches. Between 1539 and 1552, the *Sanità* prosecuted prostitues 69 times for violations of these regulations. See Michelle Laughran, "The Body, Public Health, and Social Control in Sixteenth-Century Venice," (Ph.D. diss., The University of Connecticut, 1998), 5, 61–66.

[25] See Stanley Chojnacki, "Marriage Regulation in Venice, 1420–1535," in *Women and Men in Renaissance Venice: Twelve Essays on Patrician Society*, ed. Stanley Chojnacki (Baltimore and London: The Johns Hopkins University Press, 2000), 53–75; Guido Ruggiero, *The Boundaries of Eros: Sex Crime and Sexuality in Renaissance Venice* (New York: Oxford University Press, 1985), 9; Joanne Ferraro, *Marriage Wars in Late Renaissance Venice* (Oxford: Oxford University Press, 2001), 21, 138.

as were insults which compared the insulted to animals (*cane, porco, bestia, vaccha, mullo*), in 19 cases.[26] Although women were sometimes the targets of insults, they did not appear to play a significant role as verbal aggressors. In seven cases, women claimed to have been injured by a man, in two cases women claimed to be insulted by women, and in one case, a main claimed to have been insulted by a woman, therefore making it difficult to use the records of the Avogaria to explore the relationship between gender, slander, and legal agency as other scholars have done. As with blasphemy, the reasons behind this gender distinction are unclear. We shall see in specific cases that women were equally as adept at hurling insults as men, indicating that perhaps women in early modern Venice were more confined to the domestic arena than women in other cities, though this is much debated.[27] The location where individuals unleashed insults was occasionally but not always noted. It appears to have been included in the charges when insults occurred in or around the arenas central to trade and state stability such as on galleys or in trading centers like the German warehouse, but it is unclear whether location affected monetary fines.

What many of these cases do exhibit is a profound sensitivity to obscenity and insults on the part of both judges and individual Venetians. For instance, in a dispute between two men in 1605, one of the litigants claimed that the other had said "excessive and impious words . . . that you would not say even to your worst enemy. . . . He should bridle his tongue and calm down."[28] In another case, a laborer described how he accidentally offended two prostitutes with his foul language.

> Among us workers, laughing amongst ourselves a month ago, speaking casually I said, "I am going to take a shit." Hearing these words, these prostitutes threatened to hurt me, believing that I had said these words against them. They said a thousand insults to me, calling me a son-of-a-whore and a cuckold, trying from then on to throw me into the

---

[26] Many of these same terms are noted or used by contemporary Venetian writers and chroniclers. See for instance Andrea Calmo, *Le lettere*, ed. Vittorio Rossi (Turin: Ermanno Loescher, 1888), 274; Sanudo, *I diarii*, vol. 35, 140.

[27] On debates about women's presence in the Venetian public sphere, see Chapter 4, n. 41.

[28] "Parole cosi strabochevoli, et empie che . . . non si direbono ad un capitalissimo nemico . . . doveria rafrenar la lingua et aquietar l'humore," ASV, *Avogaria di Comun, Penale*, bu. 265, fasc. 3 "Giovanni Merzari," 1 March 1605, testimony of Fabio Merzari.

water and kill me even though I really said those words casually as one is accustomed to do throughout the city, with no thought of speaking about them.[29]

In another case from 30 October 1589, Matteo Maffei denounced Girolamo Domo for verbal and physical injuries. According to Matteo, Girolamo had come to his shop complaining about the price of a tool he had bought. Girolamo called Matteo a beast, a thief, a vituperous rogue, and a son-of-a-whore. Matteo claimed, "He started to say the most violent words and insults, so I responded that we were respectable men and that he should not speak in such a way."[30] Girolamo then took out a knife and physically injured Matteo, and for these injuries, the court punished Girolamo with three years in prison, saying that "he must not molest, either in deeds or words [Matteo] nor other persons."[31]

In a somewhat unique but related example from the trials of the Holy Office, a Jew who had become Christian complained to the Inquisitor about how he had been insulted for his conversion.

Coming back from the used clothing salesman named Giovanni, a Jew named Salamon of Cesane, son of Regina the widow, both of whom live in the Ghetto and we know each other, crossed the street toward me. . . . When I saw him cross the street I withdrew into a street nearby, and Salamon followed me. He said to me in Hebrew "beast" or "big beast," and then he said that I was cursed. And then, in Italian he said I was soiled (*maltana*) and he asked me if I had lost my mind. And when I withdrew from him he said to me in Italian, "come here you big beast,

---

[29] "Stanno Anzelica et Madalena donne di partito, et ridendo sia noi lavoranti gia un mese io dissi fazo bortola parlando modestamente, et sentendo queste parole dette donne mi minacciarno di volermi far offendere credendo loro che io dicesse per elle, et mi dissero mille villanie becco fatto e ditto continuando da l'hora in poi à tentar di farmi buttar in acqua, et farmi amazzar, se bene veramente io dissi quella parole semplicemente come si suol dir per la città senza pensiero alcuno di parlar di elle," Ibid., bu. 391, fasc. 5 "Stella Angelica," 4 November 1592. Here, "fatto ditto" functions as a slightly euphemistic insult. According to Boerio, "dita a fata" was "a backhanded way of insulting someone, saying this in order not to say clearly 'son of a whore.'" See Giuseppe Boerio, *Dizionario del dialetto veneziano*, 2d. ed. (Venice: Premiata Tipografia di Giovanni Cecchini, 1856), 242. The meaning of "ditto," in effect, is a "receipt," thus the person is "done" (in the crude sense) and "paid for." I thank Linda Carroll for help with this passage.

[30] "Mi conincio à dir parole et vilanie ingiuriosissime, onde so rispondendoli che erimo huomini da bene et che *non dovea parolar à quel modo* (underlined in document)," Ibid., bu. 261, fasc. 16 "Girolamo Domo," 30 October 1589.

[31] "Non debba molestar né in fatti né in parole né lui né altri persone," Ibid., 31 October 1589.

are you afraid?" I did not say anything, but I left him barking like a
dog.[32]

The litigant was concerned enough about his fragile new religious status
that he brought his case to the Holy Office, though his complaint was
apparently not taken seriously or did not have enough evidence to pursue
and was not concluded. All these individuals and many others denounced
their fellow Venetians in reaction to being called names or hearing foul
language flung at them, demonstrating the powerful social force that
language possessed. Although words like "dog" or "cow" may not sound
so shocking today, they were quite threatening on the streets of the early
modern world and individuals reacted strongly to such threats to their
honor. Though a written rather than oral example, in his insulting poem
to Veronica Franco, Maffio Venier described her as "a cow that could
satiate the entire Ghetto (*Quella vacca che sazia tutto Ghetto*):" an insult
that was much stronger than might seem to the modern ear, because sex
with Jews was punishable by beating and exile.[33]

Many people were so attuned to the power of words that denunciations and witnesses frequently described the accused's bad character
by explicitly pointing out and focusing on obscene or offensive speech.
Denunciations often complained first and foremost about aggressive language, suggesting the prominent role of language in community as well
as the way that public speech defined a person's status. For instance,
in his denunciation against Cornelio Badoer for injury in 1597, the first
thing that the litigant Agostino Fabris mentioned was Cornelio's dirty

---

[32] "Venendo dal strazarolo che se domanda Ioe, me traverso la strada un hebreo chiamato
Salamon dei Cesane de Regina vedoa che habitano in gheto, per che io lo conosco, et lui
conosce me.... Et quando io le vidi cosi traversar la strada, io mi ritirai in una strada li
vicino, et ditto Salamone vene a trovarme. Et mi disse in hebrayico, bestia o bestion. Et poi
me disse siestu maladetto. Et poi in Italiano a me disse maltana et me domando s'io haveva
perso il cervello. Et quando io mi ritirava da lui mi diceva vien qua bestion, hai tu paura
in lingua italiana. Io non gli rispose, et lo lasseti bagiar come un cane," ASV, *Sant'Uffizio*,
bu. 52, fasc. "Georgii Neophiti, Hebreo," denunciation of 30 July 1585. I have translated the
name Ioe into Giovanni for simplicity's sake; however, this name or its abbreviation does
not seem to indicate any common name in vernacular Italian or Venetian and could be a
form of a Hebrew name. In addition, the meaning of *maltana* here is unclear; "malta" means
"mortar" and in some dialects "mud" perhaps indicating someone who is soiled, dirty, or
muddy.

[33] Maffio Venier *Il libro chiuso di Maffio Venier*, in *Contro le puttane: Rime venete del XVI secolo*,
ed. Marisa Milani (Bassano del Grappa: Ghedina e Tassotti, 1994), 71.

mouth, claiming that he did nothing but pronounce insults and blasphemy against local shop owners. When the first witness was asked if he knew Cornelio Badoer, he stated "I do not know anything except that he has a licentious tongue."[34] In another case beginning on 11 May 1620, a certain widow named Benedetta Vedova denounced two people – Angela Meronti and Angelo Faura – for verbal injury. Benedetta claimed that in front of her house in Venice, these two called her a

> fucking bugger, scoundrel, whore with a little skirt, cow, and other even more detestable injuries with the disruption of the entire neighborhood, continuing to yell at me for another half hour . . . Angelo is a most disrespectable person and has the worst manners. He usually goes around insulting and defaming this person and that person . . . defaming and offending whoever he wants.[35]

A witness testified that Angela called Benedetta a "whore, scoundrel and other dirty words – and said that she went to *osterie* to get herself buggered."[36] Other witnesses claimed that both Angela and Angelo said "up-your-ass you bugger, and the most filthy and detestable insults that I am embarrassed to say them, or even just to think about them."[37] Almost all the witnesses stated that both Angela and Angelo were known in the city for insulting a lot of people with offensive and obscene language. Despite the fact that a type of restraining order was placed on Angela and Angelo saying they were not to insult Benedetta, witnesses said they went on with their rants. Angela claimed innocence, but died of a fever before the case was decided. Even in cases with multiple crimes including

---

[34] "Non fa altro che dar asto su le proprie botteghe con vilanie, et arlassi, et biasteme horende per terrara qualche precipitio li pover botteghieri," ASV, *Avogaria di Comun, Penale*, bu. 150, fasc.1 "Badoer Cornelio," 2 June 1597; "Non so altro se non che le licentioso di lengua," 3 June 1597, testimony of Anselm Buffeli.

[35] "Una buzeruda fatta e poltrona putana gonaina vacha et con altre piu detesta de ingiurie con tumulto di tutto il vicinato continuando pur a darmi romancina per il spacio di mez'hora . . . Anzolo di pessima vita et pegior costumi solito ad ingiuriar et infamiar questo e quella . . . va per la citta infamiando et offendendo chi li piace," Ibid., bu. 462, fasc. 3 "Angela Meronti Castellan," 11 May 1620.

[36] "Putanna poltrona et altre parole sporche gli disse anco che andava sopra le hostarie a farse buzarar," Ibid., 15 May 1620, testimony of Vanzelitta Tamsello.

[37] "Buzardazza in culo et altre villanie sporchissime et detestande che mi vergono a dirle," Ibid., 16 May 1620, testimony of Barbara, wife of Francesco. "Cose neffande che mi verzogno non solamente a dirle ma a pensarne ancora," Ibid., 18 May 1620, testimony of Pasqualina Vedoa.

theft or physical injury, it was not uncommon for litigants to insist on establishing verbal offenses as the first order of business.

The insults that received the greatest attention from the *Avogaria* in terms of the number of cases, however, tended to follow two major patterns: verbal injury against nobles, and insults spoken against the interests of the state as a whole. Seventeen of these 58 cases involved insults against nobles or superiors. As one example, on 25 August 1526, the noble Galeazzo Dolfin denounced Francesco dall'Olio for both physical and verbal insults. Returning from church, Galeazzo passed under Francesco's balcony. Francesco had been watering some geraniums and managed to drench Galeazzo, and then cried, "look out you bugger" and other insulting names.[38] A witness heard Galeazzo say, "Who the devil is throwing water," and as Galeazzo looked up, Francesco responded "Are you talking to me? Look out you beast!" Galeazzo replied "Are you talking to me?" and Francesco again replied "Of course I am talking to you, you fucking bugger."[39] According to Francesco, by contrast, as his mother was watering the geraniums, she happened to spill a bit of water onto Galeazzo, who exclaimed, "get away you fucking whore who has drenched my ass." Francesco arrived on the balcony and threatened, "Look out you fucking cuckold," to which Galeazzo replied, "If I were a cuckold I would have horns! Come down here you thief and scoundrel . . . I'm going to quarter you!" Francesco then ran after Galeazzo and hit him over the head with the flat side of his sword. Afterwards, however, Francesco begged to be pardoned, stating that if he had known that Galeazzo was a noble, he would never have treated him in such a way.[40] Francesco received two drops from the cord and six months in prison for his insults and

---

[38] "Non bastandoli a ditto francesco de haverme bagnato, ma mal a mal aggiongendo me commenzo a dir villania digendomi che vardistu bardassa et altre villane parolle," ASV, *Avogaria di Comun, Penale*, bu. 213, fasc. 12 "Dall'Olio Francesco danni a Dolfin Galeazzo," denuciation of 25 August 1526.

[39] "Galeazzo disse chi diavolo geta acqua et vardo in suso et il ditto francesco dictu a mi te francesco disse che vardistu bestia et m. Galeazzo disse al ditto francesco distu a mi et francesco disse machi si che digo a ti bardassa fotua et m. galeazo disse granmerze et percorse di longo et disse al ditto francesco ti me par una bestia," Ibid., 4 May 1526, testimony of Domenego Pictor.

[40] "Via sta putana fotua in tal cul mi bagna," "Disse che zarzistu becho fotuo, et mi li rispose, s'io fusse beccho haverei le corne, et lui mi disse vien zusso ladro mariol che te voglio squartar," "Se havesse sapudo che'l fusse sta zentilhomo, non haveria fatto mai quelle materie et che li domandano mille perdonasse," Ibid., 30 May 1526, testimony of Francesco da L'Oglio.

injuries against Galeazzo.[41] Francesco's final comment is revealing. Had he known he was dealing with a patrician, he would never have used such language: a statement revealing a clear understanding of the "natural" order of the language and the verbal respect expected of social inferiors to superiors.

In another case dealing with insults against the nobility, on 10 October 1595 Giuseppe Beltrame was banned from Venice for three years for "abominable insults" spoken against both an individual young woman and the nobility in general, having said scoundrel and bugger to an actress named Giulia, and then stating that he had "it up the asses of the most excellent nobles who favored the young woman."[42] In other words, he was punished for his arrogance in claiming to have power over nobles and for making passive homosexuals of them. In this case, both masculinity and social status were therefore at stake. Similarly, in 1633, a case was initiated against Bortholomeo Malombra. This case involved no denunciation, and the court instead began by asking various witnesses if they had ever heard Bortholomeo speak out against the nobility. For instance, the judge asked the noble Gerolomo Memmo "if he had heard Bortholomeo say that he would stab the first noble – who did even the tiniest thing to him – many times in the gut until his soul came out."[43] The judge questioned witness Lorenzo Sanuto if he had ever heard Malombra "say words of hatred towards the nobility, for instance that he would like it if all of the nobility were a fresh egg that he could swallow, with other unbecoming words."[44] Neither one of these witnesses had heard such language, but the court had obviously received this information from someone and attempted to verify it. The rest of this trial has been lost and there is no sentence; nevertheless, this and other trials demonstrate the *Avogaria*'s

---

[41] Ibid., sentence of 25 August 1526.

[42] "Poltrona o buzeronna . . . dicesse di haver in culli li clarissimi nobbili che volessero favorir la preddetta signora," Ibid., bu. 33, fasc. 3, "Giuseppe Beltrame," 9 August 1595, testimony of Giovanni Zenoni; sentence of 10 October 1595.

[43] "Lo senti profferir parole di cattivo concetto e particolarmente che'l primo gentilhomo perche li facesse ogni minima cosa gli voleva cavar un stillo tante volte nella vita fino che li fosse uscita l'anima," Ibid., bu. 387, fasc. 15 "Malombra Bartolommeo sparla contro la Nobilta," 1 October 1633, testimony of Gerolomo Memmo.

[44] "Se habbi profferito parole significanti odio verso la nobilta come dir che vorrebe che tutta la nobilta fosse un ovo fresco che poterla ingiottir con altre parole indebite," Ibid., testimony of Lorenzo Sanuto.

interest in insults against the noble class and their desire to punish those who spoke them.

Cases of insults against officials and superiors were also common in the trials of the *Avogaria*, particularly on Venetian galleys. For example, on 18 August 1600 Giana da Candia was sentenced to 18 months galley service for insults and physical injury to the master of the galley where he was assigned. Giana, who was already doing galley service for another crime, entered into a disagreement with the master of the galley and yelled "you whore, I only have seven days of service left – no cuckolded, dog, son-of-a-whore is going to command me."[45] In a similar case, Marco da Candia, a galley captain, denounced the sailor Ludovico of Vicenza for insults. According to witnesses, during a disagreement, Ludovico exclaimed, "you ugly fucking cuckold, wearing your red tunic as if you were an admiral," though no sentence was pronounced for this case.[46] On 27 December 1573, Vicenzo Pililler was punished with three years galley service (and having his tongue cut out if he further disobeyed) for having insulted the captain of his galley by saying "golden beard, mustache of shit."[47] Although it is not always possible to determine the full meaning or context of these insults, their intended aggression versus superiors and the *Avogaria*'s interest in punishing them is clear. With written insults against the state and its officials as well – in particular, with a well-known libel on doge Leonardo Loredan posted on the Rialto – the state similarly was swift to intervene against its critics.[48]

At the same time that the *Avogaria* considered these cases of insults against nobles and state officials, another pressing and related problem of public language simultaneously emerged: the persistent obscenities spoken by servants and gondoliers in particular. Many observers of sixteenth-century Venetian life reported that gondoliers as a group were

---

[45] "Puttana mi manca a finir la condanna sette zorni come li havero finido nisun can becco fatto ditto mi comandara," Ibid., bu. 37, fasc. 4 "Giana da Candia," 3 August 1600, testimony of Olivier Lio.

[46] "Ah brutto becco fotudo che ti porti la casaca rossa come armiraglio," Ibid., bu. 18, fasc. 9 "Ludovico da Vicenza," 1 January 1576, testimony of Sfamali da Corfu.

[47] "Disse gridando forte verso il magnifico patron sopradetto a barba doro mustacchi di merda," Ibid., bu. 28, fasc. 17 "Vicenzo Sovolovich da Zara galleoto," 27 December 1573, testimony of Francesco Torli; sentence of 27 December 1573.

[48] See Crouzet-Pavan, "Potere politico," 59. On posters and drawings insulting the state, see also Crouzet-Pavan, *Sopra le acque salse: Espaces, pouvoir, et sociéte à Venise à la fin du moyen âge*, vol. 2 (Rome: Istituto Palazzo Borromini, 1992), 851.

remarkably insolent. Pietro Aretino wrote that he never tired of hearing boatmen's insults outside his house on the Grand Canal, laughing "at the hoots, whistles, and catcalls which the gondoliers hurled at those who had themselves rowed about by servants without scarlet breeches." In his 1585 *Piazza universale*, Tomaso Garzoni described the boatmen as "always in the public square with some lie, blasphemy, buffoonery, scandalous bad word, curse, [or] boast . . . and all of them are the lowest people. . . . They always have dirty words and vain oaths of every kind in their mouth." Thomas Coryat stated in his travel account that the boatmen under the Rialto in particular were "the most vicious and licentious varlets [sic] about the city."[49]

Legislation from the *Provveditori Sopra le Pompe*, the magistracy charged with overseeing sumptuary legislation, had long betrayed anxiety about servants' language. For instance, when the officers of the *Pompe* came to inspect banquets, they sometimes had to admonish cooks and servants not use rude language. [50] By the middle of the sixteenth century, however, the insults of gondoliers and servants had become frequent and disturbing enough to draw the attention of the Council of Ten itself.

> There are multiplying daily so many complaints to the heads of this council concerning the ill condition, the assemblies, and the gatherings that the boatmen and servants of this city continuously form and the ill words that they publicly use, besides their other insolent and dishonorable habits, showing no respect for noblemen and noblewomen, or for men and women citizens, or for other persons, and with a most evil example and little honor for the city, that if something is not done, their insolence will grow even greater as they see that it goes unpunished.[51]

---

[49] "Letter to Domenico Bolani," 27 October 1537, in *The Letters of Pietro Aretino*, ed. Thomas Caldecot Chubb (Hamden, CT: Archon Books, 1967), 84–87; Tommaso Garzoni, *La piazza universale di tutte le professioni del mondo, e nobili e ignobili*, ed. Paolo Cherchi and Beatrice Collina, vol. 2 (1585; Turin: Einaudi, 1996), 1396–97; Coryat, *Coryat's Crudities*, vol. 1, 311. See also Fabio Glissenti, *Discorsi morali contra il dispiacer del morire. Detto Athanatophilia* (Venice, 1609), 142r, cited in Denis Romano, *Housecraft and Statecraft: Domestic Service in Renaissance Venice,1400–1600* (Baltimore: The Johns Hopkins University Press, 1996), 39.

[50] "Et che li ingiuriassero di parole, over fatti, oltra che in tal caso li schalchi et cuoghi siano tenuti subito partirsi di là," ASV, *Provveditori Sopra le Pompe*, bu. 1, capitolari 1505–94, fol. 1r, 8 October 1542.

[51] ASV, *Censori*, bu. 1, capitulary dated 1541–1790, fos. 1r-1v, in Romano, *Housecraft and Statecraft*, 43.

Venice's powerful, central security council worried about servants' public speech and the effects it had on perceptions of noble status and the city itself. The Council of Ten determined that servants' public behavior had become so disruptive that on 17 August 1541, it transferred all authority over Venice's domestic servants to the magistracy of the *Censori*. Much of the work of this magistracy, in turn, was dedicated to prosecuting the perceived increase in servants' violent language, especially that of gondoliers, "who insult brides with their oars and mouths as they pass along the canals."[52] These two censors, like the *Esecutori Contro la Bestemmia*, were granted the authority of the Ten itself, including the power to inflict torture or the death penalty if necessary, attesting to the serious attitude taken towards servants' crimes. The *Censori* determined that any servant who used insulting language in public would be branded, whipped, and dropped by the cord.[53] Once again, no trial material exists from this magistracy in the sixteenth century, but this transfer of authority over servants and their language to this specific, powerful magistracy offers incontestable evidence of the significance of speech and its control to the state.

We have already seen the ways that Castiglione, Della Casa, and Guazzo insisted on the links between language and class: that nobles naturally possessed eloquence, while the underclasses did not, though could perhaps learn it. The ideas that nobles should be protected from the aggressive language of the popular classes and that the underclasses were by nature inarticulate or crude in their speech were echoed by a Venetian comportment writer – Antonino Collurafi – a teacher of rhetoric who prescribed the ideal components of noble Venetian behavior in his book *Il nobile veneto* (1623). Collurafi was not nearly as detailed or as example-oriented as his sixteenth-century counterparts; his text did not offer the sweeping and convincing models of behavior that Castiglione, Della Casa, and Guazzo had done a century before. Yet like them, he expressed the belief that Venetian nobles should (and did) possess certain social graces. They should be well versed in poetry, history, philosophy, math, languages, and military arts, as well as virtue, prudence, strength, justice, temperance, and of course, eloquence. Collurafi advised nobles to speak

---

[52] Romano, *Housecraft and Statecraft*, 246–47.
[53] Ibid., 55, 246–47.

modestly. He referred to Aristotle's claim that spoken words were outward signs reflecting the internal thoughts of the soul, the mouth being the door to the heart, so speech therefore demanded caution.

> The tongue must not come before the soul, and words must be weighed with judgment and then spoken with the tongue.... Concerning important things, speaking spontaneously cannot be without criticism for the orator or without damage to the republic.[54]

Like other books of comportment, Collurafi's text paradoxically aimed to teach nobles how to practice good public behavior at the same time that it assumed nobles would naturally possess this knowledge and had no need of instruction. The less refined language of the uneducated Venetian masses demanded surveillance and control.

> Freedom of words is denied to the ignorant who do not know what they say; to the imprudent, who do not know when to be quiet; to the miserable, who only wish to speak when it is contrary to reason. But a sage, prudent and candid citizen of a free city [i.e., the Venetian noble, emphasis added] must be able to offer his advice, opinion and truth freely.[55]

Collurafi emphasized the way that nobles naturally possessed eloquence and an understanding of how and when to speak, and this, in turn, guaranteed them the right to a political voice. By the seventeenth century, Collurafi's ideas had neatly come to reflect and re-enforce the way that various magistracies representing the republic had developed the relationship between language, class, and the state in the century before.

As we have seen, medieval statutes commonly penalized insults against both nobles and state officials, both inside and outside the Veneto; there was nothing particularly unusual about this practice in and of itself.[56]

---

[54] "La lingua non dee l'animo precorrere; ma che le parole si debbon prima librare co'l giudicio, e poi con la lingua proferire.... Nelle cose gravi orare all'improviso esser non potea senza biasimo dell'oratore, ne senza danno delle Repubblica," Antonino Collurafi, *Il nobile veneto* (Venice, 1623), 26.

[55] "La libertà delle parole e vietata a gli ignoranti, che non sanno quello, che si dice; a gli imprudenti, che non sanno, quando bisogna, tacere: ai tristi, che non vogliono, se non contra il sentimento proprio della ragione parlare: ma d'un cittadino saggio, prudente, candido, e di città libera libero esser deve il conseglio, libera l'opinione, libera la verità," Ibid., 226.

[56] On the perceived gravity of insults against superiors, see Burke, *Historical Anthropology*, 99.

Almost a third of the insult trials that the *Avogaria* processed involved such cases. However, putting this together with the fact that the *Esecutori* also (inexplicably) heard cases of verbal assaults on patricians, along with the increased punitive attention paid to servants' public language, a curious picture emerges. The combined work of the *Avogaria*, *Censori*, and *Esecutori* indicates broad concern about verbal aggression against nobles and social superiors, *by* servants and the underclasses in general, shared across a spectrum of civic magistrates. The Venetian state in the sixteenth century seemed interested in developing and enforcing a specific spoken decorum – a code of civic language – that reflected and constructed a clearly defined class hierarchy. These magistrates aimed to shield respectable ears and the honor of the state itself from the scandalous and potentially dangerous words of the lower classes.

This was especially important in Venice, where noble status had political meaning. The Venetian patriciate became a closed caste in 1297 and admission to the nobility only became more strict thereafter, especially following the creation of the Golden Book in 1506: a register of patrician lineages.[57] Stanley Chojnacki has long argued that the convergence of the state and the nobility tightened over the course of the early modern period in Venice, as patricians "assigned to the government the authority to define and attribute noble status and the responsibility of assuring them of the tangible benefits of receiving it."[58] In Venice, unlike in courtly societies, nobles represented the state. Insults up the social ladder therefore implied injuring the state itself – objectively a much more serious crime than verbally insulting any single person. In a state where the right to political participation and power hung exclusively on the ability to prove one's patrician status, insults questioning or demeaning nobles' status provoked a particularly sensitive reaction on the part of the patrician class, and therefore on the part of state magistracies that supported its interests.[59] Disciplining the tongue along class lines

---

[57] Dennis Romano, *Patricians and Popolani: The Social Foundations of the Venetian Renaissance State* (Baltimore and London: The Johns Hopkins University Press, 1987), 155; D. Raines, "Office Seeking, Broglio and the Pocket Political Guide-books in Cinquecento and Seicento Venice," *Studi veneziani* 22 (1991): 156.

[58] Stanley Chojnacki, "Marriage Regulation," 59.

[59] Though an example of written rather than verbal insults against the nobility, Venetians often blackened one another's reputations through calumny, asserting evidence of illegitimate births in the records of the *Prove di Nobiltà*, thereby questioning the credentials of young

neatly coincides with the increasing "aristocratization" of Venice in the sixteenth century. Although Venice remained a republic in name, historians have argued that the sixteenth century represented the end of "true" Venetian republicanism, resulting in the concentration of power in the hands of a few aristocrats and a more marked social stratification.[60] In effect, Venetian merchants in the sixteenth century aspired to become nobles rather than bigger merchants. The early modern period similarly witnessed a new drive to reform the justice system along more absolutist lines, as seen in Doge Andrea Gritti's attempt to introduce Roman law to Venice in the mid-sixteenth century.[61] At this time, controlling speech as a form of violence and enforcing a standard of non-criticism of the patrician class reinforced aristocratic culture and interests. This in turn also protected the unity of the state and promoted its stability.

If legislation, magistracies, and trials that correlated speech and class pointed to a specific Venetian configuration of language and statecraft in the sixteenth century, trials prosecuting insults against the state itself make this connection especially clear. All governments and regimens seeking stability sought to monitor and punish treasonous speech, including despotisms, and insulting the state had always been punished harshly in Venice. The Council of Ten had monitored civic speech since its inception. It was in fact the fear of treason and conspiracy that led to the creation of this magistracy in 1310, which was then given the task of stopping all subversive activities against the state, whether they be in action, speech, or writing.[62] The creation of the Council of Ten and its centrality in Venetian politics reflects a particular Venetian sensibility to the potential danger of verbal threats. As any student of Renaissance Italy knows, Venice was among a small handful of states including Lucca and Genoa that managed to uphold its republican constitution as one by one, other states fell victim to factional violence and became

patricians to enter the Great Council. See Alexander Cowan, "Innuendo and Inheritance: Strategies of Scurrility in Medieval and Renaissance Venice," in *Subversion and Scurrility: Popular Discourse in Europe from 1500 to the Present*, ed. Dermot Cavanagh and Tim Kirk (Aldershot: Ashgate, 2000), 125–37.

[60] See Martin, *Venice's Hidden Enemies*, 58–9; Dennis Romano, *Housecraft and Statecraft*, xv–xxvi.

[61] Shaw, *The Justice of Venice*, 207.

[62] Ruggiero, *Violence*, 127–31; Sanuto, *I diarii*, vol. 6, 258–9. See also n. 48 above.

despotisms in the later Middle Ages. Venice maintained its republican status until 1797 in part precisely because its leaders understood how powerful and divisive insults could be. As Guido Ruggiero and Edward Muir have put it, "the control of faction and speech were inseparably mixed, and speech was considered a dangerous part of the violence of factionalism." The key to preventing violent vendettas was "to silence all personal insults."[63]

In the sixteenth century, individuals continued to be punished as always for seditious speech. As Sanudo recounted, the Paduan Lorenzo di la Campana was banned from Venice for five years on 28 November 1509 "for words spoken against our *Signoria.*" On 19 November 1511, the barber Bernardin Malizia was placed on a stage between the two columns of San Marco and had his tongue cut out "for words spoken against the state." In 1584, "Several foolish and loose-tongued preachers...charged the judges of Venice with corruption and bias," laughing and carrying on in the presence of the papal nuncio and more than 4,000 onlookers. One of these preachers was banned from Venice forever as a result.[64] Like Ruggiero and Muir, Frederic Lane also related the success of Venice's great republican and cosmopolitan experiment to its success in controlling people's speech. "Men of a great variety of views," he believed, "succeeded one way or another in living in Venice pretty much as they pleased, so long as they did not attack the government."[65]

Trials from the *Avogaria* prosecuted unruly verbal outbursts rather than cases of treason or conspiracy per se; these cases were pursued by the Council of Ten itself and fall outside the central interests of this study, which does not extend to consider political plots against the government. The *Avogaria*'s work nevertheless betrays this same interest in punishing verbal violence against the state, albeit violence that was less planned, organized, or calculated. For example, in March of 1570, Nicolò Andri, a cook on a galley, was accused of insulting the state and revealing state secrets to several Turks. According to the ship's bread baker Manoli da

---

[63] Ruggiero, *Violence*, 126; Edward Muir, "The Sources of Civil Society in Italy," *Journal of Interdisciplinary History* 29 (1999): 386.

[64] Sanuto, *I diarii*, vol. 9, 353; vol. 13, 260; Alvise Michiel, *Memorie pubbliche della repubblica di Venezia*, 277r–278r, cited in Chambers and Pullan, *Venice, A Documentary History*, 84.

[65] Frederic C. Lane, *Venice, A Maritime Republic* (Baltimore: The Johns Hopkins University Press, 1973), 395.

Cerigo, although the galley was in port in Corfu – an island that was part of the Venetian empire – Nicolò was chatting with some Turks who were unloading grain. They all agreed that the Turks should not have supplied Corfu with grain because the Venetians were dogs.[66] Nicolò also discussed recent events in the fleet with the Turks, noting the fact that fifteen Venetian galleys had recently been defeated near Vallona and discussing who would next become captain of the fleet. Another witness reported that Nicolò had said "why did you bring grain to the fucking cuckolded dogs in this city?"[67] The witness Angelo da Venezia stated that Nicolò had exclaimed "that they had done badly to bring grain to the men of the Venetian empire, who were dogs and scoundrels, adding that Venetian ships had been defeated with artillery by Carracozza [a Turkish commander] – words which moved my blood."[68] Nicolò claimed innocence, but for his "many other words full of iniquity and bad spirit," was sentenced to three years of galley service and having his tongue cut out if he further misbehaved.[69] In a similar case from 1601, Giovanni Antonio Malloni was accused of physically and verbally injuring the lion of St. Mark – the symbol of the Venetian state – in Rovigo. Embittered over his gambling losses, Malloni confronted the statue of the lion over the door of the offices of taxation in Rovigo, hitting it on the eyes, nose, and head with a bucket and yelling "ugly God, dog, fucking cuckold – you give lots of money to others but none to me."[70] Malloni denied having spoken these words and claimed that such an accusation was based on the false testimonies of his enemies. The court nevertheless persisted, questioning whether or not Malloni had "committed such a detestable

---

[66] "Qual diceva al Turco, che havevano fatto male di haver portato li formenti in questo luoco, la qual cosi confirmandoli il Turco, il soggionse che questa gente erano cani, et che sapevano anco loro d'haver fatto male, dove questo Christiano li disse in conformità che veramente erano cani," ASV, *Avogaria di Comun, Penale*, bu. 141, fasc. 3 "Nicolò Andri," 13 March 1570, testimony of Manoli da Cerigo.

[67] "Perche havevano essi portato il formento in questa città à questi cani becchi fotui," Ibid., 13 March 1570, testimony of Piero da Candia.

[68] "Che si havevano diportati malamente a portar formenti alli huomini del stato del Dominio Venetiano che erano cani, et scelerati, soggiongendomi à dire che li haveva anco narrato come Carracozza haveva tirato con artigliarie alle nostre galee per le qual parole mi si comosse tutto il sangue," Ibid., 13 March 1570, testimony of Anzelo da Venezia.

[69] "Molte altre parole piene d'iniquità et mal animo," Ibid., sentence of 14 March 1570.

[70] "Dio brutto can becco fottu che tu dai tanti denari a delli altri, et a me non ne vuoi dare," Ibid., bu. 418, fasc. 4 "Malloni Giovanni Antonio," 10 June 1603, testimony of Giacomo Rana.

and abominable crime by speaking vituperous words against that image [of the lion]," and eventually punished him with 10 years galley service.[71]

Cases of insults against the state's interests often prompted the *Avogaria* to produce formal edicts and proclamations to discourage the use of violent language. For instance, after a group of people who wanted a dowry returned threatened and insulted the prioress and hospital of the *Pietà* in 1514, the *Avogaria* declared the fine of 200 *lire* or five years in prison for anyone who insulted the hospital.[72] As we have seen, insults on galleys were not uncommon. Violence among the members of the Venetian fleet particularly troubled the state, as concord and peace were necessary on the high seas to permit efficient and safe trade. In 1576, the galley worker Giovanni Albanese got drunk and insulted Giovanni da Chero by calling him a dog and a hang-man (*boia*). Then, "not content to have already insulted him once with words, he came back to say rude things to him again and to beat him."[73] Giovanni was punished with three additional years of galley service, and together with this verdict the *Avogaria* attached a separate document noting the law which had previously determined this punishment. On 28 December 1576, a month before this trial, the captain of the Venetian fleet had passed a law declaring that any insolence on the high seas, or anyone "who dares to fight or create an uproar, either in facts or in words, with anyone else from the same fleet, or from land or a soldier, will be confined to 18 months galley service."[74] On 16 January 1570, the *Avogaria* posted a proclamation over the steps of the Rialto declaring that porters and boatmen around the German warehouse had been regularly pronouncing "indecent words, and at times began to fight, which creates a notable disturbance to the calm of the merchants." The *Avogaria* declared a fine of 50 *lire* for anyone

---

[71] "Commetter cosi dettestando, et abbominevol dellitto haveste a proferir parole di vittuperio contra quell'imagine," Ibid., 10 June 1603, testimony of Giovanni Malloni; sentence of 17 September 1603.

[72] "Far diversi insolti alla casa de la pieta, ha detto vilannia ala priora piu volte perche el demanda la dota," Ibid., bu. 320, fasc. 11 "Ignoto ingiurie contra Ospitale della Pietà," 23 March 1514, testimony of Catharina uxor Ioannis; proclamation of 22 April 1514.

[73] "Non contento di haverlo ingiuriato di parole . . . torno à dirli villani et darli dei pugni," Ibid., bu. 18, fasc. 30 "Zuanne Albanese," 23 January 1576, testimony of Giovanni Albanese.

[74] "Dalli rumori et risse che talhora sogliono causare le insolenze delli galeotti . . . si fa publicamente intendere . . . che non sia alcuno di essa Armata . . . che ardisca di contrastar o far rumore ò di fatti ò di parole con alcun altro ò dell'istessa armata òdell terra ò soldato in pena di esser confinato per mesi 18 a vogar in galea sforzata," Ibid., 28 December 1576.

who dared to argue "either in deeds or in words, or in any way pronounce indecent language" around the warehouse.[75]

Not unlike insults on galleys or around the warehouses of merchants and traders, insults against the Turk were also subject to special scrutiny by the state. On 19 March 1574 two Turks – Hassan and Mostafa – complained to the Doge and *Signoria* about the "enormous injuries and insults that [Venetian] subjects had spoken . . . with insulting words offending our honor."[76] Several witnesses confirmed having heard and seen Venetian subjects insulting these Turks, and as a result, on 20 March 1574 – within 24 hours of the complaint – the *Avogaria* ordered that "no one was to dare in any way, form or manner, in words or deeds, insult, offend, or have offended or use any type of injurious words against the subjects and representatives of the most serene Lord Turk . . . with the punishment of five years galley service and three drops from the cord in public."[77] Maintaining friendly trade relations clearly necessitated the spoken propriety of Venetians and the verbal respect of visitors – behavior that a trading state like Venice demanded to protect its economic interests.

What do the sum of these laws and trials about verbal injury reveal? Early modern Venetians demonstrated a keen awareness of the boundaries separating mannered and unmannered speech, protesting when

---

[75] "Havendosi doluto li signori console della Magnifica Madion Alemana che li fachini Barcaroli, et altra qualita di gente che di servitio di detta Natione della mercantie capitano nel fontico da loro habitato contro il timore del signor Iddio e della Giustitia, et con poco rispetto sono cosi arditi che pronontiando parole indecente, et alle volte vengono alle mani, il che viene anche con notabile disturbo alla quiete di signori mercanti. . . . Non ardisca di trovar risse ne offender in fatti ne in parole alcun'altro ne in acuna maniere pronontiare parole indecenti et cio in pena di L50," Ibid., bu. 200, fasc. 11 "Boldon Antonio," 17 May 1646. This proclamation is re-issued in Italian following the original Latin proclamation from 16 January 1570. A plaque re-issuing this ordinance in 1670 still hangs in the south entrance of the *Fondaco dei Tedeschi* (now the central post office) today.

[76] "Grandissime ingiurie, et ultragii che li vostri subditi ne fanno . . . con parole ingiuriose offender l'honor nostro," ASV, *Avogaria di Comun, Civile*, bu. 279, fasc. 7 "Turchi residenti in Venezia non abbiano ad essere molestati," denunciation of 19 March 1574.

[77] "Che niuno et sia si voglia non ardiser, per alcun modo, forma over inzegno cosi in parole, come in fatti, ingiuriar, ne offender, ne far offender, o usare parole di qual si voglia sorte iniuriose o altramente contra li suditi et representanti il Serenissimo signor Turco, ma quelli ben trattar, et accarezzar, sotto pena, di servir per anni cinque in galia de condennadi, et tratti tre di corda in pubblico, et non essendo boni da Galia, di star per ditto tempo nella preson forte, et essendo donne over putti, da esser frustadi, da San Marco a Rialto," Ibid., 20 March 1574. I am grateful to Steve Ortega for pointing out this case.

an aggressor broke the rules of verbal decorum. They demonstrated what appeared to be an internalized awareness of the need for "civility" and physical, bodily control, not unlike the civility and verbal control called for in early modern books of comportment. Venetians clearly perceived verbal injury as being equally as grave as physical harm and understood language to be as forceful as action itself, seen especially in the way that the words "words and deeds" typically appeared paired together in the rote phrases of both testimony and legislation. Even though in some cases proof of bodily harm would have been more than enough to ensure prosecution, witnesses invariably included accounts of the foul language spoken against them in their accusations. To a modern individual, it would seem superfluous to mention that in addition to being physically assaulted, one was also called a dog or a cuckold, yet in early modern accounts, the verbal component of an accusation either stood on its own or further confirmed the severity of a case. The failure to protest an insult would be equivalent to admitting that the accusation was true. If insults and individuals' and officials' responses to them provide a view of community values, insights into a community's mentality, and an understanding of a community's ideas about honor and shame, then insults in early modern Venice demonstrate consistent concerns about both sexual and civil behavior. Aggressive language typically taunted individuals' sexual honor and civic respectability in general, much as in other early modern cities.

The practice of reprimanding insults, however, seemed to vary from the norm in other places in the way the *Avogaria* pursued insults endangering peaceful trade. In addition, the perceived severity of insults up the social ladder combined with an increased attention paid to servants' unruly language points to the construction of a unique, hierarchically conceived code of civic language in sixteenth-century Venice. The work of these magistracies suggests that concerns about verbal violence in the sixteenth century had less to do with medieval fears of factionalism and political vendettas and had more to do with the creation of a public language that mirrored and replicated the unique political workings of an aristocratic republic. That is to say, individuals could not insult the state or its interests, reflecting a republican order; they also could not insult its noble class, nor could the underclasses make its noble class appear dishonorable, reflecting the aristocratic component of this polity. Venetian lawmakers clearly understood Walter Ong's assertion that sound unites groups of people in a different way from the written word, in that the spoken word is at once communication and act.[78] With such a view of the word and with the experience of living in oral culture, it is possible to see the word as powerful, dangerous, divisive, and in need of surveillance.

The construction and disciplining of such spoken decorum was intrinsically related to ideas about honor. As we have seen with blasphemy, honor was clearly analyzed through acts of speech. That is to say, punishing insults served to encourage state stability not only by attempting to eradicate violence, but also by protecting the honor of the state and the honor of its patrician class as its representatives. One of the best descriptions of the way honor functioned in early modern Italy occurs in Annibale Romei's dialogue *Dell'onore* (1585).[79] Compared to virtue which is innate, internal, and rewarded by salvation at the end of one's life, honor by contrast is acquired, developed, visible, and evaluated in the public arena. It comes from what one has accomplished in life in the realms of family, friendships, and in economic and political advancement, and as Romei implies, in turn generates accomplishments in these realms as well. Most importantly, honor exists in the eye of the observer and disappears when one's reputation declines. Good opinion, in effect, was the essence of honor. According to Romei, the most common way to damage one's reputation and therefore one's honor is to fail to avenge an injury. As Edward Muir has summarized Romei, "those who truly value the honor of the world will never allow their reputation to die away by failing to redress an insult no matter what its cause."[80] Romei's ideas illustrate why it was so important for both Venetian patricians as individuals and the state at large to defend their/its honor as it manifested itself in speech. If honor served to generate social, economic, and political capital, maintaining one's honor, or at least demonstrating the appearance of defending one's honor, was crucial to patrician and civic prosperity, because once honor was lost, it was difficult if not impossible to regain.

---

[78] Walter Ong, *The Presence of the Word*, 122–31.

[79] Annibale Romei, "Dell'onore," in his *Ferrara e la corte estense nella seconda metà del secolo decimosesto. I discorsi* (Città di Castello: Lapi, 1891), 82–108.

[80] Edward Muir, *Mad Blood Stirring: Vendetta and Factions in Friuli During the Renaissance* (Baltimore and London: The Johns Hopkins University Press, 1993), 255.

Sixteenth-century efforts to discipline insults and control public speech coincided with a variety of state efforts to monitor and reduce social gathering in general. For a variety of reasons, the *Esecutori Contro la Bestemmia* and *Censori* both passed laws limiting social organization in the fifteenth and sixteenth centuries. The *Provveditori Sopra le Pompe* also passed laws to limit and monitor gatherings such as banquets and theatrical representations, because these were sites where "lascivious and disrespectable words and deeds happen."[81] Laws regulating congregation varied significantly in scope and purpose. They were aimed at preventing political insurrection, limiting sumptuary display, or simply at encouraging the flow of traffic in canals and narrow alleyways. Nevertheless, such legislation went hand-in-hand with efforts to eradicate unruly speech. As Peter Stallybrass and Allon White have suggested, "new kinds of speech can be traced through the emergence of new public sites of discourse and the transformation of old ones. . . . [T]he history of political struggle has been the history of the attempts made to control significant sites of assembly and spaces of discourse."[82] Theaters, banquets, open *campi*, *botteghe*, quays, *traghetti*, and gondolier stops were sites where exchange could easily lead to outbursts of violent language. They represented potential spaces for popular expression and protest, as evidenced by the republic's efforts to control gathering in such places. Like the prosecution of insulting language by the *Avogaria* and the *Censori*, legislation limiting social congregation also sought to discourage the spoken expression of the underclasses. The less people were permitted to gather and engage in verbal exchange, the less chance there would be for the exposure of what James Scott has labeled the "hidden transcript," or critiques of power that contested subordination.[83] Whereas social gathering around civic spectacles such as processions or coronations functioned as a means of demonstrating the unity and stability of the state, the language unleashed at informal gatherings potentially represented the more violent underbelly of civil society

---

[81] Bistort, *Il magistrato alle pompe*, 226–30.

[82] Peter Stallybrass and Allon White, *The Politics and Poetics of Transgression* (Ithaca: Cornell University Press, 1986), 80.

[83] James C. Scott, *Domination and the Arts of Resistance – Hidden Transcripts* (New Haven: Yale University Press, 1990), ix–xiii.

as it was divided by class – something the republic hoped to keep under wraps.

This is a somewhat more speculative reading of laws forbidding congregation: a reading that goes beyond their stated justification. However, magistracies punishing verbal insults specifically and social congregation more generally both conformed to the new discourse of civic order that the state was promoting in the sixteenth century. The work of all these magistracies, the *Esecutori*, the *Pompe*, the *Avogaria*, and the *Censori*, was very much in keeping with Doge Andrea Gritti's renowned efforts to create a more decorous civic center. During his term as doge (1523–38), Gritti enacted numerous architectural and civic reforms to clean up and polish the city and make it respectable in the wake of the disaster of Agnadello. In the early sixteenth century, the Piazza San Marco had been cluttered with money-changing booths, food stalls, hostels, and latrines. Gritti adhered to the tenets of Domenico Morosini's 1497 architectural treatise *De bene instituta re publica* which argued that civic beauty and decorum were political instruments that generated civic order and earned the respect and fear of enemies. Gritti hired the renowned architect Jacopo Sansovino to remove the sordid wooden stalls that had infested the Piazza San Marco and to replace dilapidated buildings with new ones, presenting a more civilized, classicizing facade to the outside world. Gritti similarly revamped carnival rites, prohibiting the vulgar throwing of pig's ears in the Piazza San Marco in favor of more noble, modest spectacles. Venice as "a new Rome" emerged out of the dark years following the League of Cambrai, and similar civic and architectural reforms continued throughout the sixteenth century.[84] Gritti's *renovatio* went hand-in-hand with sixteenth-century legislation against insults; both programs aimed to replace the unbecoming, ugly, filthy, and overflowing – whether they be bodies or buildings – with the modest, impervious, clean, and classicizing, reflecting the civilizing process as described by Bakhtin and Elias. A new aesthetic emerged for Venice: one which, equating the early modern body with Gritti's architectural

---

[84] See Deborah Howard, *Jacopo Sansovino: Architecture and Patronage in Renaissance Venice* (New Haven: Yale University Press, 1975), 11–14; Edward Muir, *Civic Ritual in Renaissance Venice* (Princeton: Princeton University Press, 1981), 163; Manfredo Tafuri, *Venezia e il Rinascimento: Religione, scienza, architettura* (Turin: Einaudi, 1985), 156–69, 244–97.

program, presented the new "impenetrable façades" of the classicizing building and the closed mouth, neatly prefiguring similar advice about hiding the tongue and closing the mouth soon to be given by Della Casa and others. The Venetian state in the sixteenth century sought to contain the body and discipline it in a variety of new ways: through legislation aimed to restrict sumptuous dress, to oversee prostitution, and as we have seen, to discipline abusive language. The tongue – which represented the site of the formation of popular/counter culture – needed to be controlled, just as squalid buildings were cleaned up and public spectacles became more decorous. Encouraging such "civility" to some extent reflected changing European attitudes towards popular culture at large, as the ethic of "reformers" across Europe encouraged "decency, diligence, gravity, modesty, orderliness, prudence, reason, self-control, sobriety, and thrift."[85] In Venice, controlling the unruly tongue went hand in hand with these other processes.

Despite their various efforts, all this is not to say that Venetian magistrates were necessarily successful in their efforts to govern the tongue, or that their ideas about the relationship between language and class were tenable. As a colorful aside and illustrative example, in a 1601 dowry dispute between the nobles Margherita Pisani and Giulio Benalio, whose children had married each other, Margherita insulted Giulio "with the most embarrassing and wicked words," calling him a traitor, an assassin, a usurer and a Lutheran, and calling his servant a whore, a cow, and a pig.[86] As a witness reported,

> this woman yelled so loudly that you could have heard her halfway up the Grand Canal, saying that Ser Giulio had ruined her and that he was a man with no conscience. . . . She continued to insult Ser Giulio, saying embarrassing words to him and vituperous words to dishonor

[85] Peter Burke, *Popular Culture*, 213. "Sul piano sociale, quest'azione moralizzatrice é rivolta decisamente ai costumi dei ceti popolari, e soprattutto della popolazione marginale. Nei confronti dei poveri per esempio, si rovescia completamente il tradizionale atteggiamento benevolo e condiscendente," Derosas, "Moralità e giustizia," 444.

[86] "S'e fatto lecito ingiuriarmi, con le piu vergognose, et nefande parole," ASV, *Avogaria di Comun, Penale*, bu. 464, fasc. 2 "Margherita Pisani" 26 June 1601; "Vechio luteran porco vituperoso userer," 30 June 1601, testimony of Zuana Grisentin; "Traditor, sassin, userer . . . diceva vilania alla massera putana, vacha, porca et altre vilanie," 3 July 1601, testimony of Geronimo Savinelo.

him, for instance that he had not confessed or had communion for fourteen years, and that he was a public usurer. She said that she was not afraid of him, since he was not man enough to lick her cunt.... I begged her to quiet down and told her it was not appropriate for a woman to use words like that. If she believed that Ser Giulio had not observed the promises from his [dowry] contract, the path of justice was open to her.... Then, she left in a boat near the warehouse of the *facina,* and continued to yell until she was half-way up the canal and you could not hear what she was saying anymore.[87]

Clearly, women could offend and insult as effectively as men, and more importantly, nobles by no means practiced the refined, modest speech that Collurafi suggested they did or should.

Furthermore, the establishment of rules to suppress base language somewhat ironically worked to open up an enlarged political space in which to unleash the tongue. Not unlike other attempts to control cultural expression, insults and foul language became all the more meaningful as means of protest after they had been specifically legislated against. As with sumptuary legislation, the more state magistrates laid down laws, the more creative and brazen individuals became in order to skirt them. In this way, placing controls on unmannered speech fundamentally worked to encourage a contest between the state and its inhabitants about the fashioning of the self and class identity. Verbal aggression functioned as a substitute for political action, as a means by which the weak and powerless could assert or avenge themselves. If Venetian magistracies sought to enforce certain standards of respectable language, insults and swearing therefore took on an increased importance as means of subversion, particularly for the popular classes potentially protecting their cultural space against encroaching sixteenth-century ideals of aristocratic

---

[87] "Questa dona cridava talmente forte, che si havrebbe sentita fin a mezo il canal grande, particularmente dicendo al s.ri giulio che l'haveva assassinata et ch'era huomo che non haveva conscientia ... continuava a vilanegiare detto signor giulio dicendoli parole vergonose, vituperose contra l'honor del detto signor giulio fra le quali fu che non si haveva confessato ne comunicato per 14 anni et ch'era publico usurer, et disse che non haveva paura di lui, perche non l'era huomo di licarghe la potifa ... io anco la pregai che la si quietasse et che non si conveniva a una dona usar parole di quella sorte et che se pur haveva qualche opinione, chel signor giulio non li havesse osservato quanto gli haveva promesso in contrato la strada della giust.a li era aperta.... l'ando poi in barca al tragheto del fontego della facina sempre cridando, et fina essendo a mezo canal l'andava cridando che non podeva intender quello la dicesse," Ibid., 4 July 1601, testimony of Antonio Boldù.

civility. Servants, laborers, and gondoliers surely gained standing among themselves for their ability to insult and swear, as insults could not only destroy honor but also create it. The records of the prosecution of crime, of course, do not clearly yield much information as to how and when this happened, because it was their purpose to prosecute foul language and not to glorify or celebrate the resistance it generated. However, we can easily imagine that the individuals whose cases are highlighted here – galley workers insulting their captains, or everyday Venetians slighting the nobility – gained a certain renown and respect in their communities as a result of their verbal prowess.

As literary evidence, Fabio Glissenti's *Discorsi morali* offers a vivid description of the life of Venetian servants and gondoliers: one that suggests that they were by no means subordinated to elite culture and that their language, in fact, made them even heroic figures in their circles. Glissenti was one of the leading physicians in late-sixteenth-century Venice and in addition, was a prolific writer. His *Discorsi morali contra il dispiacer del morire* (1596) – five dialogues that come to over 11,000 pages in length – included detailed discussions with and about servants and gondoliers in the second dialogue. Here, the interlocutors of the dialogue, a courtier and a philosopher, question a servant about whether or not he liked his job. The servant responded by claiming, with a pun, that a Venetian servant was not a "servitore" but actually a "Servito Ré" or a "served king" because he managed to turn all situations to his advantage, skimming off the household funds and visiting taverns on the clock.[88] Following this, the interlocutors engaged a gondolier in conversation, who also believed there were advantages to his trade that outsiders might not be aware of. Gondoliers expected various tips and treats from their passengers and stole from them if they did not receive them. They also received favors from courtesans. Most of all, they could often force passengers to pay more than the fixed rates, and terrorized passengers by rocking a gondola wildly if they did not agree to their fees. If all else failed, gondoliers relied on their expertise in verbal insults and dirty words to threaten their passengers. Glissenti's gondolier bragged that gondoliers learned to "curse, blaspheme, swear, reprove and

---

[88] Glissenti, *Discorsi morali*, 129v–130r. I am grateful to Dennis Romano for pointing out this text.

vituperate from childhood," illuminating how speech defined gondoliers as a proud professional group with a pronounced sense of identity.[89] Like other books of comportment and literary depictions of the lower classes, Glissenti's description of servants is one that often ridicules, criticizes, and simplifies the attitudes of the lower classes from the perspective of elites; his text is by no means a clear-cut portrait of reality. Nonetheless, he offers an understanding of how those who hurled insults the best, at least among servants and gondoliers, surely gained a certain honor in their communities.

Social inferiors such as gondoliers fought a wide variety of battles with the weapon of the tongue; they affirmed their status and increased their honor within their own social group, damaged the honor of those they insulted, and most significantly challenged the ideals of republican respectability and social hierarchy that various branches of the state were trying to enforce. With foul language, workers and servants carved out a space of resistance for popular culture. The anti-language of insults therefore suggests obvious cracks in theories of smooth, large-scale, historical transition such as that proposed by Elias, who argued for the unproblematic assimilation of elite courtly values. His explanation for change is too general and superficial, especially for an urban setting. In the end, even with the clearly organized goals of repressing foul language, state intervention was not capable of enacting change as dramatically and thoroughly as his model suggests. Individuals and their bodies were not merely inert emblems of change, but clearly possessed a dynamic agency that resisted the imposition of official culture. Control over the tongue was not merely imposed from the top down. Instead, speech was a constitutive element of power, which is, as we shall see, precisely what the Venetian practice of gossip illuminates.

---

[89] "Impercioche avezzi siamo a maledire, bestemmiare, giurare, rimproverare, e vituperare fin da fanciulli," Ibid., 142r. See also Romano, *Housecraft and Statecraft*, 221.

Appendix A: *Sample of Most Common Insults from 58 Cases of the* Avogaria di Comun, 1500–1625*

fucked/fucking cuckold (*becco fotuo*)	18
rogue/knave (*furfante*)	10
scoundrel/cheat/fraud (*mariol*)	9
whore (*puttana*)	9
dog (*cane*)	9
scoundrel/coward (*poltrona*)	8
thief/crook (*ladro*)	8
bugger (*buzerar/buzerona*)	5
rogue/rascal (*furbo*)	5
cuckold (literally goat) (*becco*)	4
whore of God (*puttana di dio*)	4
cow (*vaccha*)	4
ugly (*brutto*)	4
son-of-a-whore (*fatto e ditto*)	4
traitor (*traditor*)	4
pig (*porco/porca*)	3
pimp/procuress (*ruffiano/a*)	3
assassin (*sassin*)	2
disgraceful (*vituperoso*)	2
Jew (*giudio*)	2
dissolute/sodomite (*bardassa*)	2
beast (*bestia*)	2
pathetic (*tristo*)	2
drunk (*ubriaco*)	2
idiot (*gioton*)	2
shameful (*vergognoso*)	1
fucking cuckold (*cornuto fotudo*)	1
atheist (*ateo*)	1
Lutheran (*Luteran*)	1
usurer (*usurar*)	1
crude (*malveazzo*)	1
cuckold (*cornuto*)	1
scoundrel/villain (*scelerato*)	1
witch (*striga*)	1
little shit (*cacetto*)	1
mule (*mullo*)	1
bastard (*bastardo*)	1
fool (*buffon*)	1
villain (*briccone*)	1

*This sample was done by counting the spoken insults in trials where verbal injury was either the central accusation or figured prominently in litigation. Insults were counted whether the aggressor was proven guilty for verbal assault or not. If different testimonies reported the same insult several times in the course of a trial, the insult was only counted once.

4

Conversation and Exchange: Networks of Gossip

In January of 1567, a Dominican friar named Antonio Volpe was arrested by the guards of the Holy Office of the Inquisition in the Campo San Lio, not far from the Rialto bridge. Volpe had come to Venice from Ferrandina in the deep south of Italy. Accused of heresy, the record for his trial indicated that a wide variety of talk had circulated about his unorthodox ideas and lifestyle, eventually leading to his arrest. Some said that he did not believe in the intercession of the saints; that he had declared Saint Mary of Loreto to be the Pope's whore, or had proclaimed that Lutheran Germany was the promised land and the Elysian fields where he hoped to go and live. Others said that he wanted to give up his habit and marry a woman from Padua, or that he was already married and had a child, or even that he was in fact no longer living since he had been decapitated in Naples as a Lutheran heretic. Booksellers in particular had a lot so say about this friar. The physician Domenico della Cava testified that he had heard from the proprietor of the Salerno bookshop that Volpe owned several heretical books.

As his trial unfolded, it became clear that these and many other rumors were part of a larger plot to produce Volpe's downfall, contrived by the physician Decio Bellobuono, or at least that was what people said. Bellobuono had many reasons to dislike Volpe. Volpe had thwarted Bellobuono's brother Propertio's plans to marry a wealthy widow by revealing to the woman's family that Propertio was not the rich merchant that he presented himself to be, but just a scheming profiteer. More importantly, Fra Volpe had turned a handsome profit on the drugs for syphilis that he made in his distillery in the Campo dei Frari. He had loaned some of his riches to Bellobuono so that Bellobuono could open a distillery of his own, and when Bellobuono refused to pay Volpe back, Volpe threatened to call on civic authorities to collect his debt. Bellobuono attempted to defame the friar and spread gossip about him in order to avoid this payment, and perhaps also hoped to eliminate Volpe as a rival purveyor of cures. In a separate trial, Decio also appears to have intimidated another man, a solicitor named Annovazzo, to whom he also owed money that he refused to pay. He instead defamed Annovazzo, like Volpe, as a Lutheran. Volpe realized that two could play at the game of rumor and defamation. He claimed that the entire Bellobuono family had been banished from Naples for their involvement in a robbery and a murder. In the end, the Inquisition appears to have thrown up its hands at this case and dismissed the charges against Volpe. The court was most likely simply worn down by having to follow up on the many threads of gossip and rumor involved in the case.[1]

Volpe's trial elicited a series of elaborate stories – some around town, and others just in the courtroom – developed by both the accuser and the accused, and disseminated by a complex cast of characters. However, his trial is far from unique in how men and women used narrative and public talk to win their cases in the eyes of the community and the law. The essence of the conflict between these two men revolved essentially around quarrels over money that had nothing to do with heresy or questionable religious behavior. Bellobuono hoped to use the Inquisition to deflect legal attention from his unpaid debt by raising a daunting set of rumors about Volpe's piety. Civic and religious institutions could be turned to private ends, in this case, to defame a competitor. Savvy folk like Bellobuono knew how the courts worked: that gossip, rumor, and *fama* or public opinion not only weighed heavily as evidence, but moreover, that courts could turn up the volume of courtroom rumors to a wider civic audience. Though witnesses were admonished to keep quiet about what was said in the court of the Inquisition, we can be quite

---

[1] ASV, bu. 23, fasc. 2 "Antonio Vulpe." See also bu. 27 "Annovazzo." See William Eamon, "The Canker Friar: Piety and Intrigue in an Era of New Diseases," in *Piety and Plague in Europe: From Antiquity to the Early Modern Period*, ed. Franco Mormando and Thomas W. Worcester, Sixteenth Century Essays and Studies (Kirksville, MO: Truman State University Press, 2007), 156–76.

sure that whether or not defendants were ever punished, what was said before the Inquisitor reverberated in the city at large. In this court and others, gossip functioned as much more than mere background noise, and understanding its practice is central to understanding both group interaction, and as we shall see, both statebuilding and political culture at large in the early modern world.

If early modern Venetians used blasphemy and insults to assert their power and prerogatives, networks of verbal exchange and gossip also achieved similar ends. To the historian, gossip is in some ways more visible than blasphemy; language suggesting its practice shows up in an array of documents such as letters, chronicles, treatises, and court cases like Bellobuono's. Its ubiquitous presence suggests some questions about its practice. What was the relationship between the "informal" talk of gossip and rumor and official "public" politics, or between gossip on the street and *fama* or public opinion as defined by the law? What were the roles of men and women, nobles and non-nobles, in this practice of community talk? How did this language function in a state that was a unique mix of courtly and republican politics?

No particular people or culture possesses a monopoly on gossip, though some, including Venetians, might think that they do.[2] Venice is no exception in its practice of gossip, nor does the sixteenth century represent any clear "birth" or "crisis" in gossip. Several scholars have explored the ways in which gossip served to regulate community behavior in various geographical and historical arenas, in particular in medieval and early modern England, demonstrating how social groups constructed themselves through talk and how gossip reinforced and policed moral values.[3] While gossip in Venice mirrors much of what has been discovered

<hr />

[2] "By their own admission, Venetians take pleasure in gossip. In fact, talking about your neighbors is such an art here that there's even a term in the local dialect – "tajar tabari" – for the practice of cutting someone up behind his or her back." Elisabetta Povoledo, "Venice Bristles at the Savannah Treatment," *The New York Times*, 15 February 2006. Similarly, the Bengali claim that the practice of *adda* or careless talk and chat among friends is a particular mark of Bengali national character. See Dipesh Chakrabarty, *Provincializing Europe* (Princeton: Princeton University Press, 2000), 180–213.

[3] Bernard Capp, *When Gossips Meet: Women, Family and Neighbourhood in Early Modern England* (Oxford: Oxford University Press, 2003); Cohen and Cohen, "Camilla the Go-Between"; S. Hindle, "The Shaming of Margaret Knowsley: Gossip, Gender and the Experience

in other places; what is noteworthy about the sociology of language in early modern Venice is the way that gossip functioned within the Venetian political framework of aristocratic republicanism. In the sixteenth century, the Venetian nobility began to act and function much like other aristocrats in Europe, yet the city still remained an important center of commerce and preserved its longstanding republican institutions. As we have seen with blasphemy, territorial losses on the mainland and in the eastern Mediterranean and a fast-rising population in the first half of the sixteenth century encouraged the city to pay more attention to public morality and behavior. A heightened interest in spirituality and religious reform also wrought many changes on the lagoon city and brought the Holy Office to Venice, whose proceedings will be considered below.[4] At the intersection of the city's political, social, and religious systems existed a particular set of rules about speech and language and a particular practice of gossip that at times worked to promote political stability. In addition, gossip had a particular power in this city of travelers and immigrants who brought constant waves of news and rumor. Venice was truly a European "centre of information."[5] Its porous social and architectural space allowed not only people but also their talk to travel with ease. Although space in most medieval cities was cramped, Venetian canals and *calli* were frequently so narrow that only one person or boat could pass; tiny courtyards and windows opening near other windows or onto small Venetian *campielli* created a heightened sense of intimacy.[6] Family life and public transactions were easily seen and heard so that privacy

---

of Authority in Early Modern England," *Continuity and Change* 9 (1994): 391–419; Kamensky, *Governing the Tongue*; Susan E. Phillips, *Transforming Talk: The Problem with Gossip in Late Medieval England* (University Park, PA: The Pennsylvania State University Press, 2007); Melanie Tebbutt, *Women's Talk? A Social History of "Gossip" in Working Class Neighbourhoods, 1880–1960* (Aldershot: Scolar Press, 1995); Chris Wickham, "Gossip and Resistance."

[4] On spirituality and religious reform in sixteenth century Italy and Venice, see Chapter 2, n. 50.

[5] "Venetians produced, circulated, and received the information they deserved in the sense that in certain important respects the information structure was related to, if not a simple expression of, the economic, social and political system," Peter Burke, "Early Modern Venice as a Center of Information and Communication," in Martin and Romano, *Venice Reconsidered*, 404.

[6] See Joanne Ferraro, "The Power to Decide: Battered Wives in Early Modern Venice," *Renaissance Quarterly* 48 (1995): 504.

in early modern Venice was a luxury that even most patricians could not afford. Private life and public affairs intermingled freely in verbal exchange.

Public vox et fama – public opinion or hearsay – has a long history in Western law.[7] A consideration of *fama* in the Venetian ambit merits a closer look, however, because Venice was the only political arena on the Italian peninsula that did not clearly follow Roman law. In Venice, the only requirement necessary to become a judge was that the candidate be of the patrician class. Judges had no formal training in law.[8] Venetian legal practice may have emulated Roman tenets, but it was not bound to them, and in fact often actively excluded Roman law as a source of authority. When considering *fama*, Venetian judges decided themselves as individuals how much weight to give gossip in each given case.[9] Venetian law was an extension of the political system, and judges were not jurists but politicians who made their decisions based on their laymen's common sense and values, and as we might conjecture, on the gossip they heard. As with Roman law, *fama* in the Venetian context did not prove guilt, but it lent strength to the possibility that the accused was guilty. Legal compendia frequently prescribed investigating someone's *fama* as a means of gathering information.[10] When considering denunciations, judges were required to evaluate the reputation of the accuser. Only if a denunciation came from a person of good standing in the community

---

[7] See Fenster and Smail, "Introduction," in *Fama: The Politics of Talk and Reputation in Medieval Europe*, ed. Thelma S. Fenster and Daniel Lord Smail (Ithaca: Cornell University Press, 2003), 1–11.

[8] Shaw, *The Justice of Venice*, 12.

[9] "The jurisdictions and responsibilities of [Venice's] various councils overlapped or conflicted, and Venetian law was more "oracular" than guided by statute or precedent.... The judges in Venetian courts were politicians who lacked legal training, and their limited terms in office prevented them from relying on past experience and knowledge of precedents," Muir, "The Sources of Civil Society in Italy," 102; "[L]e regole del gioco, quelle vere, le fanno giudici e notai, caso per caso, evenienza per evenieza, emergenza per emergenza," Gianni Buganza, "Il potere della parola: La forza e le responsabilità della deposizione testimoniale nel processo penale veneziano (secoli XVI-XVII)" in *La parola all'accusato*, ed. Jean-Louis Biget, Jean-Claude Maire Vigueur, and Agostino Paravicini Bagliani (Palermo: Sellerio, 1991), 137.

[10] For a comparison, see Richard M. Frayer, "Conviction According to Conscience: The Medieval Jurists' Debate Concerning Judicial Discretion and the Law of Proof," *Law and History Review* 7 (1989): 23–88, and L.R. Poos, "Sex, Lies, and the Church Courts of Pre-Reformation England," *Journal of Interdisciplinary History* 25 (1995): 585–607.

could it be taken seriously. "If the accuser has a bad reputation, he offers no justification or proof of innocence."[11]

Gossip or hearsay – information coming from a "public and common voice" or "a voice that spread throughout the people" – proved enough to initiate an investigation and courtroom proceedings. A judge could open a case based on bad reputation alone, which manifested itself through "a public and common voice, at times from one's customs and way of life, and from the bad company kept by the person defamed."[12] Gossip always had to be checked and qualified; denouncers who claimed to have heard something had to cite, in theory, from whom or by what means they had obtained that information in order for their testimonies to be valid, though we have seen, in previous examples, that they did not necessarily do this in practice.[13] Furthermore, all who testified also had to prove themselves persons of honorable repute. In other words, public opinion and community gossip played a direct role in determining both who was accused, and who was a legitimate accuser and witness. Gossip and hearsay prompted an accuser to speak out, bringing a crime or heretic to the ears of the judge. Hearsay about an accuser or witness assayed a person's testimony. Once established as credible courtroom actors, witnesses then shared community talk as means of evidence and proof. The evidence of gossip may not have been enough to decide a case; nevertheless, the forces of *comun parlar* produced essentially all of the actors in Venetian courtroom drama aside from the judge and the notary. In trials from the Holy Office, it is not inconceivable, given the sophisticated use of Venetian court structures by the city's *popolani*, that

---

[11] "Non faccia alcuna giustificazione, o prova della sua innocenza, presumendosi questa, quando specialmente l'accusatore sia di mala fama," Ferro, *Dizionario*, vol. 1, 27. See also Priori, *Prattica criminale*, 10; Barbaro, *Pratica criminale*, 20.

[12] "L'altra inquisitione si dimanda speciale, quando il Giudice inquirisce di certo, et limitato delitto, et di ceta, et limitata persona, et in questa si ricerca la fama publica precedente . . . questa fama suol venire alle volte da una publica, et commune voce, alle volte da i costumi et modi del viver, et dalla mala conversatione della persona diffamata," Priori, *Prattica criminale*, 12. On reputation as the grounds for a trial, see also Barbaro, *Pratica criminale*, 39; Ferro, *Dizionario*, vol. 1, 30–31; Grecchi, *Le formalità del processo*, 40; Balissera Zettele, *Istrutione, et prattica criminale utilissima si alli avocati come alli cancellieri, et altri* (Venice, 1648), 41.

[13] "Nel principio del processo avertiranno di far sempre mentione da chi o per qual mezzo gi siano giunte tali notitie," Eliseo Masini, *Sacro arsenale overo prattica criminale dell'officio della S. Inquisitione* (Rome, 1705), 17.

witnesses emphasized hearsay because they knew, or thought, that that was what judges wanted to hear. Witnesses consciously played to the gallery of listeners in the courtroom, listing the names of other talkers that they thought were expected of them. A consideration of legal theory helps to explain the Inquisitors' interest in gossip in the courtroom, because as we will see in actual court cases, gossip did indeed work to provide additional witnesses, as legal theory suggested it should.

As with prescriptive literature, legal texts did not necessarily reflect legal practice, but they do offer an idea of how both contemporaries and the legal tradition continuing through the nineteenth century imagined the law should work. Venetian advocates on the one hand viewed gossip and hearsay with caution; on the other hand, they too called for, accepted, and in fact sought out gossip, *fama*, reputation, and "what people heard" as evidence central to the initiation, if not the outcome, of courtly proceedings. Litigation and exchanges in the courtroom were a test of what was known. Judges knew that gossip was a force that shaped honor and reputation and therefore they consistently sought to access networks of community information.[14] In this way, litigation effectively functioned as an extension of gossip into the courtroom – an extension, as we shall see, of the feminine and the private into the masculine and the public. What people heard became codified in the records of the church and state, validating gossip as a means of establishing honor, trust, and credit. In this context, it is important to note that *fama* is not the same as gossip. *Fama* was more formal and official, because it carried legal weight in arbitration and litigation. That is to say, *fama* represented more than gossip, as it also referred to the legal status of people and groups, as well as their wealth, power, and general prestige. The relationship between the two is always somewhat ambiguous, and "there was no simple, direct, or automatic connection between social *fama* and legal *fama*."[15] Nevertheless, Venetian cases at the very least offer a sense of the intimate connections between community and law and of the subtle play

[14] We see this in the way that Inquisitors consistently asked, "From whom did you hear this?" See also Ferraro, *Marriage Wars*, 158.

[15] Thomas Kuehn, "Fama as a Legal Status in Renaissance Florence," in Fenster and Smail, *Fama: The Politics of Talk*, 27–28. See also Antonella Bettoni, "Voci malevole: Fama, notizia del crimine, e azione del giudice nel processo criminale (secc. xvi–xvii)," *Quaderni Storici* 121 (2006): 13–38.

of legal purposes on the one side and social actions on the other. *Fama* was clearly both a legal term and a social one (its family of social terms includes *fama, infamosa, defamazione, infamante, famosa, de mala/buona fama*). In legal theory, and as we shall see, in practice, community gossip consistently wove its way from the streets to the courts through the process of denunciations, calling witnesses, and trying a criminal in sixteenth-century Venice. Though male writers condemned the female voice and theoretically labeled gossip as untrustworthy feminine speech, Sanudo, inquisitors, and Venetian advocates by contrast validated this "feminine" behavior as a legitimate social and political discourse. Even when gossip began among women, it underwent a type of "legal transubstantiation" when it entered the realm of the courtroom and the voices and records of male functionaries, becoming part of the male, citywide realm of the law.[16]

Although we can imagine that Venetians surely gossiped, what specific words, language, and events demonstrate actual incidents of such talk? Early modern definitions of types of speech and the various sins of the tongue overlap to a certain degree. There is much in common between the acts of blasphemy (*blasfemia* or *bestemmie*), cursing (*execratio* or *maledire*), swearing (*iurare* or *giurare*), rumor (*rumore* or *mormoratione*), gossip (*fama* or *petegolezze*), slander (*maledicere* or *calluniare*), and insults (*vituperium, insulto,* or *ingurie*). Gossip was distinct, however, when it involved the speech of two or more actors affecting either positively, or more usually negatively, the reputation of a third, absent party. It is not the same as idle talk, nor is it all necessarily judgmental, but rather represented a subsection of social talk about people who were absent, as distinct from face-to-face social commentary. Or, as the historian Chris Wickham has put it more simply, "gossip is ... talking about other people behind their backs," becoming rumor as its volume is turned up and it reaches a wider audience.[17] Gossip and rumor by nature remain evanescent subjects, defying the type of quantitative analysis that might apply to a study of wages or commercial exchanges. In

---

[16] See Thomas Kuehn, "*Fama* as a Legal Status in Renaissance Florence," in Fenster and Smail, *Fama: The Politics of Talk*, 34. I am indebted to Thomas Cohen's ideas and reflections on the subjects of hearsay, gossip, *fama,* and the law.

[17] Wickham, "Gossip and Resistance," 11. See also Scott, *Domination and the Arts of Resistance*, 142.

the case of early modern Venice, however, we can locate community talk through the use of specific words and language such as to gossip (*pettegole/pettegolar*), chatter (*ciance, zanze, ciacole*), or mumble, grumble, or discuss news (*mormorar*), all referring to community talk; through references to the public reputation (*fama* or *infamia*) of particular actors; through references to common talk (*comun parlar*) or what people heard or knew about others; or simply when witnesses say, "I heard that" or "it is said that" (*Ho sentito che/si dice che*). Witnesses *de auditu* – those who heard, but did not see anything – often illuminate the flow of gossip in Venetian communities.

Although much has been written about the use of language at court, language in early modern urban settings has yet to be more fully explored. As Venetian archives, legal compendia, and chronicles open a window onto the circulation of the word on the streets of the mobile city, they reveal that gossip affected individual and family honor, noble respectability, and neighborhood peace. Gossip played a fundamental role in Venetian political culture. Italian and Venetian writers alike typically construed gossip as untrustworthy, feminine speech that needed to be silenced to prevent exaggerated or false rumors from disrupting public life. Women did indeed gossip, and gossip among women functioned as a powerful means of female solidarity, as well as a tool of social management and control. Gossip gave women a type of power they did not possess in the arena of politics. Venetian men, however, gossiped as much or even more than women, indicating that actual spoken interactions did not mirror literary constructions of masculine and feminine speech. Needing to keep its political secrets and quell disruptive rumors and gossip, the state sought to silence gossiping men – in particular those who participated in the political gossip of the *broglio* that circulated around the Ducal Palace at the time of elections. Gossip however proved to be necessary to Venetian politics and daily life, as the city ultimately benefited from the fluid movement of the word on the street. Venice's unusual political mix of republicanism and aristocracy in the sixteenth century was reflected in the practice of both "masculine" rhetoric and "feminine" gossip in the city's political culture. Gossip was in some circumstances disruptive and divisive, but in other instances it served to patrol community behavior and encourage the smooth functioning of the state.

As we have seen, the Renaissance remains noteworthy in part for its "discovery" of the power of language and public speech; however, the celebration of Ciceronian rhetoric and oratory did not invite women's participation. Innumerable Renaissance treatises claimed that rhetoric was the language of men. George Trebizond and Sperone Speroni, for instance – among the best-known theorists of rhetoric in Renaissance Italy – regularly asserted that if a man wanted "to attain the glory of governing the state, then he must apply himself to rhetoric."[18] In a well-known 1405 letter to Baptista di Montefeltro, Leonardo Bruni advised women not to waste their time learning the art of rhetoric, because for women, "neither the intricacies of debate nor the oratorical artifices of action and delivery are of the least practical use, if indeed they are not positively unbecoming. Rhetoric, in all its forms . . . lies absolutely outside the province of woman."[19] Occasionally, women did present public orations; for instance, on the occasion of the consecration of new abbesses between the twelfth and sixteenth centuries, the nuns of the convent of the Virgins in Venice gave Latin orations in the presence of the doge and the senate.[20] Renaissance printed dialogues were also noteworthy for their inclusion (albeit typically peripheral) of women's voices in their texts, and numerous women furthermore composed dialogues in the early modern period.[21] We have an occasional glimpse at women's spoken eloquence in the lives of Renaissance courtesans such as Veronica Franco, who famously undertook a verbal duel with her poet-rival Maffio Venier. However, such nuns, humanists, and courtesans composing or delivering orations were rare if not exceptional, and Renaissance writers argued

---

[18] George Trebizond, "An Oration in Praise of Eloquence," in *Renaissance Debates on Rhetoric,* ed. and trans. Wayne A. Rebhorn (Ithaca and London: Cornell University Press, 2000), 31. See also Sperone Speroni, "Dialogue on Rhetoric," Ibid., 113.

[19] Leonardo Bruni, *De studiis et literis,* cited in Ann Rosalind Jones, "Surprising Fame: Renaissance Gender Ideologies and Women's Lyric," in *The Poetics of Gender,* ed. Nancy K. Miller (New York: Columbia University Press, 1986), 75. Ludovico Dolce also stated that "[M]any things are necessary to men at the same time, that is to say prudence, eloquence, expertise at governing the Republic. . . . But in the woman one does not look for profound eloquence . . . ," *Dialogo della institution delle donne,* cited in Wendy Heller, *Emblems of Eloquence: Opera and Women's Voices in Seventeenth-Century Venice* (Berkeley: University of California Press, 2003), 27.

[20] See K.J.P. Lowe, *Nuns' Chronicles and Convent Culture in Renaissance and Counter-Reformation Italy* (Cambridge: Cambridge University Press, 2003), 299–300.

[21] See Janet Levarie Smarr, *Joining the Conversation: Dialogues by Renaissance Women* (Ann Arbor: The University of Michigan Press, 2005).

insistently that silence, not eloquence, was a woman's greatest virtue.[22]
Arguments aimed at silencing women and claiming public speech as a
male prerogative – such as those made by Castiglione and Guazzo –
spanned the centuries of the early modern period and need little introduction. As late as 1663, Paolo Botti's text *The woman of few words* (*La
donna di poche parole*), offered a 300-page, 19-chapter exposition of the
variety of ways that women benefited from speaking less. He shored up
his assertions with a striking image of female speech in the frontispiece
of this work, which depicts a woman hushing her audience, as she wears
a dress embroidered with eyes and ears, suggesting how women might
see and hear but should not speak (Figure 5).[23]

Beyond simply encouraging women's silence, Renaissance writers
at large like Castiglione and Guazzo also gendered different types of
speech.[24] If rhetoric was a virtuous, masculine form of public talk, gossip
was its negative, feminine equivalent and represented a pressing problem
that women generated for their communities and states. Chatter, gossip, rumor, and excesses of speech were characterized as feminine, and a
variety of writers depicted women as whiling away their days chattering
and sharing secrets.[25] For instance, Stefano Guazzo, who as we have seen
represented one of the foremost writers on public, verbal, presentation
in the Renaissance, lamented women,

> who fall prey to other women, and after an initial greeting immediately
> begin to question, "Have you heard of the disgrace of that unfortunate

---

[22] To cite just a few examples: many Italians were surely extremely familiar with Bernardino
of Siena's idea that good wives should imitate the Virgin, who he claimed only spoke seven
times in her life. See Bernardino da Siena, *Prediche volgari*, vol. 1, 308; vol. 2, 871–74. Other
writers concurred: "E per raccoglier le molte parole in una, bellissima laude della Donna
è il silentio," Ludovico Dolce, *Dialogo della institution delle donne* (Venice, 1547), 31r; "[L]a
virtù dell'huomo, e della femina non sian la medesima; percioche la virtù della donna la pu-
dicitia; e come piacque a Gorgia, così il silentio è virtù della donna, come l'eloquenza
dell'huomo, onde gentilmente disse il Petrarca, *In silentio parole accorte, e saggie*," Torquato
Tasso, *Discorso della virtù feminile e donnesca* (Venice, 1582), 3v.

[23] Paolo Botti, *La donna di poche parole commendata* (Padua, 1663).

[24] Many sociolinguists today have considered the ways in which various types of speech are
gendered. Most notably, see Deborah Tannen, *You Just Don't Understand: Women and Men
in Conversation* (New York: Morrow, 1990).

[25] See Patricia Parker, "On the Tongue: Cross Gendering, Effeminacy, and the Art of Words,"
Style 23 (1989): 445–65; Patricia Meyer Spacks, *Gossip* (Chicago: The University of Chicago
Press, 1986), 35.

Figure 5. Frontispiece of Paolo Botti, *La donna di poche parole commendata* (Padua, 1633). Courtesy of The Newberry Library, Chicago.

neighbor of mine?" then recounting the story, relating the way in which, with the help of a servant, she had been cheating on her husband, who then caught her and took to beating both the wife and the servant. They never think of leaving out a single detail in the story, but rather embellish the tale with smaller points. And after this, another starts to say, "I too want to tell you (of course just between us) what happened in my neighborhood six days ago." Now I will let you consider how in re-telling these stories much chatter passes from one neighborhood to another, recounting other people's business.[26]

Guazzo continued that he "cannot remain quiet about the abuse in his city, where you do not see anything all day long except women out in the neighborhoods, who go chatting and sharing certain unnecessary visits from one doorway to another."[27] Alessandro Piccolomini also complained of the problem of gossip in sixteenth-century Siena.

Today our city is full of the worst tongues, and every little thing, simply stated, becomes a grand statement, and it is a difficult thing to repair. But speaking little and sagely is the best thing one can do. Coming into the disrepute of bad tongues is much to be avoided. This vice exists today in almost all women, and it is very bothersome and offensive, because women shouldn't be concerned with the affairs of others.[28]

In Venice, both Pietro Aretino and Ludovico Dolce remarked upon women's gossip. Dolce noted how "women go against the laws of nature and sin . . . by loosening their tongues in many words before they have understood, seen, or carefully considered the form and quality of their utterances."[29] Venetian proverbs pointing to women's talkativeness

---

[26] Guazzo, *La civil conversazione*, 48–49.

[27] Ibid., 236.

[28] "Hoggi la nostra città è piena di malissime lingue, et a ogni picciole cosa è semplicemente detta, si fa un commento grandissimo, et è difficil cosa a ripararsene, ma il parlar poco, e con accortezza è il meglio, che si possa fare. E molto da fuggir ancora il venir in fama di mala lingua, il qual vezzo è hoggi quasi in tutte le donne, et è pestilentissimo, e vile però una donna non ha da cercar i fatti degli altri," Alessandro Piccolomini, *Gli costumi lodevoli che a nobili gentildonne si convengono* (Venice, 1622), 258–59. For additional examples, See Alberti, *The Family in Renaissance Florence*, 210, 217; Guicciardini, *L'ore di ricreazione*, 143–44.

[29] "Di qui vi potete avedere, quanto fanno contra gli ordini di natura, et peccano stranamente quelle donne (che degli huomini non e hora il nostro ragionamento) lequali sciolgono la lingua in varie parole, prima che habbiano o inteso, o veduto, o considerato nel loro animo la forma, et qualita di quello, che vogliono profferire," Ludovico Dolce, *Degli ammaestramenti pregiatissimi che appartengono alla educatione, et honorevole, e virtuosa via virginale, maritale,*

abound – many from the first half of the sixteenth century: "No contar a la dona i to segreti" (Don't tell your secrets to a woman); "Nè femene, nè oche, no fa parole poche" (Neither women nor geese make few words); "Le done no ga altra arma che la lengua" (The tongue is women's only weapon); "I fatti i è omeni, e le ciacole i è done" (Deeds are masculine and chatter is feminine); "El segreto de le femene no lo sa nessun, altro che mi e vu e tuto'l comun" (No one knows women's secrets except for me, you, and the whole city).[30] The gossiping Venetian woman was so prominent a figure as to merit an image in Pietro Bertelli's 1591 edition of his *Diversarum nationum habitus*, which depicted a series of carnival characters, including a *petegola over rufiana*: a "gossip or procuress" shrouded in a long, dark gown and *fazzuolo* or veil covering her face, leaning over talking to (interestingly enough) a *magnifico* or chancellor from the Venetian government (Figure 6).[31]

The implications of female talk were powerful enough to attract the attention of jurists, and like comportment literature, early modern Venetian legal texts also revealed an uneasiness with the female voice. Legal writers, perhaps following Aristotelian tenets about women's weaker minds and bodies, claimed that women's spoken testimonies were necessarily unreliable. As a result, legal theorists often agreed that it took two women to produce the equivalent of one valid testimony. Though it is difficult to find this principle applied in practice, Venetian legal authorities still cited this position as part of Venetian practice in the eighteenth and nineteenth centuries.[32] Despite the fact that inquisitors and judges

---

e vedovile (Venice, 1622), 49–50. Writing to the courtesan Angela Zaffetta, Pietro Aretino claimed that "feminine gossip" was not to her taste. See Aretino, *Letters*, 122. See also Giuseppe Passi, *I donneschi difetti* (Venice, 1605), 312–416.

[30] G. Bianchi, *Proverbi e modi proverbiali veneti* (Milan: Tipofgrafia Bernardoni di C. Rebeschini, 1901), 81, 159; *I proverbi de me nono: Modi de dire e de sentenziare del veneto da na volta* (Padua: n.p., 1988), no pagination; Cibotto, *Proverbi del veneto*, 11–12. Many texts expressed the idea of words being feminine and deeds masculine; see also *Discorso intorno alla maggioranza dell'huomo, e della donna, fatto dall'accademico Bramoso dell'accademia de'solleciti di Trevigi* (Treviso, 1589), 33; *Facetie e motti arguti di alcuni eccellentissimi ingegni e nobilissimi signori* (Venice, 1550), 41v; Cortelazzo, *Le dieci tavole*, 87; Anton Francesco Doni, *La zucca*, vol. 2, ed. Elena Pierazzo (Rome: Salerno, 2003), 28.

[31] Pietro Bertelli, *Diversarum nationum habitus* (Padua, 1591), 75. On the figures "Rufiana" and "Magnifico," see Boerio, *Dizionario*, 385, 587.

[32] "Appare si dice quando vi è un huomo, e una donna tutti due giurati che fanno con qualche inditio semi prova, volendovi doi donne per far un testimonio," Zettele, *Istrutione*, 75. See also Barbaro, *Pratica criminale*, 54, and Ferro, *Dizionario*, vol. 1, 27, 717; vol. 2, 792. On women

Figure 6. Pietro Bertelli, *Diversarum nationum habitus* (Padua, 1591), 75. By permission of the Biblioteca Nazionale Marciana, Venice.

did not appear to follow this principle, such ideas nevertheless betray a distrust of women's talk, at least on a prescriptive level. Such concern about the dangerous female voice and the social problem of gossip reveals the actual power gossip possessed, suggesting that women, in fact, did not tell lies, but told the dangerous truth. Women's speech clearly had

in early modern Italian legal texts, see Buganza, "Il teste," 267; Shaw, *The Justice of Venice*, 165.

powerful connotations. The open female mouth, like an open house or the exposed female body, threatened male and family honor.[33] Gossip was "natural" to women, as nature had blessed women with power in the tongue. Typically depicted as less involved in the world of work, women had more time to share hearsay and secrets and needed to be silenced to protect male reputations.

Although the threads of gossip emerge in a variety of sixteenth-century sources, they are perhaps most visible in one particular type of archival document: court records. Among these, the records of the Holy Office of the Inquisition stand out as a font for the study of gossip. Although most courts employed scribes who transcribed proceedings with diligence and accuracy, the court of the Inquisition in Venice is renowned among historians for offering among the most exacting transcriptions of talking voices, including gestures, exclamations, pauses, and even the blushing of witnesses. In the court of the Roman Inquisition, words were not summarized, as was the practice in other magistracies, but taken down verbatim.[34] Hence, Inquisition trial records often recorded conversations or dialogues where we can hear the voices of the Inquisitor and witnesses responding to one another, or witnesses recounting conversations that took place on the street or in private homes. Although the records of the Inquisition in Venice naturally have much to tell us about heresy, orthodoxy, and reform in Counter-Reformation Venice, they also reveal a wealth of information on a wide variety of other topics such as witchcraft, the history of medicine, popular culture, and daily life in general. Established in Venice in 1547 to combat Lutheranism and other forms of heresy in the lagoon city, the Holy Office heard more than 3,500 trials before the close of the eighteenth century. These trials reveal the flow of gossip in Venetian neighborhoods and workplaces, illuminating who said what to whom and how particular people heard and communicated information.

We must note, however, that courtroom testimony is not by any means a straightforward record of public language. Many historians have debated the use of court cases as an indicator of popular mentalities and

---

[33] On connections between womens' speech and sexuality, see Chapter 5.

[34] See Anne Jacobson Schutte, "Introduction," in *Cecilia Ferrazzi, Autobiography of an Aspiring Saint*, ed. and trans. Anne Jacobson Schutte (Chicago: The University of Chicago Press, 1996), 3.

verbal expression.[35] The court was undoubtedly an unusual arena of talk, admitting a specific and very particular range of people, conversation, and controversy. It was space for formal and ceremonial presentation rather than spontaneous conversation. Court records tend to offer not what actors said to one another, but what they said to magistrates and notaries. Witnesses could not control topics of conversation and had little say over when their speech began or ended. Transcribed language may not always be an exact reflection of courtroom language as the transcription remains, to some degree, a constructed art form. Although in theory Inquisition scribes were instructed to record the exact words of courtroom speakers, this did not always occur. Even scribes for the Inquisition sometimes employed written formulas to transcribe basic, routine information, and courtroom actors also offered formulaic responses, saying what they thought the court wanted to hear and trying to answer "correctly" and avoid punishment. Perhaps worst of all for the historian, we often do not know the outcome of these cases that frequently end abruptly as a result of having been dismissed or partially lost. Though we must be aware of the various limitations of these trials as historical sources, Inquisition records still offer plentiful data for the study of unmannered speech. In particular, when a witness described a particular event, incident, or verbal exchange that could not be forced into formulaic language by either the speaker or the scribe, this more spontaneous speech immediately jumps off the page.[36] Such transcriptions probably often come close to actual verbal presentation and resonate with prescriptive meaning.

Venetians recorded in the trials of the Holy Office often confirmed the literary supposition that women were gossips. Reporting the words of Alvise Capuano, a carpenter tried for heresy in 1577, a female witness claimed that Alvise had stated, "women are gossips and should not be

---

[35] On the structure of the Inquisition in Venice, see Martin, *Venice's Hidden Enemies*. On debates about the use of court cases for historical evidence, see Burke, *Popular Culture*, 74–75; Cohen and Cohen, "Camilla the Go-Between," 57–58; Andrea Del Col, "I processi dell'Inquisizione come fonte: Considerazioni dipomatiche e storiche," *Annuario dell'istituto storico italiano per l'età moderna e contemporranea* 35–36 (1983–84): 31–49; Ferraro, *Marriage Wars*, 6; Thomas Kuehn, *Law, Family and Women: Toward a Legal Anthropology of Renaissance Italy* (Chicago: The University of Chicago Press, 1991), 96.

[36] "[W]hen they articulate ideas that take the inquisitor by surprise, then we can be confident that we are actually hearing them speak," Schutte, "Introduction," 4.

trusted. When I was going to mass, he told me that it was not neces-sary to hear so many masses – one was enough."[37] Lodovico Pico, tried for Lutheranism in 1587, was accused of yelling to several women that "going to mass was only for gossips."[38] Similarly reporting the heretical words and acts of Rinaldo Rio, a tailor from Burano, a witness stated that Rinaldo had often said to a group of women going to mass, "you are gossips – it would be better if you went to spin," suggesting that women should spin wool rather than words. Another witness reported that Rinaldo had exclaimed, "look at these geese," referring to the annoy-ing procession of chattering women who accompanied the sacrament.[39] When examined about his general beliefs and piety, Rinaldo moreover argued that Mary Magdalene herself was a gossip (*pettegola*). "She was not a good witness because women are not good witnesses. . . . She gave witness in the garden concerning Jesus Christ, whom she had seen in the garden dressed like a gardener."[40] Echoing the rhetoric of comport-ment literature and legal theory and indicating the wide diffusion of such ideas, Rinaldo believed that women were such infamous talkers that even female saints were gossips. Religious rituals such as processions and the mass were one of the regular opportunities that women had to leave

[37] "Le done erano pettegole et che non bisognava fidarle. Et quando andavo a messa, el me diceva che non bisogna udir tante messe, basta una," ASV, *Sant'Uffizio*, bu. 47, fasc. "Alvise Capuano," testimony of 20 July 1577.

[38] "L'andar à messa era cosa da petegolle," Ibid., bu. 60, testimony of 5 May 1587, fo. 1v.

[39] "Il detto Rinaldo ci diceva sette pettogole, paresti meglio andare a fillare, et queste parole ci le dicceva spesso," Ibid., bu. 55, fasc. "Rinaldo Rio," testimony of 5 November 1585. "Rinaldo diceva varda ste oche volendo intender deli done che acompagnavano [il sacramento]," Ibid., testimony of 1 March 1586.

[40] "La madalena era una pettegola, et dissi che la non era bon testimonio per che le done non son bon testimonio. . . . L'haveva fato testimonianza in horto de messer Jesu Christo che essa haveva visto in horto da hortolan," Ibid., testimony of 9 September 1586. Rinaldo here refers to John 20:11–18, "Noli me tangere," when Mary Magdalen, weeping at Christ's tomb, encounters Jesus reborn in the guise of a gardener. The speaker here seems to be reorganizing the Gospel story, as if Mary Magdalene had first seen Jesus and failed to recognize him and that is why she tells the apostles that Jesus has been taken away and she does not know where he is (the "testimonianza"). Thus, in this version, her failure to recognize that the gardener was Jesus was a good example of how women do not make good witnesses, because if she could not even recognize the Lord to whom she was devoted, how could she perceive anything or anyone else correctly? Rinaldo stretched far for an example of women as bad witnesses and his memory reorganized the story to give him one. I thank Linda Carroll for help with this translation. For other trials where men state that women are gossips or habitual talkers, see bu. 62, fasc. "Bernardina della Scala," testimony of Jacob Milano, 17 November 1588; bu. 65, fasc. "Elisabetta Stopera," 12 August 1589.

their domestic confines and exchange words with one another, explaining why men sought to limit their attendance.[41] Ceremonies and gatherings served the purpose of sharing information, news, and gossip as well as expressing religious piety and devotion, as these Venetian men noted and lamented.

Additional courtroom testimony confirms that women in fact were great gossips. For example, in 1584, a certain Elena who lived in the neighborhood of Santa Margherita was first accused of witchcraft by a neighbor Franceschina, who had heard from those who lived in Elena's house that Elena had pierced an eel with needles and roasted it under ashes as a practice of witchcraft. In particular, Franceschina claimed to have heard this from three widows named Orsola, Isabetta, and Andriana, all denizens of the house.[42] Franceschina admitted to being Elena's enemy as a result of a family squabble; though they had argued, she had never filed any formal complaint.[43] The second witness called to testify, Orsola, presented similar information, stating that she too had heard from the widow Andriana that Elena had roasted eels. Orsola added "I do not know if Andriana said this because it is the truth or out of hatred, because the

---

[41] Men speaking in the trials of the Inquisition often sought to limit the public movement of women. For instance, in a 1574 case, a woman named Giovanna claimed that Giovanni Battista Peranda told her that "one mass is enough." Ibid., bu. 37, fasc. "G.BU. Peranda," testimony of 19 October 1574. There is substantial debate about the degree to which Venetian women went out in public; whereas Dennis Romano first argued that Venetian women were normally confined to the domestic, private sphere, Monica Chojnacka and Joanne Ferraro argue that in fact women – in particular lower-class women – worked and moved about in public on a regular basis. Similarly, Mary Laven demonstrates that in order for noble nuns to be enclosed, a whole bevy of women of other social groups, including women, had to run about the city tending to their needs. See Dennis Romano, "Gender and the Urban Geography of Renaissance Venice," *Journal of Social History* 23 (1989): 341; Monica Chojnacka, *Working Women of Early Modern Venice* (Baltimore and London: The Johns Hopkins University Press, 2001), 50–80; Joanne Ferraro, *Marriage Wars*, 120–33; Mary Laven, *Virgins of Venice: Broken Vows and Cloistered Lives in the Renaissance Convent* (London: Penguin Books, 2002), 118–36.

[42] "Cognosco questa Helena Greca puol esser da 6 anni in circa, e ho inteso che l'harostido una anguilla sotto la cenere con di aghi ficadi dentro. Et che questo lo faceva per strigarie. Et questo l'ho inteso a dire da quelli che stavano in casa sua in calle del forno de Santa Margherita. Et queste persone che stan in casa sua una ha nome Orsola vedoa, l'altra do una ha nome Andriana et Isabetta, vedoa tute do. Et io ho inteso a dir le cose sopradette dala detta Andriana," ASV, *Sant'Uffizio*, bu. 52, fasc. "Elena," testimony of 2 August 1584.

[43] "Helena e mia inimiga per che le passa doi anni che la tegniva mio nevodo Zuan Antonio Vergezia per suo homo. Et per questo havemo cridado insieme, ma pero non e seguido querela," Ibid.

two of them argued together."[44] The third and final witness, Andriana, testified that she had not seen or heard that Elena practiced conjuring, "but in the neighborhood they say that she practiced conjuring. I do not know who it was that said these things."[45] The trial at this point abruptly ends. Though a mere fragment of a much larger, untold story, it nevertheless illuminates how talk functioned. Elena's neighbors appear to represent precisely the type of gossiping women frowned upon by literary culture. Their hearsay worked to construct Elena as a heretic, first in the eyes of her neighbors and then before the Inquisitors. The tribunal prioritized and sought out popular opinion and things that were known and heard. Trials such as this suggest that the developing apparatus to promote religious education, as a part of the renewed interest in spiritual reform present in the sixteenth century, perhaps had a particular interest in gossip. If religious authorities wanted to be closer to popular thought as a part of their reform programs, monitoring gossip could be seen as a very useful means of doing this – not unlike the confessional.[46]

In a similar case, when asked to describe the heretical acts of Antonia, accused of witchcraft in 1574, the witness Faustina stated, "I heard that she cures charmed and bewitched people, and it was Laura, the wife of Giacomo, a boatman, who told me."[47] A witness named Julia added that she had fought with the accused Antonia "because she had a bad tongue and went around carrying chatter here and there in the neighborhood, and she was a bad woman."[48] Another witness Magdalena added "I heard from the mouths of others that she throws wax and that she is a witch . . . I have never seen her do these things, but I have heard this from

---

[44] "Io conosco questa Helena Grecha da 3 o 4 anni in circa. Et ho inteso a dir da una madonna Andriana vedoa, che e dona di tempo che stava sul soler sora de mi, che questa Helena haveva messo una anguila piena de aghi sotto el fougo. Et io non ho inteso dir altro et non so se questa Andriana l'habia detto per la verita o per odio per che havevano cridato insieme," Ibid.

[45] "Io non ho visto ne inteso che detta Helena habia fatto herbarie o strigarie ne butar fave, ma per la contra si diseva che la feva herbarie; ma non ve so dir che le fusse queste che hano detto queste cose," Ibid.

[46] Susan Phillips has demonstrated some of the ways in which "gossip appropriates, contaminates, and . . . underlies confession." See Phillips, *Transforming Talk*, 43.

[47] "Ho sentito a dir che la varisse persone herbate, et strigate, et me l'ha ditto una Laura mogier de un Iacomo barcaruol," Marissa Milani, *Due processi per stregoneria: Venezia 1574* (Padua: Letteratura delle Tradizioni Popolari, 1993–94), 15.

[48] "Perché l'era mala lengua, et andava portando ciancie in qua in là per la visinanza, et l'era una mala femina," Ibid., 17.

many people, whose names I don't know."[49] Such testimony suggests the sensitivity of women to spoken behaviors. The accused witch Antonia developed a bad reputation as a result of her offensive speech, and the women around her also participated in neighborhood gossip – the font of their information. In this case, verbal networks among women brought to light and cemented the heretical activities of this witch, facilitating her eventual punishment and fine of 100 ducats for witchcraft.[50]

As other historians who have studied court cases have also shown, one cannot know "the truth" about these and other cases for certain; yet women clearly appeared to employ gossip as a means of revenge and community control, either over a "real" heretic, or over neighborhood misbehavior.[51] Amidst the maze of conflicting testimonies and motivations, we can never know whether Elena or Antonia actually committed the acts of which they were accused; however, both those who gossiped and those who were gossiped about were aware of the potential powers of verbal networks among women. The female solidarities found in street life were no less important than more conventional male networks of support and organization, and the neighborhood was one of the principal arenas where Venetian women typically established and defended their honor.[52] Women who wanted to win their court cases needed to be able to manipulate gossip in the courtroom. Especially in marriage litigation cases, the female gossip community provided women with witnesses for the court who would depict the woman in question in a sympathetic light and at the same time manipulate the accused's reputation and cast doubts on her enemy's honor. Women's gossip was a form of power that could shape men's honor and reputation, explaining men's fear of women's talk.[53] These examples of women sharing community information and

---

[49] "L'ho sentia per bocca d'altri che la butta cera, et che la è una striga ... Io non l'ho mai vista a far ste cose, et l'ho inteso da più persone, che'l nome non so," Ibid.

[50] Ibid., 46.

[51] See also Ruggiero, *Binding Passions*, 60; Tebbutt, *Women's Talk*, 74.

[52] See Chojnacka, *Working Women*, 51, and Romano, "Gender and the Urban Geography," 342–44. As the courtesan-writer Veronica Franco put it, "it is the act of a low and vile man to fight with a woman lacking defense or shield, except for gossip and a clever mind," Veronica Franco, *Poems and Selected Letters*, ed. and trans. Ann Rosalind Jones and Margaret F. Rosenthal (Chicago: The University of Chicago Press, 1998), 249 (*Capitolo* 24, lines 127–29).

[53] See Sandra Cavallo and Simona Cerutti, "Female Honor and the Social Control of Reproduction," in *Sex and Gender in Historical Perspective*, ed. Edward Muir and Guido Ruggiero (Baltimore: The Johns Hopkins University Press, 1990), 88–89; Joanne Ferraro, *Marriage*

then revealing this shared knowledge to the Inquisitor would suggest that women in their neighborhoods controlled specific forms of socialization and functioned as repositories of aural knowledge. To a certain degree, this afforded women a degree of power unavailable to them in the larger city space. And perhaps no less than their male republican counterparts, women who gossiped helped to shape the rules of everyday living to which all members of Venetian society were expected to conform.

Inquisition trials appear to show, however, that men gossiped as much if not more than their female counterparts. On 30 August 1582, Father Andrea Morato, the parish priest of the church of Saints Mary and Donato on the island of Murano, denounced his fellow priest Basegio Pellegrino to the Holy Office. According to Morato, "the entire neighborhood was murmuring (*mormora*)" about the fact that Pellegrino kept a concubine in his house. The sacristan of the church, Marco Bigagia, had told Father Morato that Pellegrino had come to church drunk, vomited in a sink, and then cleaned himself and the sink with a bucket of holy water.[54] Bigagia testified that many men and women said they did not want to attend the service of a skirt-chaser (*puttanier*).[55] Another witness testified that when the priest appeared to say mass, he heard people saying they were leaving to hear the mass at the church of Saint Peter the Martyr instead, because the priest at the church of Saints Mary and Donato was sleeping with a concubine. When Pellegrino said the mass, "he made groups of people grumble."[56] The rhetorical tone of this denunciation

---

Wars, 66, 124, 158; Ferraro, "The Power to Decide," 505; Mary Beth Norton, "Gender and Defamation in Seventeenth-Century Maryland," *William and Mary Quarterly* 44 (1987): 6; Ruggiero, *Binding Passions*, 72–87. Some biologists and anthropologists have argued that gossip evolved from early grooming behaviors and functions as a mutually protective ritual for members of a group. See for instance Robin Dunbar, *Grooming, Gossip, and the Evolution of Language* (Cambridge, MA: Harvard University Press, 1996).

[54] "Et detto prete concubinario levandosi de letto della concubina, in mondissimo corte subitamente a celebrar la messa, come e notorio et di cio ne mormora tutta la contra. . . . Essendo il detto padre pelegrino una matina per dover dir messa, mi fa refferto dal mio sacrestano che vene in chiesa ebriaco et vomito nel lavello, et poi pigliato il sechiello dall'aqua santa davo il lavello dall'immondicie della sua ebrieta," ASV, *Sant'Uffizio*, bu. 49, fasc. "Pellegrino Basegio," denunciation of 30 August 1582.

[55] "E assai gente non vuol odir la so messe dicendo eco qua un puttanier vuol dir la messa. Et questi sono assai peccadori e nome dei quali non me ricordo. Et sono homeni et donne," Ibid., testimony of 14 December 1582. The term *puttanier* can also be translated as pimp, depending on the local dialect of the speaker.

[56] "Et ho inteso a dire in chiesa quando questo prete se apparava per dir la messa che la zente se partivano con dir che volevano andar odir la messa a s. piero martire per che questo

and testimony indicates how Muranese churchgoers both heard and readily spread the word about Pellegrino's scandalous behavior. It was oral, community knowledge that this priest lived and worked improperly. His misbehavior was noted and shared in the spoken networks of gossip between men and women, eventually producing an official denunciation.

Individuals similarly used gossip to protect the piety of their workplace in the 1584 case of Giacomo "the Frenchman." Rinaldo Limoni, a worker in the Giuntine printing house, was sent by his confessor to denounce his fellow worker Giacomo. This case illustrates how the confessional frequently functioned as a node of gossip, because those who confessed related neighborhood and community narratives to a confessor, who in turn decided whether such tales merited being told to the Inquisitor himself. In such cases, the language of gossip moved from circulation on the street through the filter of the confessor, to be eventually codified in the written records of the Holy Office.[57] According to Rinaldo, everyone in the printing house believed Giacomo to be a Huguenot, and of the "24 or 26 who work in the shop, no one has seen Giacomo go to mass or to church."[58] Here and throughout his testimony, Rinaldo illuminates the degree to which workers discussed among themselves the reputations and behaviors of those they worked with. Giacomo's bad reputation traveled to other shops and cities and back to Venice.

> I also heard from Battista Venturino in the printing house of Tiraduro de Torchio that Lorenzo the compositor, I think he is from Piemonte, said that finding himself once with Giacomo the Frenchman in Turin and inviting him one holiday to go to mass, Giacomo responded that going to mass is all knavery and folly.[59]

Rinaldo also heard from another worker that in front of the church of San Cassiano, Giacomo would skirt the confines of the public square in order

---

prete haveva dormito con la concubina. . . . [Pellegrino] faceva mormorar le brigate," Ibid., testimony of V. Stella, 27 January 1583.

[57] See n. 46 above.

[58] "Siamo da 24 o 26 in stamparia et nessuno l'ha mai visto n'alla messa ne in chiesa, n'anco quando suona l'ave maria, mai s'ingienochia, ne si cava la bireta come fanno gl'altri nella stamperia, ne so che lui mai se sia confessato ne comunicato," Ibid., bu. 53, fasc. "Giacomo francese," testimony of 25 March 1584.

[59] "Ho inteso ancora da m. Batta Venturino nella stamparia tiraduro de torchio, che lorenzo compositor credo sia piamontese, l'ha detto che trovandosi una volta il detto lorenzo con m. iacomo francese in turino et invitandolo un giorno de festa d'andare a messa, esso m. iacommo rispose che andar a messa son tutte coionarie et menchionarie," Ibid.

not to touch the sacred ground in front of the church. Rinaldo concluded his testimony by stating that he had actually never personally heard or seen Giacomo do or say anything heretical, and he did not know who else could better inform the Holy Office of Giacomo's heretical acts – unusual coming from a printing house of only 25 workers. Rinaldo stated that personally "I have no problems with Giacomo, but because everyone in the workshop says that Giacomo is a Huguenot, I am not crazy about him."[60] The witnesses who followed Rinaldo both confirmed his statement and showed the pervasiveness of gossip in the workshop. Baptista Tentorino related that

> everyone said that Giacomo was a Huguenot . . . such as Lorenzo Dragogliare and Don Piero Codognola [who had been with Giacomo in Torino]. . . . And the cook Battista told me that during this past Lent, Giacomo ate meat. . . . I have heard that as the Holy Week approached, Giacomo pretended to want to go to France, returning after Easter week. . . . I heard this from those in the workshop of Luca Antonio, that is from Antonio the bookseller at the sign of the uncle in the Merceria, and Gasparo who works for Luca Antonio.[61]

Antonio Bragia similarly confirmed hearing from the cook Battista that Giacomo ate meat on holy days. According to Antonio, everyone in the workshop said "in one voice" that they had never seen Giacomo go to church, communion, or confession, and that everyone believed he was a Huguenot.

The final witness, Baptista Giuliani, Antonio's cook, further revealed community talk about Giacomo. Like the others who testified, Baptista claimed to have heard many things about Giacomo from the others in the workshop, but was unable to name the precise source of his knowledge. Baptista knew from others that Giacomo refused to go to

---

[60] "Io non ho mai hauto dispiacer alcuno dal detto m. iacomo, ne lui da me, ma perche si dice, che [la fatto] a praticar con li ugonotti, per questo io non m'impazzo de lui e per fa l'ordine del mio confessor, son venuto da vostra rev. et tornaro mo dal mio confessor per farme assolvere," Ibid.

[61] "Nella stamparia tuti dicevano che detto iacomo era ugonoto per che ci erano de li altri che havevano praticato detto iacomo in turino come un lorenzo dragogliare e don piero codognola. . . . Et il cuocho chiamato batta me ha ditto che detto iacomo questa quadresima prossime passata magnava la carne . . . io ho inteso a dire che detto iacomo come si avecinava la settimana santa, fingeva de voler andar in franza, et fatto l'ottava de pasqua ritornava . . . da questi de bottega del signor Lucha Antonio, cioe da Antonio libraro all'insegna del zio in marazarie et Gasparo fantor del signor Lucha Antonio," Ibid., testimony of 5 April 1584.

mass, claiming that the mass was for fools. He also heard, from someone whom he could not remember, that whenever the church bells rang, Giacomo fled to avoid participating in the neighborhood procession and the celebration of the sacraments – though again, he had never seen this. Baptista also heard that Giacomo never removed his hat in the presence of images of Christ, the Virgin, and the saints.[62] As with other cases, after the testimony of the cook Baptista Giuliani, the case ends with no decision by the court. Nevertheless, this trial highlights male gossip in the workplace. "Everyone" in the print shop of Luca Antonio, as well as bookmen from other print shops, had both talked about and heard talk about Giacomo's heretical reputation, despite a clear lack of any eyewitness evidence. The Inquisitor may never have punished Giacomo, most probably because evidence in the end was indeed lacking, but we can assume that community talk about his ritual misbehavior affected his social standing in the workshop and perhaps even worked to correct his behavior. Most importantly, the trial (or the initiation of one) is based entirely on hearsay; no one saw anything, which demonstrates the power of talk to manipulate reputations.

The 1583 trial of Father Zancharello Troiano – a priest from Burano accused of blasphemy – offers one final example of neighborhood gossip among men. The various documents and transcripts associated with this trial include a dramatic letter to the Holy Office in which a certain Francesco detailed the ways in which Troiano had used gossip and rumor to destroy Francesco's reputation as a doctor.[63] Francesco claimed that Father Troiano, together with his brother Andrea, lied and verbally persecuted Francesco; they were Francesco's enemies "in words and deeds." Francesco claimed that they were despicable people and that "the voice of the people will confirm how many disagreements, disruptions, schisms, dishonest and unscrupulous acts happen in this neighborhood" as a result of their antipathy. [64] Discord between the doctor and the priest had come about as a result of a dispute as to who should be the official church

[62] Ibid., testimony of 10 April 1584.

[63] Ibid., bu. 51, fasc. "Troiano Zancharello," letter from 18 April 1553, "Una scrittura nella quale detto medico nomina suoi nemici di Burano et la causa perche egli viene da loro calumniato et perseguitato."

[64] "A voce di populo si riferisce quante discordie, scisme, rovine, latrocinii, e ribalderie nascono, et si comettono in queste contrade," Ibid.

organist on Burano. After the doctor's candidate won, Francesco claimed that Troiano's friend Alessandro and his brothers "went around spreading the word on Burano that authorities were coming to arrest me" in the hopes of forcing Francesco to leave the island. [65] Alessandro also supposedly lied about Francesco's capacity as a doctor, stating that Francesco made the nuns pay too much for their medicine and forgot to order necessary supplies, as supported "with a thousand other pieces of chatter from lots of people."[66] Francesco continued to cite numerous other detractors on Burano who had been stirred up by Troiano's unfounded rumors. When the doctor broke up a series of social gatherings at the nunnery of San Moro, arguing that the nuns should be left alone and people should socialize elsewhere, the warden of the monastery, his wife, and others involved became incensed, gossiping to other islanders about the doctor's presumptuous reprimand. [67] Francesco complained:

> They started to hate me and to say bad things about me with whomever they wanted; they did everything possible to get me to leave the house.... Then the husband, wife and son – but mostly the wife as she is a dishonest, crazy, bewitched woman – all spoke as badly of me as possible. How many ribalds they whispered in the ears of others... and they are directly tied to the above father Alessandro, father Troiano and the majority of my enemies.[68]

Beyond his complaints about Troiano and his associates, Francesco also claimed that a certain Francesco Taiapiera, a contraband wine seller,

---

[65] "Andava seminando per Burano che havevano a venir barche de zaffi a ritener me," Ibid.

[66] "Il ditto padre Alessandro nelli monastieri massime dove io medicano et medico tutto hora con dir che facevo spender tanto a detti monastieri che non bastarebbono le loro entrate a paghar il debito et che non havevo ordinato siroppo... con mille altre cianze da soventir persone," Ibid.

[67] The way in which the doctor attracted community dislike by breaking up the social gatherings at the nunnery additionally confirms Mary Laven's ideas about gossip and the inherently social functions of nunneries. See Laven, *Virgins of Venice*, 102–17.

[68] "E Benetto Padovano, fante delle reverende monache di S. Moro, con sua moglie e figli, li quali vedendosi privi della liberta che havevano nella casa dov'io sto... cominciano a odiarmi et dire male di me con chi loro pareva et far ogni cosa acio che mi partissi di quella casa.... Onde ne seguito poi che marito e moglie, et figlio ma piu la moglie per esser donna dishonesta tenuta, et matta e spiritata, hano detto quanto male di me s'hano saputo imaginar, et quanto altri ribaldi gli hano sapputo soffiar nelle orecchie... et sono costoro stretissimi collegati del su detto padre Alessandro et di padre Troiano et della maggior parte delli miei nemicii," Ibid., bu. 51, fasc. "Troiano Zancharello," letter from 18 April 1553.

"known throughout the neighborhood as slandering scoundrel, has always said bad things about me publicly and tried with all his power together with his accomplices and my enemies to chase me away."[69] Marco Valvascione, the chancellor of Torcello, also refused to speak to the doctor Francesco and badmouthed him to other islanders. Relatives of Troiano and the warden of the monastery slandered Francesco "with their venomous and pestilent tongues." Even the island barber, Giovanni, spread rumors about Francesco among his family members and other fellow medical men.[70]

Francesco's detailed letter on the subject of gossip points to the power of the spoken word in neighborhood and community. It appears that Francesco crafted his letter to defend his name against locals who clearly resented the presence of an opinionated outsider working on the island. The changes Francesco attempted to introduce into this small community prompted a harsh and immediate verbal backlash, altering the doctor's standing to the point that he petitioned the Holy Office in the hopes of re-instating his reputation. Considering the class difference between the doctor and some of his detractors, gossip offered this community a form of retaliation that may have not been possible or easily accessible through normal legal channels. Gossip functioned as a weapon of the weak, used by these men to oust an unwanted and intrusive outsider from their community. Francesco's account also points to the complicated nature of gossip. On one hand, Francesco lamented the destructive powers of gossip, hoping to silence the gossiping tongues on Burano and reverse their effects on his reputation. Yet on the other hand, the doctor simultaneously called on public voices and on the community's verbal knowledge to confirm his complaints and vindicate his good reputation.

Trials such as these – formed around gossip and rumor – abound. Personal and neighborhood knowledge mixed and spread through the flow

---

[69] "Mostrato a dito per tutte queste contrade per uno mariolo maldicente ... sempre ha detto male di me palesemente et cercato di a tutto suo poter insieme con suoi complici e miei nemici scacciarmi di queste contrade," Ibid.

[70] "Una sua cognata detta l'Horia, moglie d'uno suo fratello detto Cristofalo, et molti altri suoi complici alli monastieri [dicono] male di me, per mettermi in disgracia di essi monastieri ma piu hano potuto gli miei buoni portamenti in essi che le vellenose et pestilenti lengue. Et questi sopra detti cio e padre Troiano, li specieri, et detto Giovanni et fratelli cappi di questa scetta con suoi complici hano piu fiate concertato come mi potesser discazzar di queste contrade," Ibid.

of talk, breaking down the otherwise insistent categories of public and private as described for instance by Guazzo. Knowledge did not necessarily reside in relations of patrons and clients or kinship alone. Instead, circuits of knowledge were constantly being made and re-made through a variety of people and relationships. There were a plethora of networks in the city outside of the traditional arena of politics – though as we will see, such networks were simultaneously connected to political culture. People actively manipulated the circles of people who knew things and treated those networks as archives of knowledge from which evidence could be extracted (or planted) when needed. Most importantly, whereas some scholars have found gossip to be a clearly gendered form of speech, this was not the case in Venice.[71] Gender is a category that cannot be sustained in the give and take of actual conversation, despite the fact that sixteenth-century writers were at pains to create rigid gender categories such as masculine rhetoric and feminine gossip.[72] Speech recorded in trial proceedings suggests that in fact there was no such thing as feminine or masculine speech; writers such as Castiglione and Guazzo constructed these categories in stark contradiction to what really happened on the street itself, as men were persistent gossips and women, especially courtesans we shall see, sometimes proved to be excellent rhetoricians. In fact, the medical man Leonardo Fioravanti – who intended to write a book on the tongue – claimed that barbers were the worst gossips, and other reports of sixteenth-century street life also observed men gossiping even more than women.[73] We could never argue, therefore, that gossip was a "feminist" practice; rather, it was a rhetorical strategy potentially

---

[71] Historians see much variation in the degree to which men and women gossip in particular places. For points of comparison, see Madeline H. Caviness and Charles G. Nelson, "Silent Witnesses, Absent Women, and the Law Courts in Medieval Germany," in Fenster and Smail, *Fama: The Politics of Talk*, 47–72; Gowing, *Domestic Dangers*, 121–23.

[72] See Wickham, "Gossip and Resistance," 11, 15.

[73] Leonardo Fioravanti, *Specchio di scienze universale* (Venice, 1567), 66 r–v. I thank Bill Eamon for this citation. On barbershops as sites for the exchange of information, see Mario Infelise, "The War, the News, and the Curious: Military Gazettes in Italy," in *The Politics of Information in Early Modern Europe*, ed. Brendan Dooley and Sabrina A. Baron (London and New York: Routledge, 2001), 230. Tommaso Garzoni also claimed that men and gondoliers in particular were infamous gossips; see Garzoni, *La piazza universale*, vol. 2, 1052, 1396–97. In England, the boatmen who carried people across the Thames were considered among the best sources for news, rumors and gossip; see Fox, *Oral and Literate Culture*, 348. Moderata Fonte also argued that "when a man has amorous concourse with a woman ... the woman always tries to disguise it as much as possible, while the man cannot wait to tell the whole world about

used to both feminist or misogynist ends by both men and women.[74] Most significantly, however, is the fact that though writers and individual Venetians may have complained about the destructive effects of chattering women and *comun parlar*, these same individuals recognized and called upon the power of gossip to establish community truths and regulate community behavior.[75] By criticizing or challenging individuals' actions, gossip at times created friction and proved socially disruptive, but by defining the parameters surrounding acceptable behavior, it also encouraged neighborhood peace and stability: effects which gossip also produced in the workings of the larger state itself.

Gossip not only impacted upon individual and family reputation but also affected civic politics as it functioned as a form of popular aggression and a means of solidarity for the politically or economically subordinated. More than just a casual force in history, rumor is often an inherent part of the political process. As such, leaders often likened rumor among the underclasses to a plague or contagion spread by word of mouth.[76] For example, on 23 June 1509, in the midst of the Venetian military crisis with the League of Cambrai, the diarist Girolamo Priuli took time away from chronicling otherwise pressing events and daily business to record a lengthy lament about the problem of gossip in Venice.

> People were gossiping and talking and spreading so many lies without any foundation in the *piazze* and under the *loggie* [of the *Procuratie*] and

it." See Moderata Fonte, *The Worth of Women*, ed and trans. Virginia Cox (Chicago: The University of Chicago Press, 1997), 90–91.

[74] This is similar to the way that Marilyn Migiel considers *The Decameron*. She argues that rather than ask whether Boccaccio's text was a feminist or misogynist one, it is more productive to observe how the speakers in his text use various rhetorical strategies to create meaning and claim authority, or how certain narrative perspectives work to gain dominance over others. See Marilyn Migiel, *A Rhetoric of the Decameron* (Toronto, University of Toronto Press, 2003), 3, 28.

[75] Pietro Aretino openly admitted to liking gossip about himself because it provided him and his publications with good publicity. He wrote to the publisher Francesco Marcolini "Even out of being blackguarded I get a certain amount of renown. For look here is my name bandied about by every idle gossiper, and you read it upon the title page of romances which could not be sold in any other way," Aretino, *Letters*, 199–200.

[76] See Nick Cox, "Rumours and Risings: Plebian Insurrection and the Circulation of Subversive Discourse around 1597," in Cavanagh and Kirk, *Subversion and Scurrility*, 43–57; Fox, *Oral and Literate Culture*, 335–405; D.V. Kent and F. W. Kent, *Neighbours and Neighbourhood in Renaissance Florence* (Locust Valley, NY: J.J. Augustin, 1982), 175; Ottavia Niccoli, *Prophecy and People in Renaissance Italy*, trans. Lydia G. Cochrane (Princeton: Princeton University Press, 1990), 23; Scott, *Domination and the Arts of Resistance*, 142; Richard Suggett, "Vagabonds and Minstrels in Sixteenth-Century Wales," in Fox and Woolf, *The Spoken Word*, 138–72.

at the Rialto and in the churches and barbershops that one could not figure out what was true. People felt as though they could say anything that they pleased; they would think up something at night and then spread it around in the morning.... Then there truly was no order at all, and it was acceptable for anyone, of any class or condition, to say whatever they wanted – whatever came to mouth in the *piazza* or under the *loggie* or anyplace ... which beyond the shame, was damaging, since whatever was spoken and said in the *piazze* was then described outside the city, since there were many diverse explorers and listeners who when they heard something, immediately described it to their *signori* and magistrates and lords outside the city, and they wrote lies and false news many times.... And other infinite disorder and ruin followed through this news and these words that were spoken in *piazze*, and everyone knows it was the worst thing for the ruin of the Venetian state.[77]

According to Priuli, the forces of gossip and the creation and spread of false rumor had been so prevalent and powerful as to weaken the republic during the disastrous summer of 1509, giving a strategic advantage to the French and Milanese forces. Neighborhood chatter is not always clearly linked to political intrigue, however Priuli's description of language running rampant decisively illuminates their connection. Private talk had clear public repercussions.

State secrecy, involving repressing gossip and stopping the leakage of secret political information, was central to the workings of the Venetian republic. The Council of Ten, for instance, required secrecy in every phase of its proceedings. The Ten had proposed, in 1425, to remove a bench in the church of San Marco near the holy water font where nobles were

---

[77] "Tante zanze et tante parole et tante nove busarde et senza fondamento se dicevanno per le piaze et per le loze et per Rialto et ecclesie et botege de barbieri in la citade predicta, che non se poteva intendere una veritade, et a tutti hera licito dire quello li piaceva et pensarssi la nocte una nova et la matina publicarla.... Ahora veramente non hera ordine alchuno, et hera licito a chadauno, de ogni grado et condictione, se fusse, dire quanto li piaceva et che li fusse venuto in bocha et in piaza et in le logiette et per ogni locho.... *ultra* la vergogna, il damno, perchè, quanto se parlavanno et dicevanno sopra le piaze, tanto hera descripto fuori dela citade, perchè heranno molti et diversi exploratori et auscoltori, che subito quello intendevanno, descrivevanno fuori ali sui Signori et magistri et patroni, et scrivevanno molte volte le bussie et nove false.... Et altri infiniti dishordeni et ruine seguite per queste nove et parole, che se dicevanno sopra le piaze, et chadauno le cognosceva che l'hera malissimo al proposito et ruina del Stato Veneto," Priuli, *I diarii*, vol. 4, 108–9. As described in greater detail by Robert Finlay, Venetians in their gossip here heaped opprobrium on a particular Venetian military commander for a defeat he had suffered. See Finlay, *Politics*, 55.

accustomed to sit and chat about state affairs.[78] Sixteenth-century doges complained of leaks of secret information from the Senate, which were then reported around town.[79] Doges themselves were in fact severely restricted in terms of their personal movement, socialization, and social talk, in part to maintain their safety but also in order to avoid divulging political information. The doge could not receive anyone in any official capacity without the presence of his advisors and could not grant any private audiences. "He could not leave the palace except for official functions," according to Alvise Zorzi, "nor could he attend the theater, go to cafes, or participate in *conversazioni*."[80] The *Inquisitori di Stato* considered the problem of state secrecy in 1481 by levying a penalty of 1,000 ducats on any Venetian who would "confer with, converse with, listen to or advise any foreigner or any ambassador who is not a subject of our *Signoria* concerning matters pertaining to our state."[81] As with blasphemy and insults, the practice of gossip seems to have been a type of speech that the state at times wanted to discipline and control. Suppressing such gossip and political chatter, however, proved to be extremely difficult. The *Inquisitori di Stato* again lamented in 1539 that "Despite all the measures taken by this council, it has still proved impossible to prevent the most important matters dealt with in our secret councils from being known and published, as we are reliably informed from every quarter."[82]

This statement by the *Inquisitori di Stato* reveals the paradoxes associated with gossip. On the one hand, they complained about political rumor, but on the other hand were informed about the problems rumor created precisely because this magistracy has obtained information through gossip itself. Gossip and rumor were potentially dangerous and destructive forces, but it proved difficult to disregard or discourage their practice as they were also useful as measures of civic opinion as well as for keeping the *popolo* under control. Marin Sanudo illustrated this

---

[78] Queller, *The Venetian Patriciate*, 221–22.

[79] Ibid., 212–24.

[80] Alvise Zorzi, *Venice 697–1797: A City, A Republic, An Empire* (Woodstock, NY: The Overlook Press, 1999), 31.

[81] Chambers and Pullan, *Venice: A Documentary History*, 80.

[82] Ibid., 81. The Cinquecento chronicler Marin Sanudo recounted the hanging of chancery secretary Antonio di Lando in the *piazza* for having revealed secret state matters; see Sanudo, *I diarii*, vol. 1, 917–19. See Burke, "Early Modern Venice," 394, for additional examples of Venetian state secrecy.

point, as his detailed and exacting chronicle relied heavily on overheard exchanges and gossip to document daily events in Venice. He frequently spoke of *mormoration* or the "gossip" he heard around the city. On 14 July 1524, he commented that "there was yesterday, in the Council of Ten, the murmurs of the majority of the land, that Alvise da Noal wants to run for Grand Chancellor." On 1 February 1499, he remarked that "this morning at the Rialto . . . there was a great murmuring in the city about the Garzoni bank."[83] Sanudo commonly included what was said (*si dice/si diceva*) on the street, such as "This morning, I heard some chatter (*zanza*) from an unclear source," or "it is said by many that Capua has been sacked by the French." Reporting the deaths of lawyer Francesco Moresini and his wife, Sanudo recounted, "it is said that they ate mushrooms and drank milk, and were poisoned by the mushrooms." At the end of a description of the trials of several witches, Sanudo closed by saying, "Here I have reported some of the many things that I have heard." On the French invasions, Sanudo related, "It is said in the city, from where this comes no one says, that the French are arriving in great numbers."[84] He often referred outright to the gossip – *zanze* or *ciancie* – he overheard in the city. "Yesterday and today there was some gossip from an un-named author that the Duke of Milan has died from the plague; but in the *Collegio* they made nothing of it." Mentioning some religious prophecy, "I cannot stop writing without recounting some gossip overheard from some Florentines about [a certain] brother Hironimo."[85] Sanudo was clearly aware of people's reputations and what Venetians thought about their neighbors and politicians, often mentioning the *fama* or commonly held reputation of various individuals. "The lawyer Venier has an awful and terrible reputation." "Tonight our doge Agustin Barbarigo died with the worst reputation any doge has had since Cristoforo Moro. . . . It was

---

[83] Sanudo, *I diarii*, vol. 36, 471; vol. 2, 391–92. Girolamo Priuli also reported the murmurings of the city: "Because of the great murmuring in Venice by every person of every sort about the declaration regarding gambling," Priuli, *I diarii*, vol. 2, 420–21.

[84] "Fo ditto questa matina una zanza incerto auctore," Sanudo, *I diarii*, vol. 33, 612; vol. 4, 76–78, *Sumario di avisi* from 27 July 1501; vol. 7, 605; vol. 25, 602–8, copy of letter from 1 August 1518; vol. 38, 295. For other examples of things that "were said," see vol. 1, 651–52, "Letter from Rome," 15 June 1497; vol. 1, 842, "Letter from Rome," 17 December 1497; vol. 8, 300; vol. 36, 339.

[85] Ibid., vol. 36, 438; vol. 1, 987–98. On gossip, see also vol. 1, 653–55, "Letter from Rome," 20 June 1497; vol. 45, 355–56.

an unbelievable thing to hear the curses that everyone gave him, for his haughtiness, greed, tenacity, and avarice."[86]

Not unlike the Inquisitor and his scribe, Sanudo codified the content of informal spoken language, recognizing that opinions, fears, and desires frequently came to the fore in the form of talk on the street. Though print culture had begun to infiltrate early modern cities, most people – even an educated, literary man like Sanudo – relied on oral transmission and rumor for quotidian information. Sanudo confirmed what Inquisition trials suggested: the marked presence of men gossiping in Venice who could have been provided with their information by either men or women, which Sanudo does not specify. Like the chronicler Priuli and the Buranese doctor Francesco, Sanudo's tone suggested that while he may have distrusted the word on the street (it was "unclear" or some people "make nothing of it"), this did not stop him from regularly including its voices in his notes, displaying a simultaneous dependence on and mistrust of gossip in his chronicle.[87] Though rumor transmitted untrustworthy talk of indeterminate origin, it was unavoidable in an account of daily events in the city. Both its message, or ignoring it, could prove dangerous to political stability.[88] Gossip was infused with power, making it a highly effective political and social tool. The information it offered could be unreliable, but it was nevertheless sought out as a litmus test of popular thought.

Sanudo's simultaneous suspicion of and reliance upon gossip is echoed in the greater workings of the Venetian state itself, as the political gossip that went along with the Venetian *broglio* illustrates the state's similar tendentious relationship to communal talk. The *broglio* was the jostling for political position and the verbal solicitation of votes that occurred in and around the Ducal Palace at the time of elections. As documented

---

[86] Ibid., vol. 36, 471; vol. 4, 113. On *fama* and reputation, see also vol. 34, 128.

[87] Elisabeth Crouzet-Pavan has noted the mistrust that Sanudo displayed for gossip and talk on the street. According to Crouzet-Pavan, Sanudo typically identified the sources of his information, yet when referring to rumor and language from the street, Sanudo's language became impersonal and distrustful, assuming gossip and rumor to be falsely founded. See Crouzet-Pavan, "Les mots de Venise: Sur le contrôle du langage dans une cité-etat italienne," in *La circulation des nouvelles au moyen âge: XXIVe congrès des historiens médiévistes de l'enseignement supérier public* (Paris: Publications de la Sorbonne, 1994), 209.

[88] "Si la *mormoratione* semble ainsi anomique, c'est que la sociabilité de la rue et de la place nourrit et diffuse aussi de véritables informations. Et le danger de ce qui est une authentique et originale mise en parole est alors bien plus grand," Ibid., 212.

and analyzed in the work of Robert Finlay and Donald Queller, the *broglio* involved malicious rumor, vote-trading, petitions for assistance, and political negotiation in and outside the assemblies of the noble class in the ambitious pursuit of office.[89] As opposed to filing quietly into the hall of the Greater Council to place their votes directly, Venetian nobles made deals, placed bets, whispered entreaties and threats, lobbied, and "moved from seat to seat with messages and gossip."[90] At the conclusion of supposedly private political debates, senators often leaked the results, extending the talk of the inner chambers of politics to the city at large. Patricians negotiated political business based on hearsay and gossip in blatant disregard for the republican ideal of the office seeking the man instead of the man seeking the office. The *broglio* involved a wide variety of activities: buying and selling votes, lining the steps of the ducal palace to chant the names of political favorites, betting on elections, following voting urns to check on political supporters, soliciting nominations, and encouraging certain candidates. Such electioneering clearly encompassed far more than gossip itself, which was just one component of this more elaborate practice. Nevertheless, it is safe to say that gossip was a significant component of the *broglio*, or that the *broglio* was a special form of gossip.

Lengthy legislation repeatedly enacted to discourage the *broglio* reveals its insistent presence. The practice extended back to the fourteenth century when Venetian territorial advances multiplied both the number of offices and the competition to hold them; the *broglio* then began when the power to name these officials passed from the doge to the Greater Council.[91] The oldest legislation against the *broglio* dates to 1303, decreeing that once the doors of the Greater Council were closed for elections, nobles had to sit quietly and vote from their respective seats, indicating that they had been doing the opposite. The following centuries passed numerous additional pronouncements against the *broglio*,

---

[89] See Finlay, *Politics*, 22; Queller, *The Venetian Patriciate*, 53. See also Ferro, *Dizionario*, vol. 1, 281; Giovanni Maria Memmo, *Dialogo nel quale dopo alcune filosofiche dispute, si forma un perfetto principe, et una perfetta repubblica* (Venice, 1563), 74. My discussion of *broglio* is entirely indebted to Finlay and Queller's research as I modestly extend the meaning of their findings and arguments.

[90] Finlay, *Politics*, 27.

[91] Queller, *The Venetian Patriciate*, 53.

resulting in harsher punishments such as the loss of office and exclusion from the Greater Council.[92] Laws aimed at preventing electoral corruption prohibited competitors from visiting one another in their homes after the Greater Council adjourned. Fifteenth- and sixteenth-century legislation from the Ten and the *Provveditori Sopra le Pompe* paid special attention to dinner parties and patrician social gatherings, attempting to limit the numbers in which patricians could meet in even private settings.[93] Though such measures were undertaken to restrict unseemly displays of private wealth, a more speculative reading suggests that they would have had the additional result of cutting down on political gossip. Legislation aimed at reducing electoral corruption went so far as to prohibit handshaking, embraces, and the extension of congratulations in an attempt to cut down on the verbal exchanges that accompanied these acts. Throughout the fifteenth century, laws repeatedly encouraged silence and restricted chatting in specified public places, such as in and around the Ducal Palace and the church of San Marco.[94] Towards the end of the fifteenth century and the beginning of the sixteenth however, the *broglio* nevertheless took on "disturbing proportions."[95] Electioneering continued to prove problematic enough to create the magistracy of the *Censori* in 1517 (the same magistracy later given jurisdiction over servants) to combat lobbying in the Senate and Greater Council.[96] These two annually elected Censors were commissioned to imprison, fine, or exile senators who solicited, lobbied, or sold their votes.

The political gossip that went hand in hand with the *broglio* was talk the government was at pains to curtail, demonstrating how the practice of gossip was inherent to Venetian political culture. Consistent and extensive legislation extending from the fourteenth to the seventeenth century reveals both the prevalence of the *broglio* and the impossibility of its eradication as election gossip persisted, if not flourished, in the face of efforts to stop it.[97] Compared to earlier legislation, assuming an increase

---

[92] Ferro, *Dizionario*, vol. 1, 281–82.

[93] Finlay, *Politics*, 203–4, 217, and Queller, *The Venetian Patriciate*, 75–78.

[94] On the extensive and varied legislation against the *broglio* in the fifteenth century, see Queller, *The Venetian Patriciate*, 51–84.

[95] Cozzi, "Authority and Law," 299.

[96] Finlay, *Politics*, 210, and Ferro, *Dizionario*, vol. 1, 372.

[97] The initial, positive results of the work of the Censors were short-lived and the magistracy eventually proved incapable of controlling electoral corruption; consequently, its functions

in this practice, sixteenth-century laws surprisingly became more lax and seemed even to accommodate the gossip of the *broglio*, suggesting an acceptance of election gossip as integral to the Venetian political process. Contemporary chroniclers, in fact, appeared to believe that the *broglio* was a "necessary evil," and "the oil that made the complex machinery of state function so smoothly for so long that it seemed that Venice was free from ambition and faction."[98] Unlike violence or dueling, the *broglio* offered a peaceful means of political decision-making. Although both Sanudo and Priuli lamented the talk of *broglio*, they both recognized its political usefulness.

> And as these intrigues and supplications will yet be the cause of Venice's ruin, so that because of them I marvel it has lasted so long. On the other hand, some have said that these intrigues, [lobbying for] offices and magistracies, and these supplications, have been the salvation of the Venetian Republic, and the principal, cause of [the nobles] not offending in tranquility, friendship and peace. So that if they were without intrigues, salutations and flattery, within a short time they would be seduced into factions and discord among themselves, as in all cities of the world, and there would be great discord among the Venetian nobility. From this the total ruin of Venice would certainly follow.[99]

As we have seen, gossip was just one component of the *broglio*. Nevertheless, these many behaviors necessarily involved the aggressive and often underhanded verbal exchange of voting patricians. Political advancement through the *broglio* demanded and appeared to legitimate the crucial practice of gossip, whose role the state reluctantly came to accept in Venetian elections.

Venice has long appeared to be different in the peaceful nature of its politics – a classic trope of the myth of Venice.[100] In fact, Venetian men significantly did not conform to some of the more violent standards of Italian masculinity. They did not exercise regular military commands

---

were turned over to the *Avogaria di Comun* in 1521, who in turn proved no more successful in stemming the practice of the *broglio*. See Cozzi, "Authority and Law," 326.

[98] Finlay, *Politics*, 221.

[99] Priuli, cited in Chambers and Pullan, *Venice: A Documentary History*, 77, and Finlay, *Politics*, 221. On Sanudo's extensive observations of the *broglio*, see Finlay, *Politics*, 23–27, 196–226.

[100] On various explanations behind the relatively peaceful nature of the Venetian republic, see Muir, *Civic Ritual*, 42–44.

on land, ride horses (at least in the city), or go about town with armed *bravi* in nearly as many numbers as mainland aristocrats.[101] Furthermore, they did not duel or participate in vendettas with the same frequency as other Italian men, and the Council of Ten passed more stringent laws prohibiting dueling than other cities. Though dueling was prohibited everywhere, there remained plenty of duels on the *terraferma* within the Venetian dominion and elsewhere in Italy.[102] If Venetian patricians dueled less, perhaps this was because they did not pursue careers as military men. However, perhaps Venetian men engaged less often in what were otherwise standard forms of early modern aggression because of the unique blending of the political practices of both formal rhetoric and oratory and informal gossip that adequately served their political needs and desires.

Gossip clearly performed myriad functions in the early modern world. It was a pastime and means of entertainment, a form of sociability, a tool of education, a source of information, and a weapon of the weak, or of women seeking success in litigation. At the level of the neighborhood, an arena of male and female honor, both men and women gossiped to patrol community behavior. At the level of the state, men gossiped as a means to political ends, to control blocks of voters or to obtain office. Though male writers condemned slippery, "feminine" gossip and praised structured, "masculine" rhetoric (we can imagine the impassioned, convincing speeches presented in the halls of the Greater Council by Venetian men schooled in classical Ciceronian oratory), the ubiquitous presence

---

[101] See Jonathan Walker, "*Bravi* and Venetian Nobles, c. 1550–1650," *Studi veneziani* 36 (1999): 85–113, esp. 86, 94.

[102] As did other states following the Council of Trent, Venetian law severely punished those who took part in duels. "La Veneta legislazione divieto severamente, e cio con moltiplici regolamenti negl'anni 1541, 1632, e finalmente nel 1739, dichiarando azione indegna ed infame anche nei nobili la sfida, privando della nobilta, cancellando il loro nome dal libro detto d'Oro all'Avogaria, privando gli stipendiati della milizia, i feudatorii di ogni titolo . . . dichiarando bandito ciascun d'ogni condizione da Venezia, e dallo stato in perpetuo, con alternativa di pena capitale," Ferro, *Dizionario*, vol. 1, 650–51. See also Jonathan Walker, "Honour and the Culture of Male Venetian Nobles, c. 1500–1650," (Ph.D. diss., The University of Cambridge, 1998), 167–72. Edward Muir points out that the Venetian printing industry produced technical literature on dueling such as Girolamo Muzio's *Il duello* (Venice, 1550) primarily for the market of aristocrats on the mainland. See Muir, *Mad Blood Stirring*, 256–61. While here I am arguing from an absence of evidence, and of course many Venetian laws were openly flouted, I know of not a single case of a duel in the city of Venice in the sixteenth century and can find no existing evidence to the contrary.

of gossip in Venetian neighborhoods and the halls of state implies that formal, republican oratory and debates were only part of the way that Venetian politics worked. The more domestic, fluid speech of gossip was its alternative, representing a more informal type of verbal negotiation that was equally as useful in political life. If male writers claimed that gossip was typically practiced by women, this suggests that women in turn were its potential instructors. That is to say, men should look to women's speech in order to be successful politicians: not unlike the advice given by Castiglione and Guazzo that unwittingly encouraged men to speak in feminine ways. Though we have no examples of such "lessons" in gossip, we can posit that the ever-present practice of gossip implies that the "domestic" was important to the "public," as private speech acts came to play a substantial role in public politics.

Republican politics were on their way out in early modern Venice; the merchant class was shrinking and Venetian patricians were becoming a landed elite. Venice had to some degree always represented a mixture of republican and aristocratic politics, but by the sixteenth century, an increasingly aristocratic state exercised its power through ever more residual republican institutions. As in courtly cultures, *comun parlar* was clearly at the core of Venice's idea of community and social capital. Individuals in other early modern states and republics gossiped, because as we have seen, comportment writers lamented the problem of loose tongues in Italy as a whole. Yet what remains noteworthy is that gossip seemed to have been a Venetian way of achieving peace and stability in this political mix of republicanism and aristocracy. Talk could curb excess and caution hasty actions. A consideration of gossip in the aristocratic republics of Genoa or seventeenth-century Holland, for example, might yield similar results. Political intrigue and neighborhood chatter – as revealed through legal testimony and Sanudo's chronicle – naturally involved different individuals aimed at achieving different social goals; yet in the case of Venice, these voices overlapped and informed each other. Historians of Venice tend to focus on the impersonal political efforts employed to consolidate Venetian authority and the Venetian state, as seen in the marked sixteenth-century increase in bureaucratic magistracies, for instance. However, the process of creating an acceptable social order also involved the conscious actions of individual Venetians themselves as they strove to maintain verbal control over their communities, tap into the knowledge residing in oral networks, and wield the power of shared, social speech to their social and political advantage. In these ways, gossip was an unofficial yet implicit practice in the workings of the Venetian state and political life. We shall see in conclusion how the speech of courtesans similarly served the state in unexpected ways, because courtesans' talk, like gossip, was a subtle but consistent component of Venetian political culture. Like gossip, courtesans' speech at times proved disruptive, but in other instances, also surprisingly contributed to the workings of Venetian statecraft.

5

The Language of Courtesans

In a letter published in 1580, the prolific Venetian poet and playwright Andrea Calmo described the way he had been bewitched by a courtesan named Basilisca. "If you could only feel the infernal fire that burns constantly in my heart," he said, "the melancholy . . . the buckets of tears that flow from my eyes. . . . I can barely eat or sleep, and I cannot remember what I'm saying when I talk. I put my socks on inside out, my jacket on backwards, and I put on two different shoes. . . . You are a bear, a tiger, a serpent, Medea, Circe, [and] Falerina."[1] Calmo's description of lovesickness is nothing unusual. In fact, he wrote similar descriptions to 49 other courtesans in the fourth book of his letters. His plea, however, presents a curious insight into women's language when he compares Basilisca to some of the greatest sorceresses of history: Medea, who used her magic to help Jason obtain the Golden Fleece and then to kill his bride with a poisoned robe; Circe, whose magical powers and poisonous herbs turned Odysseus' men into pigs; and Falerina, the enchantress who entrapped many valiant knights in the legends of Charlemagne. Calmo's comparison alludes not only to the delights of love but also to its potentially sinister side effects, or the way that love imprisons and disempowers its object through spells, incantations, and the magical language spoken by women. Enormous gaps existed between the prescriptions of Renaissance writers about how men and women should talk and the ways in which verbal exchanges actually occurred in the early modern world, and Calmo's letter is no exception. In discussions about gossip, male writers tried to construct categories for gendered speech – masculine

[1] Calmo, *Le lettere*, 266–68.

rhetoric and feminine gossip – that did not really exist. They suggested that silence was a woman's greatest virtue: advice that, as we have seen, appears to have been entirely ignored by urban women. Against this backdrop, Calmo's letter alludes to how a particular category of women was even more pronounced in skirting traditional prescriptions for women's speech and silence – the courtesan.[2]

One might well wonder, what place does courtesans' talk have in a study of language and the state? Political speech as it is traditionally cast occurred in the halls of government and the courts, far removed from courtesans' salons. Why not consider the speech of lawyers, advocates, or political men who based their livelihoods in large part on their verbal dexterity? Though courtesans' speech may at first appear unrelated to the study of speech and statecraft, when examined closely, we can see how courtesans' language played a subtle but intriguing role in Venetian society. A consideration of courtesans' speech as a facet of Venetian political culture is fitting for several reasons. Firstly, with remarkable unanimity, all scholars who have studied the lives of Renaissance courtesans agree emphatically on one point: courtesans distinguished themselves primarily through their speech and language. They asserted their power and negotiated their status through the mastery of the spoken word: an assertion that, for all its frequency, has received surprisingly little exploration or scrutiny. Secondly, and even more significantly, Italian Renaissance writers paid a truly inordinate amount of attention to the speech of courtesans. They dedicated more discursive energy to courtesans' talk than to the spoken words of any other sub-group or profession as a whole: a fact that demands examination. Because Venice was famed for

---

[2] The literature on courtesans and prostitutes in the Renaissance is vast. For Renaissance Italy and Venice in particular, the most important studies and collections of documents include: Fiora A. Bassanese, "Private Lives and Public Lies: Texts by Courtesans of the Italian Renaissance," *Texas Studies in Literature and Language* 30 (1988): 295–319; Antonio Barzaghi, *Donne o cortigiane? La prostituzione a Venezia. Documenti di costumi dal XVI al XVIII secolo* (Verona: Bertani, 1980); Rita Casagrande di Villaviera, *Le cortigiane veneziane del Cinquecento* (Milan: Longanese, 1968); Paul Larivaille, *La vie quotidienne des courtesans en Italie au temps de la renaissance* (Paris: Hachette, 1975); *Leggi e memorie venete sulla prostituzione*, ed. Giovanni Battista de Lorenzi (Venice, 1870–72); *Il gioco dell'amore. Le cortigiane di Venezia dal Trecento al Settecento*, ed. Doretta Davanzo Poli and Irene Ariano (Milan: Berenice, 1990); Margaret Rosenthal, *The Honest Courtesan: Veronica Franco, Citizen and Writer in Sixteenth-Century Venice* (Chicago: The University of Chicago Press, 1992); Ruggiero, *Binding Passions* and *The Boundaries of Eros*.

its courtesan culture, much of this discussion about courtesans' speech focused in and around the lagoon city: all reasons to look more closely at courtesans' talk.

It is important to emphasize up front that we have very few examples of courtesans' actual spoken words. Indeed, this consideration of courtesans' language rests on a slender archival and documentary base. Most historical sources that document the lives of courtesans are either legislative or literary and do not record courtesans' own voices. Historical speech, as always, proves difficult to capture. We have no records that offer us extensive transcripts of courtesans speaking, beyond what Guido Ruggiero has already explored from the records of the *Sant'Uffizio*. However, as we have seen with blasphemy, this is not necessarily a block to gaining insight into courtesans' language, because much can be learned from looking closely at peripheral evidence. In this case, we know an extraordinary amount of information about what people *said* about their speech. Such reflective or secondary evidence tells us little about courtesans' agency, but it has a lot to say about their perceived roles in Venetian society as well as the complex connections and interactions that existed between speech, gender, sexuality, and the state.

Both Guido Ruggiero and Margaret Rosenthal have examined the dual, paradoxical nature of the perceptions of courtesans as both dangerous threats to civic stability and honored arbiters of social status. Courtesans ingeniously appropriated the symbolism of both Venus and the Virgin from Venetian iconography in their self-fashioning. Ruggiero has demonstrated how prostitution was "potentially subversive . . . in a society that saw itself based upon marriage and the family," and yet courtesans flourished in sixteenth-century Italian cities because they "satisfied new social imperatives."[3] In her magisterial study of Veronica Franco, Rosenthal has similarly noted how courtesans "embodied a city immersed in luxury, spectacle, disguise, commercialization, voluptuousness, and sensuality" while at the same time offering proof of the republic's progressive social policies and tolerance.[4] These scholars have explored a great

---

[3] Ruggiero, *Binding Passions*, 26, 38. See also Guido Ruggiero, "Who's Afraid of Giuliana Napolitana? Pleasure, Fear, and Imagining the Arts of the Renaissance Courtesan," in *The Courtesan's Arts: Cross-Cultural Perspectives*, ed. Martha Feldman and Bonnie Gordon (New York: Oxford University Press, 2006), 280–92, esp. 281–82.

[4] Rosenthal, *The Honest Courtesan*, 3.

variety of topics associated with courtesans and their lives, including how courtesans were made, how prostitution was disciplined, and how these women served as both symbols and anti-symbols of the Venetian republic. In doing so, neither has by any means ignored the importance of spoken language and conversation; both point to eloquence as one of the skills courtesans employed to survive and advance in society. As Ruggiero puts it, "power over words implied in many ways power in the world and over men."[5] However, both Ruggiero and Rosenthal use the term "words" broadly to mean written language, including poems and letters, as much as speech. I would like here to add a new dimension to their work by paying specific attention to courtesans' talk, or at least as much of it as we can glean from extant records. Doing so deepens our understanding of courtesans' lives and position in society. Namely, when examined through the lens of their linguistic practices and their talk, we can see how courtesans occupied a small but consistent place in Venetian political culture.

Many have noted the ways in which courtesans served as commercial assets to the Venetian state.[6] Here, I would like to emphasize the degree to which, as Ruggiero has put it, courtesans were selling more than just their bodies. Throwing this point into even higher relief allows us to assert that courtesanry was a Venetian industry driven by the profits of not just sex, but of conversation and verbal exchange, or the language that courtesans sold as entrepreneurs or gave as gifts, sometimes to the benefit of the state. Courtesans were subtly yet powerfully connected to Venetian civic identity and the Venetian economy itself through their mastery and sale of *language* in particular. If Venice had become noted throughout the sixteenth-century world for its illustrious courtesans and courtesans were famed for their eloquence, this in turn suggests that Venice's public image and economic strength were derived in part from the witty speech of this select group of women.

---

[5] Ruggiero, *Binding Passions*, 45.

[6] Ann Rosalind Jones, "City Women and Their Audiences: Louise Labé and Veronica Franco," in *Rewriting the Renaissance: The Discourses of Sexual Difference in Early Modern Europe*, ed. Margaret W. Ferguson, Maureen Quilligan, and Nancy J. Vickers (Chicago: The University of Chicago Press, 1986), 303; Ruggiero, "Who's Afraid of Giuliana Napolitana?" 282; Rosenthal, *The Honest Courtesan*, 22.

And yet, as with gossip, there existed conflicting and often contradictory connections between courtesans' language and Venetian political culture. Like the Jews, courtesans embodied both the evils and dynamism of a mercantile society concerned with turning a profit. They traded both sex and words for financial gain, and in doing so fit into the classic conflation of the lure of the marketplace, sexual seduction, and moral outrage.[7] Read together, literature, legislation, and trial testimony highlight the unstable nature of courtesans' talk. Their words were beautiful, but dangerous. Courtesans' speech commanded fascination and admiration, but sometimes condemned them to persecution and marginalization. It was precisely this varied and fluctuating nature of their speech that allowed courtesans to play a peculiar role in Venetian political culture. The nature of power and agency has long been understood as shifting and unpredictable, as varied and often surprising, and the Venetian promotion of courtesans' language to the wider world illustrates this phenomenon. Although their speech frequently condemned them within the city – Venetian magistracies at times focused their disciplinary powers on courtesans' language to promote civic stability – an admiration for their eloquence simultaneously promoted them when projected to the wider world. That is to say, it was this perception of their language as mutable and unstable, as eloquent but also offensive and sinful, that allowed them to function simultaneously as victims and agents. Courtesans were both sexualized demons and eloquent humanists, sinful deviants and savvy economic agents, who both suffered and profited from the use of their eloquence and witty speech. Most significantly, the inherent tension around courtesans' language made it possible for them to assume an emblematic, diplomatic importance in the city's promotion of itself that other Venetian women could not assume.

Many sixteenth-century writers considered courtesans' speech dangerous because of its sexual nature: a concept that was rooted to some degree in the idea that speech itself was sexual. Anatomists and medical men, for instance, depicted the mouth as a sexual orifice and the tongue as a phallus. The renowned sixteenth-century anatomist Berengario

---

[7] See Evelyn Welch, *Shopping in the Renaissance: Consumer Cultures in Italy, 1400–1600* (New Haven: Yale University Press, 2005), 32.

da Carpi concluded in his 1522 *Isagogae* that the tongue, "like the penis . . . has more and larger pulsating and quiet veins than any other member equal to it in size."[8] In his 1535 treatise *Anatomica methodus,* Andrés de Laguna provocatively asserted that

> the tongue, like some stern doorkeeper . . . is quite spongy so that it draws and attracts to itself whatever moisture there may be, like some old drunken woman. . . . [I]t often happens that the tongue admits some harmful medicines. . . . Thus it happens that the tongue is very frequently deceived. . . . Under the tongue there is something called a frenulum (little checkrein); if by chance this becomes more loose than is convenient or reasonable in any person, as may be seen in women who are more talkative than any turtle-dove, you should not expect silence. . . . One must, however, note carefully that nature has attached such a checkrein only to the tongue and to the private parts, for in these organs especially she has desired that men should be modest.[9]

Two sixteenth-century Venetian proverbs highlight this association: "The mouth and the asshole are brothers" (*La bocca e'l cul son fradei*), and "All mouths are sisters, but those of the asshole and the cunt are the closest" (*Tutte le bocche son sorelle, ma quella del cul e della pota son più felle*).[10] Lastly, while we have seen that rhetoric, in theory, was often described as masculine speech that was off limits to women, Renaissance writers also at times described rhetoric and oratory as sexualizing or feminizing practices. Cicero and Quintillian were decidedly nervous about the potentially feminizing aspects of rhetoric because they believed Roman men ought to define themselves through action rather than talk. Copying a passage from the third book of Cicero's *De oratore*, Pico della Mirandola condemned the rhetor as a sodomite, and a man who behaved like a woman.

> Who would not approve the soft step, the clever hands, the playful eyes in an actor and a dancer, but in a citizen or a philosopher, who would not disapprove, censure, and abominate them? If we see a girl graceful

---

[8] Berengario da Carpi, *Isagogae breves,* in Lind, *Studies in Pre-Vesalian Anatomy,* 122.

[9] Andrés de Laguna, *Anatomica methodus,* in Lind, *Studies in Pre-Vesalian Anatomy,* 266–67. Francesco Sansovino also argued that male and female tongues were anatomically different. See Sansovino, *L'edificio del corpo humano,* 15v–16r. I am grateful to Cindy Klestinec for this citation.

[10] Cortelazzo, *Le dieci tavole,* 91, 129.

in her manners and talkative, we will praise her, will kiss her. These things we would condemn and prosecute in a matron. Therefore, it is not we, but they [the rhetoricians], who perform Bacchanalias at the feet of a Vestal, who dishonor the gravity and chastity of philosophical matters as if with games and curling irons.[11]

Similarly equating rhetoric or public speech with sexuality, Pietro Aretino claimed in his satires that procuresses and pimps quoted Petrarch with ease.[12] This feminization of rhetoric is an especially intriguing concept for Venice, where more so than in many other cities, rhetoric remained a real skill that was actively used in day-to-day political negotiation in the halls of government.[13]

According to Pico and Aretino, rhetoric and public speech were associated with enticement and magical allure, which are figured as feminine and thus implicitly threaten any male-dominated society. Ioan Couliano has noted the close connection "between the five senses, the production of the voice, and the secretion of sperm. The last two are closely allied in Renaissance medicine, because they represent the only two modalities through which the spirit leaves the body in an observable way."[14] If we take these ideas a step further, cutting out the tongue would represent a type of castration. Similarly, laws against insults and blasphemy would have undertones aimed at creating civic sexual respectability. As we have

---

[11] Giovanni Pico della Mirandola, *Epistola Hermolao Barbaro*, in Giovanni Pico della Mirandola and Gian Francesco Pico, *Opera omnia* (Basel, 1557), in Wayne A. Rebhorn, *The Emperor of Men's Minds: Literature and the Renaissance Discourse of Rhetoric* (Ithaca: Cornell University Press, 1995), 135.

[12] Arturo Graf, "Una cortigiana fra mille," in *Attraverso il Cinquecento* (Turin: Ermanno Loescher, 1888), 231, n. 1. Similarly, Aretino's Nanna equates sex and conversation when she states that "if I were a man, I would like to bed down with a woman who has a honied instead of a learned tongue; and I would be happier to hold in my arms an experienced slut than Messer Dante himself." See Pietro Aretino, *Aretino's Dialogues*, trans. Raymond Rosenthal (New York: Stein and Day, 1971), 200.

[13] See Virginia Cox, "Rhetoric and Humanism in Quattrocento Venice," *Renaissance Quarterly* 56 (2003): 652–94.

[14] Ioan P. Couliano, *Eros and Magic in the Renaissance* (Chicago: The University of Chicago Press, 1987), 101–2. On the connection between sexual ejaculation and speech in Renaissance medical theory, see also Allison Coudert, "Some Theories of a Natural Language from the Renaissance to the Seventeenth Century," in *Magia Naturalis und Die Entstehung der Modernen Naturwissenschaften: Studiea Leibnitiana* 7 (Wiesbaden: Franz Steiner Verlag GMBH, 1978), 63–64. Couliano's statement is not entirely correct, because early modern medicine held that the spirit could also leave the body through bloodletting and female sperm in menstruation; nevertheless, the connection between the voice and sexuality remains strong.

seen with sexual insults, the eradication of such speech had a particular resonance in republican societies. Republics, unlike courts, did not tolerate illegitimate birth.[15] Unruly sexuality undermined the institutions of marriage and the family, while a disciplined sexuality preserved family, community, and republican order. The desire to control the social body legitimated controlling the actions of the physical body, and patrolling speech as a facet of sexuality would work to shore up such connections.

Most importantly, however, as the physician de Laguna indicates, the tongue was feminine in nature and represented a type of female penis. Female silence was equivalent to chastity and a loose tongue to sexual licentiousness. In an often-cited chapter on "Speech and Silence," Francesco Barbaro made the connection between sexuality and speech especially clear. "It is proper," he wrote, "that not only the arms but indeed also the speech of women never be made public; for the speech of a noble woman can be no less dangerous than the nakedness of her limbs."[16] Stefano Guazzo similarly employed the word *conversazione* to equate chat and women's sexuality, observing that "la conversazione delle donne" meant both men's sexual relationships with women and masculine discussion with women.[17] In another passage well-known among feminist historians, the humanist educator Guarino claimed in 1438 that Isotta Nogarola's sexual deviancy matched her public speech, as "the woman of fluent speech is never chaste."[18] Feminine speech clearly proved problematic in the early modern world. Normally, women "belonged" to men – to their fathers or husbands – who controlled their sexuality. A woman who "spoke" therefore took possession of her own body and sexuality – a dangerous notion in a society based on chastity and patriarchal control. Women's public language symbolically equaled prostitution. Female

---

[15] Jacob Burckhardt claimed that in the dynasties of the Renaissance, there was a "public indifference to legitimate birth." For instance, "when Pius II was on his way to the Congress of Mantua (1459) eight bastards of the house of Este rode to meet him at Ferrara, among them the reigning Duke Borso himself and two illegitimate sons of his illegitimate brother and predecessor Leonello." Burckhardt, *The Civilization of the Renaissance in Italy*, vol. 1, 38. On sexuality and republicanism, see Ruggiero, *The Boundaries of Eros*, 9.

[16] Francesco Barbaro, *On Wifely Duties*, trans. Benjamin G. Kohl, in *The Earthly Republic: Italian Humanists on Government and Society*, ed. Kohl and Ronald G. Witt with Elizabeth Welles (Philadelphia: University of Pennsylvania Press, 1978), 205.

[17] See Jones, "Surprising Fame," 77–78.

[18] Cited in Lisa Jardine, "Women Humanists: Education for What?" in Hutson, *Feminism and Renaissance Studies*, 56.

speech, on the one hand, represented one axis of a wider, more sweeping critique of women's nature in general. On the other hand, early modern individuals suggested that loose tongues metaphorically led to the next step of prostitution. Such perceived connections between speech and sexual promiscuity therefore left women faced with a series of paradoxes. If women were not respected or respectable, they could not be heard; if they spoke, they were by definition unrespectable and opened the door to a barrage of criticism of and attacks on their virtue.

Similarly, injunctions against women's speech placed them in a political bind. According to male writers dating from the ancient world through the Renaissance, including Giovanni Della Casa, women by nature were not capable of speaking "well," "respectably," or "safely," so they were not considered political actors; yet because they were not recognized as political actors, they were effectively denied a voice. Humanists like Juan Luis Vives and Leonardo Bruni excluded rhetoric from women's education because it belonged to the public realm or the spheres of law, politics, business, and diplomacy, which were strictly off limits to women. Renaissance pronouncements on women's speech obsessively dictated that speech and chastity were mutually exclusive: an opposition that remains fascinating in that it was by no means self-evident. As Ann Rosalind Jones has suggested, "the link between loose language and loose living arises from a basic association of women's bodies with their speech: a woman's accessibility to the social world beyond the household through speech was seen as intimately connected to the scandalous openness of her body."[19] Many literary scholars have noted the ways in which discussions of sexuality in the Renaissance were infused with ideas about language; many Renaissance writers linked language and desire.[20] Courtesans' public speech was clearly constructed as dangerous because

---

[19] Jones, "Surprising Fame," 76.

[20] Much has been written, especially by literary scholars, on the relationship between speech and sexuality. See Margaret W. Ferguson, "A Room Not Their Own: Renaissance Women as Readers and Writers," in *The Comparative Perspective on Literature: Approaches to Theory and Practice*, ed. Clayton Koelb and Susan Noakes (Ithaca: Cornell University Press, 1988), 93–116; Jonathan Goldberg, *Sodometries: Renaissance Texts, Modern Sexualities* (Stanford: Stanford University Press, 1992); Madhavi Menon, *Wanton Words: Rhetoric and Sexuality in English Renaissance Drama* (Toronto: The University of Toronto Press, 2004), 4–34; Patricia Parker, *Literary Fat Ladies: Rhetoric, Gender, Property* (New York: Methuen, 1987), 8–35; Peter Stallybrass, "Patriarchal Territories: The Body Enclosed," in Ferguson et. al., *Rewriting the Renaissance*, 123–42.

of the ways in which it laid bare the sexual nature of their bodies and their trade.

Against this general cultural background, courtesans came to embody literally this link between speech and sexuality in the early modern period. The term "honest courtesan" first appeared in the second half of the fifteenth century. Whereas prostitutes in the late Middle Ages were referred to more generally as *peccatrici* or *meretrici*, the emergence of this new term, *cortigiana onesta*, indicated a change in cultural perceptions away from the universal, moralistic condemnation of all prostitutes to the praise and even glorification of a select group of them.[21] The term courtesan, derived from the term *cortigiano*, denoted a mannered and educated group of women – elevated above the ordinary working prostitute – who circulated among the ranks of humanists, artists, and the papal court. The courtesan's lifestyle typically involved luxurious physical surroundings, an intellectual life, music, and knowledge of the literature of ancient Greece and Rome.[22] She distinguished herself from the common prostitute, in part, through spectacular appearances at banquets, high fees, musical abilities, dress, and an elite clientele. For example, when the Venetian courtesan Andriana Savorgnan was 22 and at the height of her career, her lovers included the *crème* of the Venetian aristocracy, including Nicoletto Corner dalla Ca'Granda, Filippo da Canal, Lorenzo Celsi, Santo Contarini, Alessandro Contarini, and Scipione Avogadro.[23]

Venice and Rome represented the two Italian cities particularly noted for the sale of sex in early modern Italy, and many writers and chroniclers noted the large numbers of prostitutes in Venice. Although such figures are regularly cited in almost all existing studies on courtesanry, a review of these numbers will help emphasize the connections between gender, speech, and the state. Marin Sanudo meticulously noted in his

---

[21] See Graf, "Una Cortigiana fra mille," 224, 227. See also Barzaghi, *Donne o cortigiane,* 41, and Villaviera, *Le cortigiane veneziane,* 25. Not everyone acknowledged such a great distinction between prostitutes and courtesans; see Alessandro Citolini, *La tipocosmia* (Venice, 1561), 443.

[22] In one of his novelle, Matteo Bandello describes the room of the Roman courtesan Imperia as being so beautiful that rather than spit on the floor and soil the luxurious surroundings, the Spanish ambassador instead spit in the face of a servant. See Matteo Bandello, *La terza parte de le novelle,* ed. Delmo Maestri (Alessandria: Edizione dell'Orso, 1993), 193–94.

[23] See Marisa Milani, "Cortigiane e inquisizione a Venezia nel secondo '500," in *Stregoneria e streghe nell'Europa moderna,* ed. Giovanna Bosco and Patrizia Castelli (Pisa: Ministero per i Beni Culturali, 1996), 311, and Ruggiero, *Binding Passions,* 32–33.

chronicle that among Venice's 300,000 inhabitants in 1509, of 48,346 women and children, there existed 11,654 *femene da partido* (women who were shared/*partirsi* among many, or prostitutes). Excluding children, noblewomen, and citizens, this figure suggests that the number of prostitutes could have been as high as one-third of the female population.[24] In fact, these figures were exaggerated, for Venice had only 115,000 people in 1509 and reached its highest population in 1563 with 168,000 inhabitants. Nonetheless, it is still probable that a large number of women were prostitutes.[25] As many as one in every 10 inhabitants (or one in every five women) in sixteenth-century Venice might have made their living from prostitution, and even a figure of half these numbers would be remarkable.[26] Legislation from the *Provveditori alla Sanità* described the "infinite number of the many infamous *meretrice* that exist and are growing by the day in this city," and many literary descriptions confirmed this depiction of the city.[27] Of perhaps thousands of prostitutes, there were many fewer women who could be considered courtesans; nevertheless, courtesans were also particularly numerous in Venice. The English traveler Thomas Coryat put their number at 20,000 (showing how exaggerating numbers is a topos of male rhetoric). The *Catalogo di tutte le principale et più honorate cortigiane di Venezia* (1565) listed 210 names, and Michel de Montaigne suggested a figure of around 150 such women in his travel journals.[28] Even later in the middle of the eighteenth

---

[24] Sanudo, *I diarii*, vol. 8, 414; Marisa Milani, "Cortigiane e inquisizione," 307.

[25] See Daniele Beltrami, *Storia della popolazione di Venezia dalla fine del secolo XVI alla caduta della repubblica* (Padua: CEDAM, 1954), 59.

[26] See See Paula Findlen, "Humanism, Politics, and Pornography in Renaissance Italy," in *The Invention of Pornography: Obscenity and the Origins of Modernity, 1500–1800*, ed. Lynn Hunt (New York: Zone Books, 1993), 357, n.120. It is important to note that Findlen's figures, also, are questionable, because no statistics record whether women earned a living from prostitution; they only record whether a woman had sexual relations outside of marriage. Many of the women referred to as *meretrice* earned their living by working as laundresses, spinners, or domestic servants.

[27] *Leggi e memorie veneti*, 105. Niccolò Franco said that prostitutes in sixteenth-century Venice numbered in the thousands, Matteo Bandello described Venice as having "an infinite number of whores," and Ortensio Lando agreed that to try to count them "would be like trying to count the stars in the sky." See Niccolò Franco, *Le pistole vulgari* (Venice, 1542 edn.), 187v–188r; Bandello, *La terza parte delle novelle*, 31; Ortensio Lando, *Sette libri de cataloghi* (Venice, 1552), 23.

[28] Coryat, *Coryat's Crudities*, vol. 1, 402; Michel de Montaigne, *Journal de voyage en Italie*, ed. Maurice Rat (Paris: Editions Garnier, 1955), 73. See also Giovambattista Giraldi Cinthio, *Hecatommithi, overo cento novelle* (Venice, 1593), vol. 2, 91v.

century, Carlo de Brosses still found there were twice as many courtesans in Venice as in Paris, and expressly noted that Venetian courtesans were "well employed."[29] Venice was clearly renowned as a lascivious and alluring city that offered the sale of sex in abundance.

Scholars have long studied courtesans' lives, and yet any attempt to study courtesans as a group distinct from prostitutes as a whole poses several obstacles. There were numerous synonyms for prostitutes in the sixteenth century, and the prostitute and the courtesan were both commonly referred to as a *meretrice, bagascia/baldracca, bardassa, sgualdrina, mondana, donnaccia, a donna di malavita,* or sometimes even so simply as a *signora.* In many cases, it was a fine line that separated them, as the vocabulary that defined them and its connotations blurred. Sixteenth-century Venetians themselves often referred to them as distinct groups, but also sometimes grouped them together or continued to refer to prostitutes and courtesans as a whole as *meretrice,* or women who simply had sexual relations outside of marriage.[30] Distinguishing courtesans as a group is also challenging because Venetian legislation did not always do so. The language of the *Provveditori alla Sanità* and the *Esecutori Contro la Bestemmia* – the two magistracies assigned to oversee various aspects of prostitution in the city – frequently combined and conflated these terms, as did Venetian men and women themselves.[31]

Scholars tend to agree, however, that courtesans distinguished themselves in large part through their great skills in the art of conversation. As insulting drawings and gestures have shown us, communication involves action as much as language, and courtesans were no exception to this idea; their dress and lifestyles were also important to their success. Their spoken language, however, appeared to play a special role in their careers. Courtesans were Renaissance versions of the classical *hetairie,*

---

[29] Graf, "Una cortigiana fra mille," 288.

[30] "Quelle veramente si intendino meretrice quale non essendo maritate haverano comercio et praticha con uno over più homeni . . . quelle che havendo marito non habitano con sui mariti, ma stanno separate et habino comercio con uno over più homeni," ASV, *Senato Terra,* 12 February 1543, cited in *Leggi e memorie,* 109.

[31] On similar questions of naming and vocabulary and the various levels of prostitution that existed across the social spectrum, see Elizabeth Cohen, "'Courtesans' and 'Whores': Words and Behavior in Roman Streets," *Women's Studies* 19 (1991): 201–8; Jones and Rosenthal, "Introduction: The Honored Courtesan" in Franco, *Poems and Selected Letters,* 2–3; Ruggiero, *Binding Passions,* 35–36.

or "women friends" called on for spiritual and aesthetic enjoyment in *symposia* or intellectual conversations in the Hellenist circles of Greek antiquity.[32] Courtesans sold their sexual services, but what differentiated them from the common prostitutes, besides their glamour, grace, and beauty, was their eloquence. A man in search of sex alone sought out a prostitute, but paid more for the refined experience that included a stimulating (or erotic) conversation. Many contemporary descriptions of courtesans emphasize their mastery of the spoken word, their linguistic skill, and their conversational bravura. For instance, when instructing her daughter in the arts of courtesanry, Pietro Aretino's Nanna tells Pippa that "noblemen are accustomed to great ladies and derive more pleasure from gossiping and chitchat than from other things. So you must know how to talk." If not with gossip, the courtesan had to be prepared to "put on a show of reading *Furioso*, Petrarch and Boccaccio's *Hundred Tales*, which you should always keep in full view on your table."[33] The courtesan Giulia da Brolo was famous for reciting comedies, and Lucrezia Squarcia for walking around, Petrarch in hand, reading poetry and debating Homer, Virgil, music, and the *questione della lingua* at social gatherings.[34] The character Ludovico commented on the courtesan Matrema-non-vole in the satirical prose dialogue the *Ragionamento del Zoppino* (1539) for appearing to be a "new Cicero" and for memorizing all of Petrarch, Boccaccio, and numerous Latin verses. "I know 25 gentlemen," he claimed, "who are professional orators who know less about talking than she does."[35] Although we can never know the exact words of conversations that took place in the private boudoirs of Venetian courtesans, many men described the scintillating conversation that occurred there. Eloquence functioned as courtesans' cultural passkey,

---

[32] See Pio Pecchiai, *Imperia* (Padua: CEDAM, 1958), 6.

[33] Aretino, *Dialogues*, 181, 233.

[34] Maffio Venier, "Daspuò che son entrà in pensier sì vario," in Milani, *Contro le puttane*, 66; "Lucrecia Squarcia, che di poesie/Finge apprezzar e seguitar gli studi/... Recando spesso il Petrarchetto in mano/Di Virgilio le charte et hor di Homero/Spesso disputa del parlar Thoscano," *La tariffa delle puttane di Venegia*, reprinted in Barzaghi, *Donne o cortigiane*, 173.

[35] *Ragionamento del Zoppino*, ed. Mario Cicognani (Milan: Longanesi, 1969), 42. Ercole Bentivoglio sent a courtesan named Angela (perhaps Angela Zaffetta) a chapter of his concerning the *questione della lingua* entitled *Della lingua tosca* and expressed his own desire to learn Venetian dialect from her. See Graf, "Una cortigiana fra mille," 230. For similar descriptions of courtesans' eloquence, see Aretino, *Letters*, 249, Calmo, *Le lettere*, 278–80; 290, 297, 309, 334.

and it was through the manipulation of language that courtesans gained entrance to the elite world and made their living.

Although Renaissance culture dedicated much discursive energy to controlling and minimizing women's speech in general, a truly surprising amount of legal and literary attention was paid to controlling the language of courtesans as a specific group. Courtesans' speech was often singled out as particularly unruly. A law passed in 1571 by the *Provveditori alla Sanità* prohibited courtesans from attending church on major holidays under a fine of 200 *lire di piccoli*, so that among their many disruptive forms of behavior, their "many lascivious words do not provide a negative example to others who attend church."[36] A second law from 1578 remarked on the verbal commotion caused by prostitutes and courtesans who attended city churches dressed as married women or widows, and a third law from 1582 reiterated concerns about the uproar caused by the scandalous language of courtesans and prostitutes that resulted in "*mormoratione universale*".[37] Calmo described the courtesan Meneghina Cinqueta as "an evil tongue... full of slander and wanton words... always assassinating and destroying the honor of others." Tomaso Garzoni noted how prostitutes and courtesans regularly duped unwitting young men with their seductive words, and many other writers reiterated similar ideas about courtesans' unruly tongues.[38] As a living example of the verbal deception of courtesans, many sixteenth-century Venetians surely either recalled or knew of the spectacular case of Antonio di Landi,

---

[36] "Che alcuna meretrice over cortesana sia di che conditione esser si voglia, non possano ne debbano de cetero andar in chiesa alcuna il zorno della festa et solenità principal di quella, acciò non siano causa di mali esempii con molti et parole lascive a quelli over quelle che vanno a buon fine in ditte giesie con vergogna di questa città," ASV, *Provveditori alla Sanità*, Capitolare 1, 1485–1574, carta 157, 10 March 1571.

[37] "Nelle chiese di questa città a tempo che si celebrano li santi officii vano diverse meretrice e cortesane in esse chiese vestite da maridate e da vedove facendo atti disonesti con mal essempio e mormoratione," Ibid., Capitolare 2, 1574–1689, carta 37, 20 December 1578; "Cosi per terra come per barca, si come si ha inteso, vestite con diversi habiti lascivi et facendo molti chiassi et usando termini inhonesti con mormoratione universale et contaminatione delle persone da bene che vanno a dette chiese et luochi per devotione," Ibid., Notatorio 11, carta 112, 2 December 1582.

[38] Andrea Calmo, *Le bizarre, faconde, et ingeniose rime pescatorie* (Venice, 1553), 44; Garzoni, *La piazza universale*, vol. 2, 951–65. See also Aretino, *Letters*, 122; Mattio Pagan, *Pronostico alla villota sopra le puttane* (Venice, 1558); Passi, *I donneschi difetti*, 158–77; *Ragionamento del Zoppino*, 37; Francesco Sansovino, *Ragionamento, nel quale brevemente s'insegna a giovani huomini la bella arte d'amore* (Venice, 1545), 19v; Venier, *Il libro chiuso* in Milani, *Contro le puttane*, 68–69.

a state secretary who was betrayed by a courtesan in matters of state in 1498.[39] It is interesting to note that, for all this concern, the records of the *Sanità* indicate that one prostitute, Catharina Zotta, was punished for foul language in the sixteenth century, and the *Esecutori Contro la Bestemmia* banned one prostitute for blasphemy in 1551.[40] Despite the fact that both legal and literary discourse aggressively argued that courtesans and prostitutes were particularly obscene talkers, the low number of them prosecuted for verbal crimes in the sixteenth century – two – once again suggests a disconnect or slippage between the way that male authorities described female speech and the way courtesans actually spoke, at least in the public realm.

If there was any one label consistently applied to courtesans that captured their role as temptresses and their alluring, wicked voices, it was their frequent description as Sirens. Although we have already seen this term used by both Castiglione and Guazzo to describe outspoken women in general who threatened the natural order with their loquacity, Niccolò Franco, Girolamo Parabosco, Perissone Cambio, Francesco Pona, Tomaso Garzoni, and others all applied this term to courtesans.[41]

---

[39] The courtesan Laura Troylo had the suspicion that Antonio Landi had been revealing state secrets to a Trevisan named Giovanni Battista. Troylo invited a friend named Gieronimo Amai to hide behind the bed during one of these secret exchanges, and then Troylo and Amai denounced Landi for his crime, who was then executed and hung from gallows between the columns of San Marco. While this case could appear the results of the honorable, patriotic efforts on the part of Troylo to preserve state secrets, the rhetorical tone of its interpreter Sanudo, as well as the nineteenth-century historian Giusseppe Tassini, suggests that it was yet another example of a deceptive, chattering courtesan who could not keep quiet. "Ed ditta Laura non li bastò l'animo andarli ad accusar; ma mandò questo Hironimo," Sanudo, *I diarii*, vol. 1, 917–18. "La donna, incapace di tacere, comunicò il fatto ad un altro suo amico, per nome Girolamo Amai," Giusseppe Tassini, *Alcune delle più clamorose condanne capitali eseguite in Venezia* (Venice: Tipografia di G. Cecchini, 1866), 115–16. The poligrafo Niccolò Franco similarly argued that prostitutes used their beauty to overhear secrets and strategically employed such knowledge to gain profit and reputation. See Franco, *Pistole vulgari* (Venice, 1539 edn.), xxiv–xxv.

[40] ASV, *Provveditori alla Sanità*, Notatorio 6, carta 231v, 20 August 1552; *Esecutori Contro la Bestemmia*, Libro 1, Raspe, 1548–70, carta 30, 7 April 1551. While he does not mention any specific name or magistracy, Pietro Bembo found the case of a prostitute who blasphemed in 1512 significant enough to mention in his *Della historia vinitiana*: "In Vinegia I Signor Dieci bandirono una meretrice, che Dio et Santi sozzamente bestemmiato havea, e s'era fuggita, postale questa conditione, che se ella in luogo alcuno della Republica presa fosse, la testa le fosse tagliata e ella abbrusciata," Pietro Bembo, *Della historia vinitiana* (Venice, 1552), 176–77.

[41] Franco, *Le pistole vulgari* (Venice, 1542 edn.), 220v; Girolamo Parabosco, *Quattro libri delle lettere amorose* (Venice, 1611), 38; Perissone Cambio, *Primo libro dei madrigale* (Venice, 1547),

Recounting his travels to Venice at the end of the sixteenth century, Thomas Coryat emphasized the dangerously seductive tongues of Venetian courtesans.

> Moreover shee will endevour to enchaunt thee partly with her melodious notes that she warbles out upon her lute, which shee fingers with as laudable a stroake as many men that are excellent professors in the noble science of musicke; and partly with that heart-tempting harmony of her voice. Also thou wilt finde the Venetian cortezan (if she be a selected woman indeede) a good rhetorician, and a most elegant discourser, so that if she cannot move thee with all these foresaid delights, shee will assay they constancy with her rhetoricall tongue. And to the end shee may minister unto thee the stronger temptations to come to her lure.

For these reasons, Coryat goes on to warn the traveler not to enter into conversation with the Venetian courtesan and to "furnish they self with a double armour, the one for thine eyes, the other for thine eares . . . against the attractive inchauntments of their plausible speeches."[42] It is interesting to note in passing the Siren that graces the frontispiece of Aretino's *Stanze di M. Pietro Aretino* (1537) (Figure 7). Often attributed to Titian, this image depicts Aretino as a rustic shepherd singing to his love Angela Sirena, who emerges from the clouds as a winged Siren in the heavens. Angela Sirena was not (that we know of) a courtesan, but was the wife of Gian Antonio Sirena. Nevertheless, Aretino like other writers of his generation sometimes referred to courtesans as Sirens and Titian's image works to visualize the ideas of this group of writers.

Literary references to the Sirens – to the enchantresses whose songs threatened to shipwreck Odysseus and his crew off the coast of Italy – imply various layers of meaning. Courtesans were indeed sexualized women, but descriptions of them as Sirens suggest that narrative or

dedication (no pagination); Francesco Pona, *La lucerna*, ed. Giorgio Fulco (Rome: Salerno, 1973), 108; Garzoni, *La piazza universale*, vol. 2, 965. Though not connected to courtesans per se, on a related note, the late sixteenth-century Paduan professor of rhetoric Antonio Riccobono claimed that the enemies of rhetoric denounced rhetoricians for clinging "to the allurements of words as to the rocks of the Sirens." Antonio Riccobono, *Oratio pro studis humanitatis*, in Giancarlo Mazzacurati, *La crisi della retorica umanistica nel Cinquecento (Antonio Riccobono)* (Naples: Libreria Scientifica Editirice, 1961), 171.

[42] Coryat, *Coryat's Crudities*, vol. 1, 406.

STANZE DI M. PIETRO ARETINO.

Figure 7. Frontispiece of Pietro Aretino, *Stanze di M. Pietro Aretino* (Venice, 1537). The Metropolitan Museum of Art, Harris Brisbane Dick Fund, 1937 (37.37.2). Image © The Metropolitan Museum of Art.

poetry and song – not sex – was true source of their power.[43] Courtesans embodied the idea that narrative and language itself could be seductive

[43] On the courtesan's voice in Renaissance music, see the articles by Feldman, De Rycke, Flosi and Davies in *The Courtesan's Arts*, 105–60.

and harmful, in the same way that the Sirens tempted Odysseus with a complete knowledge of all events, especially those at Troy, but only at the price of his life. If courtesans were indeed Sirens, this meant that their powers of speech were linked to that of the Homeric Muses themselves. That is to say, courtesans were not simply "monstrous" females; they possessed the divine powers of speech, song, and epic poetry: the language of culture par excellence. At the same time, while the Muses commanded the language of poetry from Zeus for the posterity of the Western world, Sirens and courtesans commanded it for their own inscrutable purposes. In this way, courtesans were anti-Muses; they threatened to destroy, instead of preserve, one's honor and identity.[44] In the Venetian context, courtesans, like Sirens, offered knowledge – a knowledge specifically of sexuality – and many patrician youths visited them to gain access to this world. However, their speech also threatened the loss of men's constructions of themselves as husbands, fathers, undertakers of lucrative professions, and civic politicians: in effect, the loss of male identity if men became obsessed or subsumed by their relationships with courtesans.

While some portrayed courtesans as Sirens, many went a step further and labeled them as witches. The 1531 poem *La puttana errante* – an epic Rabelaisian fable inspired by Aretino's pornographic writing, or perhaps assembled by Pietro Aretino and Lorenzo Venier together to mock the courtesan Elena Ballerini – offers a vivid portrayal of the courtesan as a witch. It describes a parade of courtesans as a crowd "of witches, enchantresses and Erinys (*megere*), with each harpy holding that which she needs for charms and curses," such as fingernails, hair, the skin of an unborn fetus, or the bones of the dead.[45] In describing courtesans as *megere*, a term that means both one of the three furies and a prostitute, the poem plays up the connection between prostitution and the enchanting speech of witchcraft. The *Ragionamento del Zoppino* similarly recounts

---

[44] See Lillian Eileen Doherty, "Sirens, Muses and Female Narrators in the *Odyssey*," in *The Distaff Side: Representing the Female in Homer's Odyssey*, ed. Beth Cohen (New York: Oxford University Press, 1995), 81–92.

[45] "Di streghe incantatrici e di megere/Et ha ciascuna in man di queste arpie/Cio che bisogna a incanti et a malie/Unghie, capegli e funi d'impiccati/E di non nato fanciullino pelle/Ossa di morti dal vivo cavati/Grassa di donne giovenette e belle/Vasi pieni di lagrime e stillati/D'herbe colte a splendor di certe stelle/Che disperdan I parti et il cervello/Tolgan spesso a quest'amante e a quello," *La puttana errante*, reprinted in Alessandro Luzio, *Pietro Aretino nei primi suoi anni a Venezia* (Turin: Ermanno Loescher, 1888), 118.

the various acts of sorcery that courtesans undertook to cause someone to fall in love with them, and the character Zoppino claims that their magical words and incantations are so frequent and lengthy that it would take a month to recount them.[46]

While the terms siren and witch functioned as metaphoric descriptions, witchcraft was a real legal and spiritual problem in early modern Venice and the Holy Office sometimes tried courtesans and prostitutes for witchcraft.[47] Many historians – Ruth Martin and Guido Ruggiero in the case of Venice, Robin Briggs in France and Lorraine, and Lyndal Roper in Germany – have long studied the gendering of witchcraft, emphasizing that most accused witches were women, and many at least in Northern Europe were midwives and healers.[48] The accused in approximately 18 inquisition trials for witchcraft in sixteenth-century Venice were labeled *cortigiane* or *meretrice*, and trial content reveals additional courtesans who practiced *stregoneria*.[49] Although this remains a small

---

[46] *Ragionamento del Zoppino*, 20–22. Pippa similarly asks Nanna if she should learn to use spells, sorceries, and witchcraft as part of her trade as a courtesan. See Aretino, *Dialogues*, 226. Maffio Venier also referred to Veronica Franco as "Quella solene strega, quella erbera," Maffio Venier *Il libro chiuso*, in Milani, *Contro le puttane*, 71.

[47] It is difficult to know exactly how many trials of courtesan-witches the Venetian Inquisition initiated because many trial records are incomplete and have been lost, dispersed, or ruined. However, in the second half of the sixteenth century, approximately 1500 trials took place, and of these, about 150 were for witchcraft, magic, and divination – 98 percent of these witchcraft trials were of women, tried primarily in the 1580s. These trials began with the first trial for witchcraft in 1552 against Lucrezia (bu. 10) and ended with the trial of Angela Manza in 1592 (bu. 69). See Marisa Milani, *Piccole storie di stregoneria nella Venezia del '500* (Verona: Essedue Edizioni, 1989), 16, and Marisa Milani, "L'incanto di Veronica Franco," *Giornale storico della letteratura italiana* 162 (1985): 251, n. 5.

[48] Ruth Martin, *Witchcraft and the Inquisition in Venice, 1550–1650* (Oxford: Blackwell, 1989); Ruggiero, *Binding Passions*; Robin Briggs, *Witches and Neighbors: The Social and Cultural Context of European Witchcraft* (New York: Penguin, 1996); Lyndal Roper, *Oedipus and the Devil: Witchcraft, Sexuality, and Religion in Early Modern Europe* (London: Routledge, 1994), esp. 199–225.

[49] A precise count remains elusive. On the one hand, many *meretrice* were surely accused of sorcery as a rote accusation, suggesting that such numbers may be inflated. See Martin, *Witchcraft and the Inquisition*, 234–38. These numbers may be an underestimate, on the other hand. Lucia Furlana (bu. 49) for instance, tried for witchcraft, is referred to as a "dona di pessima et cativa vita," which is often used synonymously to mean a *meretrice*. Also, several trials reveal several courtesans or *meretrice* who are not being tried themselves. For instance, the trial of Girolamo Zago (bu. 49) discusses four *meretrice* who participated in witchcraft; the trials of Faustina (bu. 57) and Elisabetta Greca (bu. 66) reveal several courtesan witches working together, though only one is principally accused. A complete reading of all the sixteenth-century trials of the Holy Office would most likely reveal additional courtesan witches.

number, the content of these trials often reveals a perceived cultural con-nection between courtesans and witchcraft. Some of these trials, such as that of Emilia Catena (1586) and Isabella Bellocchio (1589) resulted in whipping and various forms of public humiliation that would have made a strong impression linking courtesans and witchcraft in the minds of contemporary Venetians.

This linkage is significant because witchcraft was fundamentally a spo-ken, verbal practice and a crime of language.[50] In early modern Europe and Venice in particular, the practice of witchcraft involved a variety of arts ranging from bean-throwing (*butta fave*), conjuring the devil with tarot cards (*il tarocco*), boiling bones or making a type of witches' stew (*la pignatta*), or seeing the future or past in a jar of holy water (*l'inghistara*). Though diverse in practice and often focused on the imme-diacy of material objects, almost all these acts of witchcraft necessarily employed incantations in order to make the magic work. Many rituals involved complex mixtures of words and actions: an object, movement, or gesture whose magical powers were brought to life by an oration. Without these spoken words used to activate the magic, the action or object alone had no effect.[51] For instance, someone hoping to make a fickle lover return might turn to a witch for the *tarocco*. This required directing prayers and reciting formulas to the tarot card of the devil with a candle lit in front of it, usually at dawn or sunset, so that the devil would enter the heart of an unfaithful lover and convince him to return to his partner. Or, someone like the famed courtesan Veronica Franco, trying to locate a lost or stolen item, might ask for an *inghistara*. Here,

---

[50] Because the boundaries between saints and heretics or witches were often quite blurry in the early modern world, it is interesting to note the degree to which those supposedly possessed by the devil emphasized orality and spoken language in their revelations. Armando Maggi describes some visionaries and demonically possessed as "obsessed with orality." See Armando Maggi, *Satan's Rhetoric: A Study of Renaissance Demonology* (Chicago: The University of Chicago Press, 2001), 144.

[51] See Ruggiero, *Binding Passions*, 92, 99–109. In his encyclopedic *La tipocosmia*, a text pur-porting to describe all the actions existing in the world, Alessandro Citolini, a Venetian resident and writer interested in language, considered necromancy and witchcraft actions undertaken above all by the mouth. See Citolini, *La tipocosmia*, 539. On spells and witchcraft as a crime of speech, see also Stuart Clark, *Thinking with Demons: The Idea of Witchcraft in Early Modern Europe* (Oxford: Oxford University Press, 1997), 282–84; Marisa Milani, "Cortigiane e inquisizione," 313; Thomas, *Religion and the Decline of Magic*, 183, 502–12.

the witch would recite a series of *pater nostri, ave marie,* or incantations to a jar of holy water to locate the missing goods.[52]

Inquisition records are often frustratingly thin on the actual spells and incantations pronounced by these women, and testimony only reveals a fleeting glance at such language. However, the vast majority of witchcraft trials indicate the regular use of magical words even when they were not directly transcribed. Witnesses called to testify often commented on the "diabolical words" they heard the witch pronounce, or claimed that the witch spoke something softly as she enacted her magic.[53] These trials often point to the close association of courtesans and magical language, demonstrating how people believed that courtesans wielded a particular power over spoken words. During the trial of a certain Bianca Lando, for instance, Bianca's servant Ancilla unwittingly revealed the common cultural connection made between courtesans, orations, and magic. "My mistress pronounces orations using the fabric from church altars," Ancilla remarked, "and this is how she practices witchcraft. But even though she does these little things as all women do, she is a saintly, Catholic woman and she is not a courtesan."[54]

As Keith Thomas has argued, in an age when doctors were unable to treat most illnesses, when poverty, sickness, fire, famine, and sudden disaster or death were common experiences, people often turned

---

[52] For instance, Veronica Franco recited the words "Anzolo santo, anzolo biancho, per la tua santità et per la mia verzinità mostrame il vero et la verità chi ha tolto la tal cosa cioé le forfette et l'officio," ASV, *Sant'Uffizio,* bu. 46 "Veronica Franco" 8 October 1580. The trial of Gabriele da Venezia (bu. 65) illustrates the practice of the *tarocco,* and the trial of Camilla Milanese (bu. 65) also illustrates the practice of the *inghistara.* The wetnurse and midwife in Pietro Aretino's *Dialogues* describe the orations associated with throwing beans; see Aretino's *Dialogues,* 379–80. For the various techniques and practices of witchcraft, see Marisa Milani, "L'incanto di Veronica Franco," 250–63.

[53] "Et non sentiva ciò che dicessero quelle done che le buttava, perché parlavano pian pian et non volevano che si sentisse la lor virtù," Ibid., bu. 53, "Magdalenam Bradamonte," 21 June 1584, 25v. See also the trials of Catterina Furlana, Ibid., bu. 55, testimony of Marina, 16 February 1585, 5r. The trials of Latisana and Benedetta Maranese (bu. 68), while not of courtesans per se, offer good examples of witches' orations.

[54] "Mia madonna attende a far delle orationi, delli panni de altari per le chiese, e queste sono le sue strigarie. È una donna santa, una donna catholica, save che tutte le donne fa qualche coseta, ma la non e cortegiana," ASV, *Sant'Uffizio,* bu. 65, "Bianca Lando" 16 November 1589. The speakers in Moderata Fonte's dialogue *The Worth of Women* similarly indicate a commonly perceived connection between courtesans, spells, and magic when one woman describes how a prostitute cast a spell on her husband. See Fonte, The *Worth of Women,* 69–70.

to either religion, magic, or both, for help, healing, or hope. That is to say, they invoked the magical words of the mass and the prayer, or the spell and the incantation, to assist them in times of need. According to Thomas, churchmen and magicians possessed similar and parallel powers.[55] Prayers and spells were two sides of the same coin: magical words pronounced either to supplicate or control. They were types of speech that were not incompatible, even in the years after the Reformation, as there were magical elements that survived in religion (prayers and masses continued to have an incantory character) and religious tendencies that survived in the practice of magical speech (*pater nostri* and *ave marie* were regularly used in the orations of Venetian courtesans). If blasphemy, rhetoric, and the magical words of the mass tended to be represented as masculine forms of speech, this suggests that the spells and incantations of witches and courtesans were their feminine counterpart, and male religious authorities aimed to silence such challenges to their voice in the age of the Counter-Reformation. The patriarchal powers of this repressive culture aimed at clarifying the difference between the masculine prayer and the feminine spell. Not all witches were courtesans, but many courtesans practiced witchcraft and believed in the magical power of their spoken words. The prosecutions of courtesan-witches, albeit relatively small in number, therefore revealed a competition between men and women over the control of magical speech. This gendered contest over language was certainly not the most central one in Tridentine culture in which male authorities were concerned about the regulation of many kinds of irregular speech and action, including that of men. Yet the prosecution of the courtesan-sorceresses demonstrated how the Inquisition in Venice functioned as an arm of the state attempting to silence the unruly language of these women.

As an interesting, but related aside: archival documents from a variety of magistracies also suggest that the Venetian state linked courtesans, foul language, and immigration together as a nexus of immorality and vice that needed patrolling, not unlike connections state magistracies perceived between blasphemy and immigration. The *Esecutori Contro la Bestemmia* was originally given jurisdiction over the crime of blasphemy in 1537. It was given additional jurisdiction to serve as the appellate court

---

[55] Thomas, *Religion and the Decline of Magic*, 41.

for the *Provveditori alla Sanità* in cases involving prostitution in 1553, and these powers were confirmed and amplified in 1578, followed by jurisdiction over the registration of foreigners in 1583. That is, to repeat: the state placed jurisdiction over blasphemy, foreigners, and prostitution under one magistracy designed to oversee civic morality. On 16 September 1539, the *Provveditori alla Sanità* passed a law stating that "all foreign prostitutes who have lived in Venice for under two years ... must leave the city within fifteen days." Those who did not were punished with whipping from San Marco to the Rialto, six months in prison, the fine of 100 *lire di piccoli*, and banishment. The Council of Ten repeated a similar law in 1572, suggesting that during the sixteenth century, many courtesans and prostitutes were foreigners.[56] If courtesans were known for their lascivious tongues, enough to prompt the passing of laws that specifically took note of their language, and if many courtesans came from outside the city, this suggests that when it remarked on courtesans' language, civic legislation once again had the collateral effect or intention of disciplining the tongues of immigrants to conform to civic standards of respectability.

Courtesans certainly had vehement and often violent detractors. Aggressive diatribes against their entire existence – let alone their speech and language – abound. In his famous attack on Veronica Franco, Maffio Venier stated that it would take thousands of pens and an infinite number of poets to be able to sing all her vices and defects.[57] While courtesans

---

[56] "Che tutte le meretrice forestiere che da anni doi in qua sono venute ad habitare in questa Città (sic), etiam che fussero de terre et lochi subditi a questo illustrissimo Dominio, debbono in termine de giorni XV proximi partirse immediate da questa città sotto pena de esser frustade da S. Marco a Rialto, stare mesi sei in preson serrate et pagare lire cento de pizoli," ASV, *Provveditori alla Sanità* capitolare 1, carta 45, 16 September 1539. See also *Consiglio dei Dieci, Misti*, libro 13, 12 September 1539; *Consiglio dei Dieci, Comuni*, registro 30, 1571–72, carta 101v, 28 March 1572. Michelle Laughran has argued that "immigration generated not just the demand for prostitution but the prostitutes themselves," and many prostitutes in both Venice and Europe at large came from outside their resident cities. See Laughran, "The Body, Public Health and Social Control," 62–64. The trial of Sofia Solarin before the Holy Office similarly suggests the large number of foreign prostitutes present in the city. One witness described her as a "ruffiana che allogia tutte le meretrici thodesche che vengono qua a venetia e sempre ne ha tre o quattro," ASV, *Sant'Uffizio*, bu. 65, fasc. Sofia Solarin, 10 December 1589.

[57] Maffio Venier, *Il libro chiuso*, in Milani, *Contro le puttane*, 68. No one was more explicit about the perilous aspects of courtesans' existence than Veronica Franco herself, who described the life of a courtesan as one that "always turns out to be a misery. It's a most wretched thing, contrary to human reason, to subject one's body and labor to a slavery terrifying even to think of," Veronica Franco, *Poems and Selected Letters*, 39 (Letter 22).

may have possessed a mastery of language, their livelihoods necessarily entailed the stigmatized commerce of the body and sex, and it is important not to overstate their agency. Courtesans' lives were difficult, and as Rosenthal has demonstrated, they were often victims of the attacks of envious men who vied with them for patronage. Rosenthal, however, tends to depict male writers as discussing the courtesan with an almost exclusively negative tone. According to Rosenthal, writers described courtesans as objects of "abject servility" who were "seldom championed by their fellow citizens" and "frequently were the victims of envious men who competed with them for public attention." She claims that "rather than being championed by many male contemporaries, the courtesan was used . . . as a satirical outlet" and that male authors demonstrated "a growing mistrust and hatred of the courtesan."[58] This description of courtesans as universally disparaged, however, only begins to scratch the surface, and examining a variety of depictions of courtesans' speech reveals a more complex picture of their position in society. Courtesans occupied a more complicated position in the minds of Venetian writers. Although writers like Andrea Calmo, Sperone Speroni, or Pietro Aretino expressed criticism of courtesans in shocking and often vulgar language, it does not necessarily follow that such writers were consistently courtesans' antagonists. In fact, a select group of Venetian writers – the poligrafi – at times appeared closer to courtesans as a group than to any other subset of Renaissance culture.

The poligrafi were group of literary odd-job men who rejected conventional careers as servants of the courts to work in the relative intellectual freedom of Venice. In the 1530s and 1540s, vernacular literature was becoming increasingly popular. As a result, Venetian printers who published vernacular works like Gabriel Giolito de' Ferrari and Francesco Marcolini profited from this trend and the tremendous expansion of printing in Venice in general. Such printing houses encouraged the production of non-scholarly texts for more popular consumption and employed the poligrafi as editors, translators, and writers during this period of growth. The poligrafi authored a wide variety of texts, including poetry, plays, fables, travel literature, satires, letters, and burlesques.

---

[58] Rosenthal, *The Honest Courtesan*, ch. 1, "Satirizing the Courtesan: Franco's Enemies," 11–57, esp. 33, 15, 17, 19.

Many of these texts were incredibly popular and went into multiple editions; some were reprinted every three or four years for half a century. The poligrafi were a diverse group in terms of their social class and literary output. Ludovico Dolce, Lodovico Domenichi, Giuseppe Betussi, and Pietro Aretino especially came from moneyed backgrounds, whereas Niccolò Franco and Anton Francesco Doni did not.[59] The fantastical works of Franco and Doni contrast sharply with the more sober writing of Dolce and Domenichi.

Their diversity aside, the poligrafi also had much in common. They were famous for their critical approach to much of Italian society, including ancient and modern learning, the vast majority of Italian professions, and Italian social organization. They were especially disparaging of humanists, Petrarchists, and Renaissance grammarians. Many of them ridiculed those who worried about accents, vocabulary, sentence structure, and parts of speech in an effort to revive classical eloquence instead of simply expressing themselves clearly. They thought writers should be more concerned about other more pressing issues such as political power and morality.[60] The poligrafi also had much in common with courtesans. If courtesans sold conversation, the poligrafi were the corresponding vendors of the printed word. Like courtesans, the poligrafi were immigrants (Dolce was the only native Venetian among the group) who made their living in a foreign city through trade in language. Most importantly, as merchants of words, the poligrafi appeared to appreciate courtesans deeply, and often included courtesans' writings in their collections. Their relationship suggests a nexus of conversation and print that publicized courtesan's voices to the wider world.[61]

Niccolò Franco, for instance, credited courtesans with having reintroduced otherwise lost cultural delights back into Italian society – including, we can imagine, conversation. Courtesans evoked a golden

---

[59] While Aretino was not a poligrafo per se, he may, for convenience, be grouped with these writers because of his close association with this group and the way he helped establish many of them as writers.

[60] Grendler, *Critics of the Italian World*, 154.

[61] On the poligrafi, see Claudia di Filippo Bareggi, *Il mestiere di scrivere: Lavoro intelletuale e mercato librario a Venezia nel Cinquecento* (Rome: Bulzoni, 1988); Giovanni Aquilecchia, "Pietro Aretino e altri poligrafi a Venezia," in *Storia della cultura veneta*, vol. 3:2, ed. Arnaldi and Stocchi, 61–98; Paul Grendler, *Critics of the Italian World, 1530–1560: Anton Francesco Doni, Nicolò Franco, and Ortensio Lando* (Madison: University of Wisconsin Press, 1969).

age, he claimed, by using their social graces to bring the glories of the ancient world into the modern one.[62] Anton Francesco Doni celebrated the courtesan Francesca Baffo in his *Pistolotti amorosi* and included a copy of a letter to her in his *Tre libri di lettere*: a collection of letters addressed to the likes of Michelangelo, Tintoretto, Sansovino, and Aretino, and very few other women besides Baffo. Lodovico Domenichi and Giuseppe Betussi also included Baffo's poems in their printed collections, and both Domenichi and Girolamo Parabosco also dedicated sonnets and letters to her.[63] While Sperone Speroni brutally denounced an imaginary courtesan in his *Orazione contro le cortegiane* (1575), he too had once written in praise of courtesans. This later diatribe reflected a reaction to the repressive, moralistic climate of the Counter-Reformation. Scholars often consider Speroni to be among the harshest of courtesans' attackers, yet Speroni was an arch-sophist practicing his argumentative style and cannot necessarily be taken at face value: an important point to keep in mind for discussions about courtesans in general.[64]

Of all those who commented on the lives of courtesans, it was Pietro Aretino and his ribald tales, recounted in a brothel among prostitutes, that perhaps best exemplified the relationship between courtesans and the *poligrafi*.[65] Like other Venetian writers, Aretino was highly critical

---

[62] Franco, *Le pistole vulgari* (1542 edn.), 223v–224r.

[63] Anton Francesco Doni, *Pistolotti amorosi* (Venice, 1552), 12v–14r; *Tre libri di lettere* (Venice, 1552), 73r–v. While the *Pistolotti* is a satyrical take on Petrarchism and sixteenth-century love treatises, it nevertheless represents the respect Doni held for Baffo. Though biographical information about Baffo is scarce, many assume that she was a courtesan. See C. Mutini, "Franceschina Baffo," in *Dizionario biografico italiano*, vol. 5 (Rome: Istituto della Enciclopedia Italiana, 1963), 163. For a lengthy list and discussion of all the poems and sonnets written both by, for, and in praise of courtesans, by various members of Venetian literary circles, see Bareggi, *Il mestiere di scrivere*, 17–29, 104, n. 20, and Villaviera, *Le cortigiane veneziane*, 143–91.

[64] See Rosenthal, *The Honest Courtesan*, 25. Virginia Cox emphasizes the fact that while some dialogues, such as Bembo's *Prose della volgar lingua*, are indisputably monological and advance a single point of view, others are much more ambiguous and create "almost endless possibilities for creative manipulation of the relations between reader and text." Speroni's dialogues, she argues, belonged to the second category; they do not attempt to promote any one single opinion. See Cox, *The Renaissance Dialogue*, 5, 64–65, 84.

[65] On Pietro Aretino and his commentary on courtesans, see Christopher Cairns, *Pietro Aretino and the Republic of Venice: Researches on Aretino and His Circle in Venice, 1527–1556* (Florence: Leo S. Olschki, 1985); Giulio Ferroni, "Il teatro della Nanna," in *Le voci dell'istrione: Pietro Aretino e la dissoluzione del teatro*, ed. Giulio Ferroni (Naples: Liguori, 1977), 136–202; Paul Larivaille, *Pietro Aretino: Fra Rinascimento e manierismo*, trans. Mariella Di Maio and Maria Luisa Rispoli (Rome: Bulzoni, 1980); Rosenthal, *The Honest Courtesan*, 11–57.

of the courtesan, who he believed represented the moral, economic, and social decay of sixteenth-century Italy. He depicted courtesans and prostitutes as among the most foul-mouthed of women, and Nanna, Antonia, and Pippa, the courtesans whose dialogue forms Aretino's *Ragionamenti* and *Sei giornate*, appear no more than calculating swindlers who excel in the arts of deceit, flattery, and lying. However, Aretino's words, like those of Speroni and other Venetian *poligrafi*, maintain an underlying complexity. Although Aretino's dialogues took place in Rome, because he was active as a writer in Venice, his dialogues also reflect ideas that he likely thought applied in Venice as well. A close look at his portrayal of courtesans' language reveals a nuanced understanding and often profound admiration of their speech.

Like the *poligrafi* that he supported, Aretino ridiculed the literary norms of the day such as the reverence of the Platonic dialogue, the prevalence of books on manners, and the Renaissance culture of politeness. Rebelling against the standards of Renaissance humanism and respectability, Aretino dedicated his *Dialogues* to a monkey rather than a prince, and employed courtesans' voices in these dialogues rather than those of courtiers and ladies as a means of ridiculing these figures. Sarcastically mimicking advice from comportment literature, Aretino has the courtesan Nanna – rather than a respectable lady – advise her daughter on the importance of manners and conversation. She tells Pippa to use a "gentle voice" and "make an effort to say something that doesn't stink of the brothel" and remember that "good manners are the best go-betweens to help you rise in the world."[66] However, this is advice given from one prostitute to another, not with the aim of social or cultural edification but with the goal of how to best cheat clients out of as much of their fortune as possible. In this way, Aretino ridiculed both courtesans and their more respectable, upright counterparts: he criticizes social climbers who hope to improve their status through manners as being no better than the prostitutes, or the dregs of society.

However, Aretino also argued that compared to nuns and wives, courtesans were the only truly honest women whose actions, for once, matched their words (158). In addition, his letters betrayed a profound admiration for the courtesans Zufolina and Angela Zaffetta. He praised

---

[66] Aretino, *Dialogues*, 169–70, 220.

their speech, and in one letter invited Angela to dine with himself, Titian, and Sansovino: a sure sign that she was a delightful conversationalist.[67] He typically depicts Nanna – the main protagonist in his dialogues – as a dynamic and engaging speaker, and the responses of the other interlocutors in his dialogues consistently underscore – albeit obscenely – just how compelling her words are. For instance, Antonia responds to Nanna's speeches by saying "I'm waiting for you to get to the heart of your story, and I feel just like a baby waiting for his wet nurse to shove her tit in his mouth."[68] Antonia believes that Nanna's words "should be inscribed in letters of gold" (62). Nanna's speech is so vivid and persuasive that it produces immediate physical and erotic results.

> Pippa: Oh, you are a wonderful painter with words; and as I listened to you, I got all excited. I had the feeling that the hand you described touched my nipples and was just about to feel . . . I won't say what.
> Nanna: I saw the passion on your face, which changed completely, then blushed red while I was showing you what one does not see. (200–1)

Antonia similarly comments that when she listens to Nanna, what happens to her is "what happens to someone who smells a purge and, without even taking it, goes twice or three times to move her bowels" (52–53). Pippa and Antonia's responses to Nanna's speech illuminate Aretino's thoughts on courtesans' language. He may or may not have respected courtesans in terms of their morality, piety, or social respectability, but they were clearly fascinating to listen to. Their speech commanded attention so well that he used them as his mouthpiece for pornographic expression. Though Aretino never states this outright, it is implicit that erotic language such as Nanna's served not only to seduce but also to assert female agency and social mobility, as courtesans used their alluring talk to attract their noble clientele and make a living.

More importantly, Aretino also chose a courtesan to express his views on contemporary debates about language itself, as Nanna repeatedly ridicules the ways in which Renaissance men spoke. She tells her daughter not to imitate the affected language of princes and courtiers. "I beg you" she says "my dear daughter, do not forsake the speech which your

[67] Aretino, *Letters*, 120–22, 272.
[68] Aretino, *Dialogues*, 26.

dear little mother taught you; leave all 'in such a manner's' and 'directly's' to affected courtiers." Instead, Nanna says that she remains herself when she speaks. "I say the words as they trip to my tongue; I don't lift them out of my mouth with a fork, because they are words and not confectionaries; when I speak, I resemble a woman, not a magpie" (182–83). Nanna emphasizes that when she talks, she is spontaneous and avoids the affectation commonly described by humanist literature.

> I make it all up as I go, I improvise and don't drag things out by the hair, I say them right off in a single breath and not in a hundred years, as do certain worn-out style-doctors who teach us how to write books, taking a lifetime on their "so-to-speaks," "as-it-weres," and "as-to-shits," composing comedies out of speeches more constipated than constipation; and that's why everyone rushes to look at my gossip, printing it right away as if it were the *Verbum Caro*. (213–14)

Nanna's chatter is by no means a simple feminine annoyance; rather, it is a theatrical spectacle that forces her audience to listen. Publishers rushed to capture and print her words, she claimed, in the same way that Aretino's texts flew off the presses. In this way, through Nanna – the voice of a courtesan – Aretino scathingly criticized the social and cultural practices of Renaissance literary speech and flaunted literary convention by ridiculing Bembo's contemporary advice to follow archaic linguistic models. Like other poligrafi, Aretino did not describe courtesans simply as "corrupt," but also as remarkable for their verbal prowess.[69]

Despite their criticism of humanists as ridiculous and useless pedants, it remains important to note that the poligrafi could not resist the debates surrounding the *questione della lingua*; many of them composed texts on language and grammar.[70] Although such interests by no means indicate concrete links between the poligrafi and the speech of courtesans, they demonstrate how this group of male writers who were either intrigued by or critical of contemporary debates about language appeared to value the verbal arts of courtesans as a group. The poligrafi admired courtesans as examples of both frankness and eloquence. As we have seen,

---

[69] See Rosenthal, *The Honest Courtesan*, 34, 42.

[70] The third book of the 1552 edition of Anton Francesco Doni's *Tre libri di lettere* is a book of grammar. See also Ludovico Dolce, *Delle osservationi* (Venice, 1556); Sansovino, *L'arte oratoria* and *Le osservationi della lingua volgare* (Venice, 1562).

courtesans' language was noted for both its beauty and its obscenity, and insult, slander, and obscenity were also common in writings of poligrafi, as Aretino especially made clear. Poligrafi at once expressed an interest in linguistic debates while simultaneously flouting the conventions of grammar, language, and the courtly, Ciceronian dialogue that such debates established.[71] Such contradictory interests in language may explain why courtesans' speech appealed so much to the poligrafi, as courtesans were both positively and negatively renowned for their tongues. The poligrafi represented a distinct, popular, and highly published arm of Venetian literary culture that appreciated courtesans' language and turned up the volume of their words. Aretino was especially fundamental in generating a new, international marketplace for the obscene. The written or printed versions of courtesans' voices from his and other poligrafi's sixteenth-century texts spawned additional waves of interest in such language – particularly obscenity and pornography – and set the stage for its more widespread diffusion, especially in seventeenth- and eighteenth-century France.[72]

In many ways, courtesans disrupted the categories of masculine and feminine and sometimes even represented a third sex, both in terms of their behavior and depictions of it. As Nanna succinctly put it, "Whores are not women: They are whores."[73] They were women who borrowed the idioms of traditional Petrarchism developed by male writers and composed themselves as the erotic projections of male fantasies. Writers often described them scandalously adorning themselves with male attire, and Venetian legislation and literature illustrated this practice as well.[74] Most importantly, they were women who needed masculine virtues to survive, especially verbal expertise. Unlike other women whose honor was more regularly defined by silence and chastity, courtesans, like men, needed eloquence for their livelihood and survival and used their mastery

---

[71] See Cox, *The Renaissance Dialogue*, 18, and Grendler, *Critics of the Italian World*, 7.

[72] Aretino's *Ragionamenti* became the prototype for seventeenth-century pornographic writing, both in Italy and France. See Paula Findlen, "Humanism, Politics, and Pornography."

[73] Aretino, *Dialogues*, 135.

[74] "Hanno trovato questo novo et non più usato di vestirsi con habiti de homo . . . sia proibito alle meretrici et cortigiane sopradette l'andar per la città vagando in barca vestite da homo," ASV, *Consiglio di Dieci*, Comuni, Registro 33, 1577–78, fo. 167v, 14 July 1578. See also Aretino, *Letters*, 249; Alessandro Fabri, *Diversarum natioun ornatus* (Padua, 1593), 7–9; Cesare Vecellio, *Habiti antichi e moderni* (Venice, 1598), 114.

of words to create their public personas. The figure of the courtesan especially disrupts the categories of masculine and feminine speech in the writings of Aretino. Aretino places vulgar, aggressive language into the mouths of courtesans: a deeply unfeminine and transgressive subversion of typical structures of gender and speech as defined by the likes of prescriptive moralists. As Bette Talvacchia has pointed out, especially in his *Sonetti lussuriosi*, he allows women "to indulge in vulgar speech, to state their sexual desires, and to command their partners in sexual performance, all of which is transgressive for a female voice."[75] Aretino blurs the boundaries of masculine and feminine by narrating an erotic story through women's voices, by empowering a female voice and then endowing it with a content that conveys masculine desire. All this is to say that representations of the unstable nature of courtesans' speech and their sexually ambiguous nature granted them a particular voice in Venetian culture and Venetian political culture more specifically. Courtesans could speak more, and more frankly, than other Venetian women: a skill that, as we shall see, worked to enable and empower their roles as entrepreneurs and diplomats in Venetian political culture.[76]

In addition to the poligrafi, travelers regularly expressed their fascination with courtesans and publicized them so that Venetian courtesans enjoyed wide fame in other Italian cities and abroad. Thomas Coryat remarked that "the name of a cortezan of Venice is famoused over all Christendome." One of the most discussed and debated documents regarding courtesans in sixteenth-century Venice, *La tariffa delle puttane di Venegia* (1535), is a dialogue attributed to both Aretino and Lorenzo Venier in which a Venetian gentleman describes they city's women to a foreigner who comes specifically to visit its courtesans. The visitor boasts, "For Venice, I left my patria, and I do not regret it, because [now] I never have a famine for fornication." In one of his *novelle*, the Milanese writer Matteo Bandello similarly recounts the way that courtesans lured foreigners to Venice, and according to a letter

---

[75] Bette Talvacchia, *Taking Positions: On the Erotic in Renaissance Culture* (Princeton: Princeton University Press, 1999), 96–99.

[76] "Their membership in the so-called third sex gave them a privileged view of the practices of others and, thus, empowered them to speak, quite literally to 'authorize' a portrait of society," Findlen, "Humanism, Politics and Pornography," 107.

reprinted in Sanudo's chronicle, the French ambassador announced to other travelers at the dinner table in 1531 that in Venice, one can find "perfect merchandise," naming Cornelia Griffo, Julia Lombardo, Biancha Saraton, Elena Ballerina, and other Venetian courtesans.[77]

The fact that so many foreigners came to Venice to find courtesans is not surprising; much scholarship, including that of Margaret Rosenthal, has noted this to be the case. What is more remarkable, however, is the degree to which various writers, travelers, and observers of Venice claimed to want to come to Venice for the *specific* experience of courtesans' conversation. For instance, in one of his *novelle*, Celio Malespini described two gentlemen who went to Venice expressly "to enjoy some of the beautiful and pleasing conversation of the graceful young girls that exist in such large numbers."[78] Montaigne intriguingly remarked that rather than be shocked by their wanton nature, he was more taken aback by the efficient organization of courtesans who charged a standard sum for the "whole deal" or a different fee for conversation alone, suggesting that this explicit service was so regularly sought out that courtesans distinguished its charges in their accounting practices.[79] In fact, one of the most consistent tropes in sixteenth-century literature about courtesans is the idea that courtesans talked people, including their numerous foreign clients, out of their money. The *Tariffa delle puttane* and the *Ragionamento del Zoppino* both claim that courtesans emptied the purses of their clients with their verbal dexterity and seductive speech. Maffio Venier described Franco as sweetly talking the money out of the bag of Henry III.[80] Although courtesans' income was not taxed monthly

---

[77] Coryat, *Coryat's Crudities*, vol. 1, 401; "Per Venegia io lasciai la patria mia. E no men pento, purche qualche volta non havessi di fotter carestia," *La tariffa delle puttane di Venegia*, reprinted in Barzaghi, *Donne o cortegiane*, 169; Bandello, *La terza parte de le novelle*, 152; Sanudo, *I diarii*, vol. 54, 421, 6 March 1531, letter of Francesco Mazzardo.

[78] "Per godere della bella e soave conversazione delle leggiadre giovanette che vi sono in copia grandissima," Celio Malespini, *Ducento novelle* (Venice, 1609), vol. 1:4,19r. The poligrafo Ortensio Lando, when thinking about leaving Venice in the imaginary voyage recounted in his *Commentario*, lamented the idea of missing "the sweet conversation of the virtuous Giulia Ferreta and Francesca Ruvissa," Ortensio Lando, *Commentario delle piu notabili, et mostruose cose d'Italia, e altri luoghi, di lingua aramea in italiana tradotto, nel qual s'impara, e prendesi istremo piacere* (Venice, 1550), 38v.

[79] Montaigne, *Journal de voyage en Italie*, 72.

[80] *La tariffa*, reprinted in Barzaghi, *Donne o cortigiane*, 184–85; *Ragionamento del Zoppino*, 18–19; Maffio Venier, "Daspuò che son entrà in pensier sì vario," in Milani, *Contro le puttane*, 65.

as it was in Florence, the Venetian republic did impose a tax on courtesans in 1514 that benefited the *Arsenale* and its harbor, from which it received "a great quantity of money."[81] Courtesans were generally prosecuted less often in Venice than in Rome and Florence, and Thomas Coryat remarked that one of the reasons that the Venetian state tolerated the presence of so many courtesans was "the revenues which they pay unto the Senate for their tolleration, doe maintaine a dozen of theeir galleys, (as many reported unto me in Venice) and so save them a great charge."[82] An elite caste of both Venetian men and foreigners involved in politics, trade, or industry such as the printing industry had the financial capabilities to maintain courtesans and in doing so, "fill[ed] the coffers of the Republic."[83]

Courtesans clearly commercialized language: a business that was both culturally associated with the city and contributed significantly to its economy. This is especially evident in the way that writers exploited courtesans and their eloquence as a tourist attraction, and more indirectly, in the textual sales of the poligrafi, who successfully sold works often based on or related to the language of courtesans. In short, like shipbuilding or glass-blowing, the sale of sex and more importantly, conversation, came to be closely associated with the lagoon city and defined it in the minds of both locals and foreigners as a mark of Venetian culture. Courtesans provided Venice with several cultural services; for instance, it was normal that patrician men around the ages of 14–15 would begin to visit courtesans for early sexual experiences, and courtesans served

---

[81] See L. Menetto and G. Zennaro, *Storia del malcostume nei secoli XVI e XVII* (Abano Terme: Piovan Editore, 1987), 17.

[82] Coryat, *Coryat's Crudities*, vol. 1, 403. See also Jones, "City Women and Their Audiences," 303. In 1514, Marin Sanudo also recorded the taxes collected from Venetian prostitutes and courtesans in his diaries, stating that they helped pay for the construction of the Arsenal. See Graf, "Una cortigiana fra mille," 288–89. Graf cites no page or column number in Sanudo, and I have been unable to find this reference. Unfortunately, because of the stigma attached to the sale of sex and a lack of data demonstrating how much courtesans earned and how much they may have contributed to the fiscal economy, we can speculate only on the symbolic significance of such taxation.

[83] Lynn Lawner, "Gaspara Stampa and the Rhetoric of Submission," in *Renaissance Studies in Honor of Craig Hugh Smyth*, ed. Andrew Morrogh, Fiorella Superbi Gioffredi, Piero Morselli and Eve Borsook, vol. 1 (Florence: Giunti Barbèra, 1985), 347. See also Georgina Masson, *Courtesans of the Italian Renaissance* (London: Secker and Warburg, 1975), 10–11, and note 6 in this chapter, on the courtesan as a commercial asset.

to drive men away from the vices of sodomy and homosexuality.[84] In addition – recalling the fact that Giovanni Della Casa described conversation as fundamentally resembling a commercial transaction – courtesans provided a great commercial asset based in part on the marketing of their conversation and language. This was especially the case because ordinary, "respectable" Venetian women could not have undertaken the commercialization of language. In an age that represented the expansion of markets and early capitalism in both Europe and the world at large – an age that promoted the development of individualism through taste and purchasing power as many historians have argued – Venice was among the premier cities whose economy was driven by consumption.[85] As Evelyn Welch has stated, it "was exceptional in its commercial sophistication and specialisation," and despite potential moral injunctions against courtesans, Venice as a capitalist city made a place for courtesans as entrepreneurs – a place for them to sell their bodies and their words.[86] Courtesans may have been despised for their sexual nature, but were empowered by the fact that they were economic agents: a figure that, again like the Jews, the Venetian state often sought to promote for its own benefit.

More than any other single example, the life and writing of Veronica Franco (1546–91) illuminates the lure of the courtesan's conversation to foreign visitors: a lure which benefited not only the Venetian economy, as we have seen, but also Venetian diplomacy. At the height of her career, Franco attended the well-known literary salon of Domenico Venier, and published her volume of *Terze rime* in 1575 and a collection of 50 letters in 1580. Famous for her beauty, wit, and sexual prowess, Franco became one of the most celebrated courtesans in the Renaissance world; her life has been well studied and she needs little introduction. Her use of spoken

---

[84] Ruggiero, "Who's Afraid of Giuliana Napolitana?" 286.

[85] On consumption in early modern European historiography, see N. McKendrick, J. Brewer, and J. H. Plumb, *The Birth of a Consumer Society: The Commercialization of Eighteenth-Century England* (Bloomington: Indiana University Press, 1982), and D. Roche, *A History of Everyday Things: The Birth of Consumption in France, 1600–1800* (Cambridge and New York: Cambridge University Press, 2000). On Italy in particular, see R. Goldthwaite, *Wealth and the Demand for Art*, and Lisa Jardine, *Worldy Goods: A New History of the Renaissance* (New York: Doubleday, 1996). Some have argued by contrast that consumption was not as significant a force in the early modern world as we might think. See L. Martines, "The Renaissance and the Birth of Consumer Society," *Renaissance Quarterly* 51 (1998): 193–203.

[86] Welch, *Shopping in the Renaissance*, 8–9, 191.

language, however, merits a second glance, and one episode from her career in particular sheds additional light on the relationship between courtesans, speech, sexuality, and the state: her famous meeting with Henry III, the heir to the throne of France.

The 23-year-old Henry III of Valois, traveling back from Poland to claim his crown as the king of France in the summer of 1574, sent a letter to the *signoria* of Venice requesting permission to visit the city he had heard so much about.[87] His eight-day stay in Venice prompted the state to produce the most spectacular series of celebrations that the city had perhaps ever put on for a visitor. Rowed into the city on a galley of 400 men, Henry was escorted under a triumphal arch built by Palladio and painted by Tintoretto and Veronese. He was treated to fireworks, processions, boat races, musical and theatrical productions, and a banquet for 3,000 people in the Hall of the Great Council. Venetian dignitaries escorted him on a visit to the aging Titian's studio, and perhaps most incredibly, to a breakfast composed entirely – food, goblets, tableware, and all – of sugar. Henry toured the marvels of Venice, including its churches, palaces, shipyards, and villas on the mainland. Yet, perhaps the height of his sojourn, measured by his own enthusiasm, was his visit to Veronica Franco, who entertained him for an evening at her house. Their meeting was secret, however, he was most likely guided there by patrician officials, including perhaps Marco Venier or Andrea Tron or both. Franco made the secret public by circulating a letter and two sonnets in his honor, as well as by giving him a portrait of herself in enamel upon his departure. Though Henry III's visit to Franco was unofficial, it remains striking that patrician representatives of the Venetian state would have encouraged a courtesan to entertain a powerful visiting monarch. The courtesan Angela Zaffetta – the same courtesan whose conversational skills were deeply appreciated and admired by Pietro Aretino – similarly entertained Ippolito dei Medici when he was the Spanish ambassador's guest in Venice in 1530. Why were courtesans brought out to participate in stately politics? Why was it not enough for Henry III or Ippolito dei Medici to dance and speak with Venetian patrician women – the 200

---

[87] For a more complete account of Franco's visit with Henry III and Henry III's triumphal visit to Venice in 1574, see P. Nolhac and A. Solerti, *Il viaggio in Italia di Enrico III, re di Francia* (Turin, 1890); Rosenthal, *The Honest Courtesan*, 102–11.

or so noble women who were in fact specifically trotted out to meet Henry III at the celebratory ball in his honor?

One reason Franco represented a highlight of Henry's visit had likely to do with sexual pleasure. But another explanation links perhaps in the nature of diplomacy in the early modern world. Margaret Rosenthal has suggested that courtesans functioned as "a cultural code or cipher through which Venice, the secular city, publicized itself in the sixteenth century."[88] Rosenthal demonstrates how Franco accomplished a degree of civic patriotism through her written texts, especially her sonnets and letters, but how did courtesans also serve the city with their talk? As both Castiglione and Guazzo pointed out, court society tended to offer women a position as arbiters in taste and courtly politics – a voice that was traditionally denied to republican women. These writers hardly offered an accurate guide to reality because, as we have seen, Castiglione gave women little voice in his text. Nevertheless, women's personalities, like that of Isabella D'Este in Ferrara, often appeared to shape life at their courts more so than women in republics, and courtly settings put women in positions of power as conversationalists.[89] Courts were famously sites of spectacle and display and were well versed in the arts of wooing visiting dignitaries with the feminine splendors of court society – clothing, dancing, dining, courtly games, music, and talk.[90] Early modern courtly diplomacy functioned not unlike a marital wooing process. Marriage and diplomacy were in fact inherently linked in the courts of early modern Italy and Europe, as courts married their princes and duchesses off to one another in large part as a means of establishing political alliances.

The Venetian republic, by contrast, did not marry its patrician women off to mainland courts, and Venetian social life did not revolve around a central court in which high-ranking women participated. With perhaps the great exception of Caterina Corner who was married to the King of Cyprus in 1468 so that Venice might gain control over the island, the Venetian state did not employ women and marriage for the purposes of diplomacy. Venetian women were contained in the city and according to many writers, either stuck in nunneries or physically enclosed in their

---

[88] Rosenthal, *The Honest Courtesan*, 3. See also 64, 73.

[89] See Larner, "Europe of the Courts," 669.

[90] See Stephen Kolsky, "Graceful Performances: The Social and Political Context of Music and Dance in the *Cortegiano*," *Italian Studies* 53 (1998): 1–19.

homes before marrying back into the Venetian patriciate to perpetuate the ruling class. The more staid republic of Venice, which was famous for wearing black, for enacting sumptuary laws restricting the display of luxury and magnificence, and for keeping its women behind closed doors, was not in the regular habit of pulling out all the stops for royal visits or of allowing its women to woo visiting dignitaries. But Venice in the sixteenth and seventeenth centuries was one of the lone republics in an increasingly courtly and absolutist environment; it desperately needed to court the king of France to counter the political ambitions of Phillip II of Spain in an age of dramatic Hapsburg advances on the Italian peninsula. Though it could try to do so in part through pure spectacle and its own patrician women as it did in the official festivities it held for Henry III, at least some Venetian nobles recognized that the "courtly" conversation and talents of its most renowned courtesan might also prove politically useful as a bridge between republican Venice and this visiting monarch.

It was this liminal position of Venetian courtesans – who were good conversationalists like Castiglione's courtly lady and wore fashionable, sumptuous, clothing but were outside the rigid honor code that restricted Venetian noble women's physical and verbal presentation – that enabled them to function as a liason in political interactions between the republic and its courtly visitors. In the Roman context, in a discussion of "The Power of Speech in Love," Pierre de Brantôme, a sixteenth-century traveler and writer, commented that Roman courtesans "make great mock of the gentlewomen of the same city, which are not trained in witty speech like themselves." According to Brantôme, Roman ladies copulated "like bitches, but are dumb of mouth like sticks and stones." These wives were "without soul, wit, or conversation," and therefore held no more attraction than a marble statue, illuminating perhaps a need for conversation filled by the courtesan, who replaced courtly wives on the Venetian social scene.[91] In Venice, Thomas Coryat similarly described the difference between wives and courtesans when he tried to explain the abundance of Venetian courtesans by remarking that Venetian nobles "coope up their wives alwaies within the walles of their houses for feare of these inconveniences. . . . So that you shall very seldome see a Venetian

---

[91] Pierre de Brantôme, *Lives of Fair and Gallant Ladies* (New York: Liveright Publishing, 1933), 166.

gentleman's wife but either at the solemnization of a great marriage, or at the christening of a Jew, or late in the evening rowing in a gondola."[92] There is considerable debate regarding the numbers of women who regularly walked on the streets. As we have seen, many scholars now argue that Venetian public spaces were regularly inhabited by a wide variety of women.[93] Nevertheless, statements like Coryat's and Brantôme's suggest that Venice's own republican women could never be such good socialites and conversationalists – a necessary skill in the ambassadorial wooing process – as their more courtly counterpart, the *donna di palazzo* or courtesan.[94] As Rosenthal and Ruggiero have both noted, the Venetian courtesan's profession should not be understood as limited to her sexual activity or her body; her work was also "socially and intellectually defined."[95] Here, I would add that as a result of their eloquence, courtesans' work was also politically defined; it played a role in the political culture of the lagoon city, especially when it served diplomatic ends.

We will never know the private words exchanged between Franco and Henry III, and can never hear the exact language of what might have been the studied or sexualized speech of Franco or any other courtesan in her private quarters. Despite the centrality of conversation to courtesans' livelihood, any study of courtesans' speech can, at best, work only from an essential absence of evidence and circle around an empty, unknowable center. For this reason, as we have noted, much of this discussion has been based on constructions or descriptions of courtesans' language, typically by male writers. What can we glean, however, from written examples that come as close to speech as possible? Although such discussion springs from the printed page and not from examples of spontaneous, spoken language, the textual forms Franco employed lend themselves, at least to some degree, to scrutiny as a spoken voice. Many scholars have demonstrated the often fine lines that existed between the oral and the written and have argued for the myriad ways in which printed and spoken language have directly influenced one another.[96] The form of the *capitolo*

[92] Coryat, *Coryat's Crudities*, vol. 1, 403.

[93] On this debate, see Chapter 4, n. 41.

[94] Andrea Calmo also alluded to the appeal of courtesans to ambassadors. See Calmo, *Le lettere*, 364.

[95] Rosenthal, *The Honest Courtesan*, 4; Ruggiero, "Who's Afraid of Giuliana Napolitana?" 282.

[96] See Chapter 1, n. 4.

that Franco used showcased poetic debate in which poets answer one another in a sparring dialogue. It represented a type of dramatization of speech in a conversational manner, and both Ann Rosalind Jones and Margaret Rosenthal agree that Franco's letters also evoked a decidedly conversational tone.[97] Franco herself noted the conflation and overlap of speaking and writing, as she referred to the parallel expressions or "appeals through my voice or in ink."[98]

Franco's letters and *capitoli* in *terza rima* reveal and even showcase her spoken, verbal dexterity. Many of her letters and poems allude to "pleasant" and "sweet" conversations with various men, and we can imagine that many other courtesans similarly shared this type of talk with their lovers and clients. One letter specifically stated that one of the main talents it took to succeed as a courtesan was "grace and wit in conversation."[99] Other letters refer to instances in which Franco was insulted, and in her famous response to such insults, Franco asserted that if language was a weapon, women were no less agile than men in launching verbal attacks.

> The sword that strikes and stabs in your hand – the common language spoken in Venice – if that's what you want to use, then so do I: and if you want to enter into Tuscan, I leave you the choice of high or comic strain, for one's as easy and clear for me as the other. . . . Whichever of these you wish to use, as you do elsewhere, to speed on your arrows in a contest of insults exchanged between us, choose the language that you prefer, for I am equally happy with them all, because I have learned them for exactly this purpose. (167)

In response to a lover who has offended her, she retorted that "the deceiving tongue that lies to do me harm I will tear out by its root, after it's been bitten against the palate with repentant teeth" (133). In her writing, Franco displayed her rhetorical skill in contests with men, as her confident voice forcefully asserted itself in her written words. In addition to demonstrating her abilities as a verbal combatant, Franco further underlined her expertise in oratory by arguing that she, unlike her male

---

[97] Jones and Rosenthal, "Introduction: The Honored Courtesan," 7; Rosenthal, *The Honest Courtesan*, 123, 133.

[98] Franco, *Poems and Selected Letters*, 100–101 (*Capitolo* 8, line 54).

[99] Ibid., 39 (Letter 22). See also 32 (Letter 13), 42 (Letter 37), 152–53 (*Capitolo* 15, line 95).

counterparts, also understood the strategic value of verbal restraint and silence. Discussing verbal dueling, she stated that:

> An inexcusable wrong is committed by a man who defames a woman in her absence, even if what he says is obviously true.... And one advantage my opponent used was to spread rumors while I was away, false tales untouched and unmixed with truth. And yet for all this I did not rise in anger but rather rejoiced when, by keeping silent, my truth prevailed over what he had said.... This is what I did, for most unfairly defamed and blamed by a cowardly man, I consoled myself with higher thoughts. (235–37)

Franco argued, as comportment writers had long suggested, that effective speech involved not only verbal assertiveness but responsivity and a tactical knowledge of when gains in reputation and status could be made through simple silence and verbal control. And yet, Franco's eroticism and eloquence set her apart from the chaste, silent women of the Venetian patriciate and the idealized woman described by prescriptive writers.

In her speech, writing, and public presentation, Franco occupied a political position – one that Venetian patrician women never did – as the state's feminine voice, going so far as to state that she defended and spoke "for all women."[100] As the republic showed its allegiance to the French leader Henry III by handing him the more staid, republican gift of "the keys of the city" by permitting him to participate in civic affairs (for instance, by allowing him to attend a voting session of the Great Council), some of its representatives offered up Veronica Franco to extend to Henry III the more courtly, feminine gifts of sex and conversation that its patrician women were not in a position to offer. In other words, courtesans replaced wives as the conversational, feminine, representatives on the social scene, and through her own literary self-fashioning, Franco drew on "a pool of positive associations with the feminized city-state and [raised] her status as a courtesan by demonstrating her participation in a patriotic discourse to which distinguished male writers from Petrarch and Aretino to Domenico Venier had contributed."[101] Though Veronica Franco and Angela Zaffetta represent only two cases of courtesans wooing foreign dignitaries and Franco's moment with Henry III was but a fleeting

---

[100] Franco, *Poems and Selected Letters*, 164–5 (*Capitolo* 16, line 79).
[101] Jones and Rosenthal, "Introduction: The Honored Courtesan," 11.

one, these examples nevertheless point to a Venetian need to create patterns of verbal exchange and political sociability not based on kin, lineage, or republican political organization. Through these meetings, courtesans profited by drawing attention to themselves and elevating their social status; the state profited by forging a diplomatic link with other European states.

Venetians formed myriad connections between speech, gender, and political culture in the ways in which they discussed, disciplined, and promoted courtesans and their language. Through punitive laws and magistracies, tourists and travelers, the *poligrafi*, the sale of conversation, and through the occasional diplomatic voices of its courtesans, various aspects of Venetian society both criticized and exalted the words of these women. For this reason, the role of courtesans' language in political culture ultimately cannot be characterized in any single manner. As with the language of gossip, Venetians reacted in a variety of ways to the language of courtesans. It was at times appreciated and sought out, and at other times condemned and persecuted. In the interstices of such tensions, however, it is clear that courtesans' verbal prowess at times benefited the civic arena, economically, culturally, and politically.

In this way, though courtesans were consistently labeled as sorceresses and Sirens whose seductive language threatened male identity, courtesans would perhaps more correctly be understood as Odyssean. Odysseus, like courtesans, commercialized language by trading songs as commodities, turning a profit as he crossed the Mediterranean by offering his poems and stories in exchange for riches and supplies.[102] The business of courtesanry and Venetian political culture might seem unlikely bedfellows, but courtesans' language clearly made positive contributions to the Venetian economy and Venetian civic identity as courtesans functioned for both locals and foreigners as a symbol through which Venice publicized itself. The fact that courtesans provided a model for another female voice poised to emerge in Venice in the seventeenth century – the opera singer – underlies this idea of the verbal economy, or the exchange of spoken or

---

[102] There are many examples of the exchange of words for goods or profit in the *Odyssey*. For instance, In Book 11:339–53, Odysseus agrees to tell the court of Alcinuous the story of his journey in exchange for more loot to take home; in book 14:507–14, Odysseus receives clothing from the swineherd Eumaios in exchange for the telling of his "blameless fable."

sung words for money.[103] For the Homeric hero, poetic performance was not just a part of aristocratic ritual or gift exchange but represented a commercial transaction, much as it did for Venetian courtesans whose linguistic expertise was the root of both their disparagement and their promotion as entrepreneurs who traded on their words.

[103] Heller, *Emblems of Eloquence*, 14–15.

Conclusion

In a 1607 manuscript attacking Venice in the name of the pope and the Jesuits, a Catholic writer named Antonio Persio listed every offense that the republic of Venice had ever committed against the papacy or the church, devoting two chapters to the city's sins. His discussion of Venetian lasciviousness included a damning description of the Venetian theater. "At the time I lived in Venice," Persio recounted,

> comedies were introduced in such a way that an expensive building like an amphitheater was constructed where almost all the nobility gathered, and there were nobles who begged the comedians to say the worst and dirtiest things they knew how to say, and these nobles brought their wives and children to this corruption. . . . Noble women went with their shoulders and chest bared to the stomach, showing their breasts.[1]

The Jesuits harshly condemned such a display of sex and impropriety. For Persio, dirty words and physical exposure almost seemed equivalent to incest and rape. At the same time, however, Persio described how nobles hungered for the delights of foul language and actively sought out its

---

[1] "Al tempo ch'io quivj dimoravo v'erano introdotte le Comedie in modo, che per esse era stato fato un'edificio dj gran spesa aguisa d'un anfiteatro ove si riduceva quasi tutta la nobilta, et v'erano nobili che pregavano li Comedianj che diccesero le piu grasse per non dire piu sporche cose che mai sapessero, et essi ci menavano poj le mogli et le figliuole alla quale corruttela . . . .le nobile Venetiane andar con le spalle e con il peto igude sino all'ombelico mostran le mamelle," Antonio Persio, *Trattato de'portamenti della repubblica di Venetia verso la Santa Chiesa*, Biblioteca Nazionale di Napoli, MS XI E. 40, cc. 134, (Naples, 1607), 38 r–v, cited in *Inventari dei manoscritti delle biblioteche d'Italia*, 131, Marciana mss. italiani, Classe 7 (nn.1–500), ed. Pietro Zorzanello and Giulio Zorzanello (Florence: Olschki, 1956), 104. Little or nothing is known about the life of Antonio Persio. I thank E. J. Johnson for pointing out this source.

pleasures, salivating at the idea of this theatrical diversion that perhaps offered a release from aristocratic ideals of discipline and control. Persio's description of Venice surely contained exaggerations used to shore up the papacy's stance against the corruption of Venice, but his comment about nobles' enjoyment of obscenity offers some indication of how Venetian attempts to control foul language were far from effective. His observations demonstrate one of the great paradoxes of the relationship between language and society: language builds communities while simultaneously encouraging interventions to control its expression.

While this study has not explored Venetian theater explicitly, a brief consideration of the history of theater in the sixteenth century offers a useful point for conclusion. The theater represented a forum for the display of public speech with which, as we have seen with other forms of talk, the state had a long, thorny, and conflicted relationship. Where the theater was concerned, comedies proved particularly worrisome and problematic. The government legislated to control all theatrical performances beginning in 1508. According to this ruling passed by the Council of Ten, because many of the comedies that had come to Venice had contained "many lewd, lascivious and most unwholesome words and acts," no performance was to be given in the city without the express permission of the Ten itself.[2] While the state was clearly concerned that bawdy language was corrupting public morals, this law was not systematically observed. Sanudo recorded on several occasions the "very dirty words" (*parole molto sporche*) associated with the performances of the notorious Paduan playwright Ruzante. On 5 May 1523, Sanudo noted that a comedy of Ruzante's was "highly improper for performance in the presence of the Signoria." Audience indignation resulting from another play performed on 9 February 1525 was so strong as to call for a substitute show for 13 February.[3] By 1526, Ruzante's Venetian performances came to an end, suggesting that many Venetians had no tolerance for the unruly language and behavior associated with comedies. As a letter to the doge remarked in 1585, people knew that "the performance of the comedies

---

[2] "Multa verba et actus turpia lascivia et inhonestissima," Giovanni Sforza, cited in Eugene J. Johnson, "The Short, Lascivious Lives of Two Venetian Theaters, 1580–85," *Renaissance Quarterly* 105 (2002), 939.

[3] Sanudo, *I diarii*, vol. 34, 124; vol. 37, 559–60.

with licentious and unwholesome words have disturbed the public order."[4]

However, in the same way that the language of courtesans was useful for diplomatic purposes, the state similarly relied on the raunchy language of the comedy to woo important visitors to the lagoon city. In 1529, the Ten were forced to permit the offensive comedy of the *compagnia dei reali* to be performed because the courtiers of the Holy Roman Emperor Charles V were in town, and would have been sorely disappointed had the performance been canceled. In the following century, the Ten allowed the performance of a comedy during Lent to entertain the bored diplomats who accompanied the French ambassador.[5] Persio indicated that Venetian enjoyment of foul language continued unabated into the seventeenth century. Like that of Aretino, the vulgar language of Ruzante, whose plays frequently employed words such as *cancaro* (canker or pox) or *pota* (twat), remained incredibly popular: so popular that Galileo Galilei, a long-time resident in nearby Padua, collected Ruzante's work and read it aloud to his friends.[6] By the eighteenth century, Luigi Riccoboni claimed that Ruzante had introduced to the stage "all of the most barbarous languages in Italy."[7] Despite all the state's efforts to control it, foul language remained as popular as ever. The elite's love of bawdy language, far from extinguished, was in fact creating a bigger marketplace than ever before for the obscene in print in the seventeenth century.[8] Any process of verbal sanitizing that the state may have attempted was never fully achieved nor perhaps ever fully desired, even among the upper ranks who had frequently complained about having been affronted by dirty words. In fact, as Edward Muir has argued, libertine behavior (and, we can imagine, the foul language associated with it) became even more widespread at the start of the seventeenth century when a period of free

---

[4] ASV, *Consiglio de'Dieci*, Parti Comuni, Filze 161, 1585 November-February, cited in Johnson, "The Short, Lascivious Lives," 953.

[5] Ibid., 940.

[6] Nancy Dersofi, "Translating Ruzante's Obscenities," in *Studies for Dante : Essays in Honor of Dante Della Terza*, ed. Franco Fido, Rena A. Syska-Lamparska, Pamela D. Stewart, and Dante Della Terza (Fiesole: Cadmo, 1998), 105.

[7] L. Riccoboni, *Discorso della commediia all'improvviso e scenari inediti*, ed. I. Mamczarz (Milan: Edizioni Polifilo, 1973), 28, cited in Dersofi, "Translating Ruzante's Obscenities," 105.

[8] See Lynn Hunt, "Introduction: Obscenity and the Origins of Modernity, 1500–1800," in Hunt, *The Invention of Pornography*, 26–27.

speech, following the expulsion of the Jesuits in 1606, permitted a more open form of intellectual politics, resulting in the performance of more public comedies, and as he argues, the rise of opera in Venice.[9]

The Venetian state had a capacious appetite for controlling and repressing disquieting talk, yet official campaigns achieved decidedly mixed results. This is not to end our story with the simple conclusion of institutional failure; instead, we see the fruitful reality of contradiction. Venetian authorities addressed their fears through regulating speech, but also knew, if even just implicitly, that such talk had a necessary and sometimes empowering place in the proud peculiarities of they city's political life. The control of speech ultimately involved reciprocity between the authorities and the community rather than the simple imposition of elite, aristocratic, or religious standards on popular speech.

This study has shown the ways in which speech codes originally developed in an aristocratic context echoed, co-existed, and played themselves out in the urban republic of Venice. Sixteenth-century literature devoted an attention to spoken language that had never been seen before in Europe. Writers like Castiglione, Della Casa, and Guazzo were taxonomists who sought to locate and categorize the infinite varieties of mannered and unmannered speech according to time, place, age, gender, and social station. They argued on the one hand that different parameters governed men's and women's speech and that everyone's speech was necessarily determined by their social class; at the same time, however, they often contradicted these prescriptions, illuminating debates about class and gender in the Renaissance world. Such texts, in any case, exemplified the increasing degree of control placed on the early modern body and the tongue that Elias defined as the civilizing process. To some extent, these categories reflected and constructed the ways in which the republic of Venice patrolled spoken language. Discourses about speech and class were inherently bound up with one another in Venetian politics, because magistracies more often punished underclass language when it overstepped the boundaries of respectability. In addition, like their literary counterparts, everyday Venetians had clear ideas about how men and women, nobles and commoners should and did speak.

---

[9] Edward Muir, "Why Venice? Venetian Society and the Success of Early Opera," *Journal of Interdisciplinary History* 36 (2006): 331–53.

However, the motivations for controlling public speech in early modern Venice, as well as the means for doing so and the results these attempts produced, were much more complex and went far beyond the ideas and prescriptions laid out by comportment writers, let alone the theories of the likes of Elias or Foucault. As we have seen, a unique mixture of aristocratic and republican cultures existed in sixteenth-century Venice. While Venice still remained an important center of commerce and republican politics, Venetian nobles began to act and function more like other European aristocrats. Venetian mercantile, maritime activity was not nearly as great as it had been in the fourteenth and fifteenth centuries and Venetian nobles were slowly becoming a landed, aristocratic elite. At the intersection of these two cultures existed a particular set of rules about speech and language. On the one hand, as a commercial republic, the Venetian state sought to punish and eliminate all the unruly verbal outbursts that threatened civic order such as blasphemy, insults, and to some extent, the language of gossip. On the other hand, in order to satisfy an increasing need to engage in courtly politics, its patriciate purchased Palladian villas and styled itself increasingly as aristocrats over the course of the sixteenth century. Along these lines, the state also often permitted or even encouraged other more provocative and entertaining forms of language, such as the speech of courtesans or the raunchy language of comedy.

This study has grouped various types of foul or disorderly language together as a whole because considering different forms of disruptive speech as a group allows us to grasp more clearly how state interventions regarding language represented a coherent, institutional program. What can we deduce, however, about the differences between these various speech acts? What were the boundaries between them, and what different conclusions can we draw from having investigated different types of talk? Blasphemy was intrinsically related to socialization, because the acculturation of foreigners into the Venetian way of life – including courtesans – involved learning to avoid dangerous and indecorous expressions. An examination of insults demonstrates the link between civic and architectural cleanliness, as well as how individuals creatively substituted verbal aggression for political action. Understanding the flow of gossip in Venice allows us to begin to see Venetian justice in a new way, as an extension of a kind of popular justice that paid careful attention to reports about reputation as they filtered up from the street. While historians have long pointed to the power of ideas about honor and reputation in the pre-modern world, an examination of both insults and gossip nevertheless underscores the truly remarkable attention that individuals paid to these concepts. Early modern men and women understood perhaps more profoundly than any of us moderns ever will the degree to which precious honor is easily lost and almost impossible to regain. In addition, the prosecution of insults and the workings of gossip also demonstrate the impacts that different types of state structures may have had on their citizens. The use and abuse of gossip and insults illuminate that it did in fact matter whether early modern individuals lived in republics or courts. Republicanism was a real, lived experience in Venice – not just a rhetoric or façade – because the republic of Venice clearly attempted to resolve social or political conflict through politics rather than through the more violent means of dueling or bloodshed as in other political arenas. This is made visible in both the continuous legislation against insults, which otherwise unchecked would lead to increased physical violence, as well as the permitted practice of the *broglio* in lieu of more violent means of political decision making. Lastly, the speech of courtesans, for all that it was destabilizing or transgressive, surprisingly ended up serving the needs of statecraft that was otherwise conservative, elitist, and patriarchal.

What becomes of this story of public speech and of the relationship between language and the state? Did patterns of speech or its control undergo any noticeable changes after the sixteenth century? In many cases, they did not. For instance, comportment writers continued to produce similar exhortations regarding decorous and unruly speech into the seventeenth century. Giuseppe Passi's *Discorso del ben parlare per non offendere persona alcuna* (Venice, 1600), for example, sustained many of the ideas of Castiglione and Guazzo regarding the powers and dangers inherent in men and women's speech. Manuals of civility and behavior continued to be printed and read, though the center of their production shifted to France and England as seventeenth- and eighteenth-century writers developed the traditions of writing about the *honnête homme* and the gentleman.[10] Would hurling the words "cuckolded dog" at your

---

[10] Burke, *The Fortunes of the Courtier*, 124–32.

adversary have earned you a fine or galley service in 1650 or 1700? The answer to these questions is undoubtedly yes. The idea of the dangerous utterance or harmful insult remained intact after 1600, as the *Signori di Notte al Civil* and the *Esecutori Contro la Bestemmia* continued to process hundreds of cases regarding foul language in the seventeenth century. As Persio's description of Venice suggests, however, such patrols continued to remain only partially effective. Did gossip continue to function as effectively as a political tool? Filippo de Vivo has shown that public talk continued to be an important function of statecraft into the seventeenth century as the popular masses, barred from traditional political action, regularly participated in "political communication" through rumor and gossip.[11] While not clearly connected to the state per se, it is nevertheless intriguing to note how various observers through the nineteenth and twentieth centuries continued to comment on the excessive degree to which Venetians gossiped. William Dean Howells, Abraham Lincoln's appointed consul to Venice in the 1860s, strikingly noted that

> There may be much corruption in society, but there is infinitely more wrong in the habits of idle gossip and guilty scandal, which eat all sense of shame and pity out of the heart of Venice. There is no parallel to the prying, tattling, backbiting littleness of the place elsewhere in the world. A small country village in America or England has its meddlesomeness, but not its worldly, wicked sharpness. Figure the meanness of a chimney-corner gossip, added to the bitter shrewdness and witty penetration of a gifted roué, and you have some idea of Venetian scandal.... [T]he people, shut out from public and free discussion of religious and political themes, occupy themselves with private slander, and rend each other in their abject desperation.[12]

Even today, in the twenty-first century, the Venetian editor Franco Filippi notes that "gossip, backbiting, and at times defamation are still well-rooted habits in the city."[13]

Although these aspects of oral culture and its interaction with the state remained fairly stable, other aspects of this relationship began to

[11] Filippo de Vivo, *Information and Communication in Venice: Rethinking Early Modern Politics* (Oxford: Oxford University Press, 2007).

[12] William Dean Howells, *Venetian Life* (Boston: Houghton Mifflin, 1896), 363.

[13] Franco Filippi, *Anche questa è Venezia* (Venice: Filippi Editore, 2005), 133.

change by the seventeenth century. For instance, while the theater would remain a popular site of social gathering and exchange until Napoleon's arrival in 1797, several new spaces for public speech developed during the course of the seventeenth and eighteenth centuries that changed the way public discussion took place, including the salon, the *ridotto*, and the coffeehouse.[14] Like inns and taverns, the seventeenth-century coffeehouse in particular became a place where inhabitants of Italian cities delivered, collected, and discussed news. Coffee along with tobacco first made its appearance in Venice in the late sixteenth century. In 1640, the first "coffee shop" opened in Venice. The famous Caffé Florian, still operating in the Piazza San Marco today, opened in 1720, and by 1763 Venice had over 200 cafes. Adam Fox has demonstrated how, at least in the case of London, cafes became the most dynamic market places for the exchange of print and speech, as well as their cross-fertilization.[15] The growth of coffee houses was accompanied by the growth of the *ridotto* or gambling house, which also became a popular place for social gathering in the seventeenth and eighteenth centuries. The *ridotto* in fact became so frequented and so feared as a site for sharing political information that the doge ordered these gambling houses closed at the end of the eighteenth century out of fears of political conspiracy. In addition, the end of the sixteenth and the beginning of the seventeenth century in Venice witnessed the rise of the earliest type of printed news in the form of *avvisi*. These were newssheets – the prototype for modern newspapers – containing information about military and political events that started to be distributed on a regular basis, even up to once a week. By the 1630s, coinciding with the Thirty Years' War, periodical political news came to be regularly printed in Italy.[16] This meant that while oral news and exchange remained important, it now increasingly competed and mixed

---

[14] Much has been written on the growth of public speech in early modern France, especially on salon conversation. See for instance Benedetta Craveri, *The Age of Conversation*, trans. Teresa Waugh (New York: New York Review Books, 2005); Arlette Farge, *Subversive Words: Public Opinion in Eighteenth-Century France* (University Park, PA: Pennsylvania State University Press, 1992); Arlette Farge and Jacques Revel, *The Vanishing Children of Paris: Rumor and Politics Before the French Revolution* (Cambridge, MA: Harvard University Press, 1991); Lisa Jane Graham, *If the King Only Knew: Seditious Speech in the Reign of Louis XV* (Charlottesville: University Press of Virginia, 2000).

[15] Fox, *Oral and Literate Culture*, 376, 404.

[16] Mario Infelise, "The War, the News, and the Curious," 216.

with news arriving through print, altering the flow and importance of gossip and rumor as the range and quantity of "news" grew as a result of print.

Amidst these continuities and changes, this book has attempted to demonstrate how the Venetian state in the sixteenth century enhanced its power to control disruptive speech and in doing so established patterns that would last through most of the early modern period. Alongside new mechanisms for patrolling talk, the state demonstrated a new interest in speech: an awareness of its powers and capabilities and how they could both threaten the unity of the state or be harnessed to its benefit, as in language of gossip or courtesans. In other words, the punishment of the tongue in early modern Venice translated into action that centuries earlier had only existed in a more virtual way: in texts, frescoes, sermons, treatises that depicted God's punishment for bad language, or in statutes that were not prosecuted in any systematic manner. When authorities in sixteenth-century Venice intervened by creating new laws and decrees about speech, they gave the condemnation of speech an entirely different social meaning with real consequences. This attention to public speech ultimately demonstrated that constructing a normative language, like building a bureaucracy or increasing military conscription, was a useful tool in the practice of statecraft. As Gramsci suggested, "correct" grammar and language

> is always a "choice", a cultural trend, and always a cultural-national-political act. One can debate the best way to present the "choice" and the "trend" in order to have them accepted willingly, that is one can debate the best means to achieve this end; but there can be no doubt that there is an end to be reached that necessitates fitting and consistent means. It is a question of a political act.[17]

That is to say, early modern Venetian directives about speech and talk had less to do with concerns about manners or medieval fears of divine punishment – though they may have occasionally been couched that way – than with using language to produce civic and political unity in a way that affected everyone who lived in Venice.

---

[17] Gramsci, *Quaderni del carcere*, 2344.

Was this complex and often paradoxical relationship between language and statecraft unique? Certainly, no one single case can provide overarching rules for other cities or states; there are major differences in politics and social life not only from country to country but from region to region. Nevertheless, while Venice was distinctive in ways that led to an increased control of language – namely, its permeable urban space that allowed for the free movement of people – it was not so different as to prevent us from imagining similar links between language and state-building elsewhere. This book has been dedicated to the historical case study of Venice, and linking history to the present always carries some risk of anachronism. Nevertheless, in terms of comparison, it is hard to think about the relationship between language and the state without calling to mind a range of contemporary discussions and battles about language that echo the Venetian case. Most obviously, the *Académie française* – the official French authority on the French language – has long considered Anglican words unwelcome in French and often suggests French alternatives to Anglo-Saxon words. While the *Académie* is only an advisory body and has no official, authoritative role in the French government or state, its pronouncements on the infiltration of English words into the French language clearly demonstrate that many clearly view the use of English words as a corruption of French culture if not a watering-down or attack on French identity. Similarly in the United States, discussions about bilingualism and the place of Spanish in American culture have long sparked heated debates. Such discussions – not unlike in Venice, linked to immigration – have raised numerous questions about the relationship between language and citizenship. Can or should the American national anthem be sung in Spanish? Should election material or ballots also be in Spanish? Should bilingual education in America receive federal funding, or should such programs be replaced by immersion in English alone? There may have been unique aspects to the Venetian patrolling of unruly speech in the early modern period; we no longer have civic officials patrolling the streets today on the lookout for foul language or blasphemy. Nevertheless, worries about how changes in language represent potential threats to states and their cultures occur in a variety of political and historical settings.

I have attempted to show how the tenets outlined by literary discourse were not always maintained in spoken interaction, and similarly, that rules established by the state often went unheeded. To a certain degree, Elias was correct; early modern Venetians appeared to internalize emerging ideas about modest behavior and the control of the body. However, the civilizing process that Elias imagined clearly did not occur in any smooth or teleological manner, because the unfolding of this process was coupled with contradictions and resistance. Power did not simply radiate down from above. Public speech also helped to define one's place in the community and social hierarchy so that the use and discipline of language was not just a tool of the government but a constitutive element of power, for use not only by the state but also for individuals within it. The act of blasphemy, for instance, inherently challenged both temporal and spiritual hierarchies as a blasphemous utterance typically depicted the divine as human and placed the blasphemer in a position of power over the Creator and the State. Gondoliers and servants who flung insults at their masters turned the tables on their superiors and exhibited their verbal prowess, thereby enhancing their honor in their communities. Marginalized, underclass actors who had no official voice in the Venetian government were able to establish a degree of control over their neighborhoods and communities by participating in networks of gossip. Politics clearly remained a contested arena in the early modern city. In this way, the humble voices of Venetian bread bakers and gondoliers illuminate the complex relationships between men and women, between superiors and inferiors, and between Venetians at large and the state they lived in. Their stories demonstrate how ideas about social and political order were founded upon and enacted through ideas about language. Individuals and various branches of the state engaged in a contest over what citizenship in that state entailed: a contest that often played itself out in battles over public talk. In early modern Venice, both mannered and unmannered speech vied for different kinds of power in a complex social landscape of overlapping voices.

Bibliography

PRIMARY SOURCES

ARCHIVAL SOURCES

Archivio di Stato, Venezia

Avogaria di Comun, Civile.
Avogaria di Comun, Penale.
Censori.
Cinque Anziani alla Pace.
Consilio di Dieci: Misti, Parti Comuni.
Esecutori Contro la Bestemmia.
Provveditori Sopra le Pompe.
Sant'Uffizio.
Senato Terra.
Signori di Notte al Criminal.

PRINTED SOURCES

To eliminate excessive irregularities, all books printed before 1850 have been cited by city and date alone.

Alberti, Leon Batista. *The Family in Renaissance Florence.* Translated by Renee Neu Watkins. Columbia, SC: The University of South Carolina Press, 1969.
Andreolli, Bruno, Stefania Manente, Ermanno Orlando, and Alessandra Princi-valli, eds. *Statuti di Ala e di Avio del secolo XV.* Rome: Jouvence, 1990.
Aquinas, St. Thomas. *Summa theologica.* Allen, Texas: Christian Classics, 1981.
Aretino, Pietro. *Aretino's Dialogues.* Translated by Raymond Rosenthal. New York: Stein and Day, 1971.
————. *The Letters of Pietro Aretino.* Edited and translated by Thomas Caldecot Chubb. Hamden, CT: Archon Books, 1967.
————. *Stanze in lode di Madonna Angela Sirena.* Venice, 1537.

Aristotle. *The Politics.* Translated by Horace Rackham. London: Heinemann, 1932.

Ascheri, Mario. *Bucine e la Val d'Ambra nel Dugento.* Siena: Biblioteca Comunale di Bucine, 1995.

Augustino, Padre. *Lamento di Padre Augustino che si duole della sua sorte che lo habbia fatto imperator senza imperio, e messagli la lingua in giova per biastemmar, e al fin l'hanno messo in chebba condannato a pane e acqua.* N.p.[Venice?], 1542.

Avarucci, Giuseppe, ed. *Lo statuto comunale di Monte San Pietrangeli.* Padua: Editrice Antenore, 1987.

Bandello, Matteo. *La terza parte de le novelle.* Edited by Delmo Maestri. Alessandria: Edizione dell'Orso, 1993.

Barbaro, Antonio. *Pratica criminale.* Venice, 1739.

Bembo, Pietro. *Della historia vinitiana.* Venice, 1552.

Bertelli, Pietro. *Diversarum nationum habitus.* Padua, 1591.

Bicchierai, Marco, ed. *Statuto et ordinato è . . . Torri in Val di Pesa, una comunità fiorentina nei suoi statuti quattrocenteschi.* Scandicci, Florence: Centrolibro, 1995.

Bistort, G. *Il magistrato alle pompe.* Venice: Miscellanea di Storia Veneta, vol. 5, 1912.

Boccaccio, Giovanni. *The Decameron.* Translated by G.H. McWilliam. London: Penguin Books, 1972.

Bonifaccio, Giovanni. *L'arte de'cenni.* Vicenza, 1616.

Botti, Paolo. *La donna di poche parole commendata.* Padua, 1663.

Brantôme, Pierre de. *Lives of Fair and Gallant Ladies.* New York: Liveright Publishing, 1933.

Britti, Francesco. *Ammaestramento de figliuoli.* Venice, 1573.

Cabei, Giulio Cesare. *Ornamenti della gentildonna vedova.* Venice, 1574.

Caggese, Romolo, ed. *Statuti della repubblica fiorentina.* 2 vols. Florence: Olschki, 1949.

Calmo, Andrea., *Le bizarre, faconde, et ingeniose rime pescatorie.* Venice, 1553.

———. *Le lettere.* Edited by Vittorio Rossi. Turin: Ermanno Loescher, 1888.

Cambio, Perissone. *Primo libro dei madrigale.* Venice, 1547.

Camporesi, Piero, ed. *Il libro dei vagabondi.* Turin: Giulio Einaudi, 1973.

Castiglione, Baldesar. *The Book of the Courtier.* Edited by Daniel Javitch and translated by Charles S. Singleton. New York: W.W. Norton, 2002.

———. *Il libro del cortegiano.* Edited by Carlo Cordié. Milan and Naples: Riccardo Ricciardi, 1960.

Ceppari, Maria A., Erminio Jacona, and Patrizia Turrini, eds. *Bucine e la val d'Ambra nel Dugento: Gli ordini dei conti Guidi.* Siena: Biblioteca Comunale di Bucine, 1995.

Chambers, David, and Brian Pullan, eds. *Venice, A Documentary History.* London: Blackwell, 1992.

Cinthio, Giovambattista Giraldi. *Discorsi*. Venice, 1554.

———. *Hecatommithi, overo cento novelle*. Venice, 1593.

Citolini, Alessandro. *La tipocosmia*. Venice, 1561.

Collurafi, Antonino. *Il nobile veneto*. Venice, 1623.

Colombo, Realdo. *De re anatomica*. Venice, 1569.

Contarini, Gasparo. *De magistratibus et republica venetorum libri qinque*. Venice, 1551.

Cortelazzo, Manlio, ed. *Le dieci tavole dei proverbi*. Vicenza: Neri Pozza, 1995.

Coryat, Thomas. *Coryat's Crudities*. 2 vols. Glasgow: James Maclehose and Sons, 1905.

da Certaldo, Paolo. *Libro di buoni costumi*. Edited by Alfredo Schiaffini. Florence: Felice le Monnier, 1945.

Della Casa, Giovanni. *Galateo*. Translated by Konrad Eisenbichler and Kenneth R. Bartlett. Toronto: Centre for Reformation and Renaissance Studies, 1986.

———. *Galateo*. Edited by Giuseppe Prezzolini. Milan: Rizzoli, 1995.

Della Riva, Bonvesin. *Le cinquanta cortesie da tavola*. Edited by Mario Cantella and Donatella Magrassi. Milan: La Spiga, 1985.

Discorso intorno alla maggioranza dell'huomo, e della donna, Fatto dall'accademico Bramoso dell'accademia de'solleciti di Trevigi. Treviso, 1589.

Dolce, Ludovico. *Degli ammaestramenti pregiatissimi che appartengono alla educatione, et honorevole, e virtuosa via virginale, maritale, e vedovile, libri tre*. Venice, 1622.

———. *Delle osservationi*. Venice, 1550.

———. *Dialogo della institution delle donne*. Venice, 1547.

Doni, Anton Francesco. *Pistolotti amorosi*. Venice, 1552.

———. *Tre libri di lettere*. Venice, 1552.

———. *La zucca*. 2 vols. Edited by Elena Pierazzo. Rome: Salerno, 2003.

Doria, Gianni Penao, ed. *Statuti e capitolari di Chioggia del 1272–1279*. Venice: Il Cardo, 1993.

Droandi, Attilio, ed. *Statuto del comune di Arezzo*. Arezzo: Alberti and C. Editori, 1992.

Erasmus of Rotterdam. *The Collected Works of Erasmus*. Edited by Elaine Fantham and Erika Rummel. Toronto: The University of Toronto Press, 1989.

Ercolani, Girolamo. *Le eroine della solitudine*. Venice, 1655.

Fabri, Alessandro. *Diversarum nationum ornatus*. Padua, 1593.

Facetie e motti arguti di alcuni eccellentissimi ingegni e nobilissimi signori. Venice, 1550.

Falloppia, Gabriele. *Observationes*. Modena: S.T.E.M. Mucchi, 1964.

Ferraris, Vittorio, ed. *Gli statuti criminali del comune di Mombaruzzo nell'anno 1322*. Turin: Edizioni dell'Orso, 1994.

Ferro, Marco. *Dizionario del diritto comune e veneto*. 2 vols. Venice, 1842.

Fioravanti, Leonardo. *Specchio di scienze universale*. Venice, 1567.

Firenzuola, Agnolo. *Delle bellezze delle donne*. Venice, 1622.

Fonte, Moderata. *The Worth of Women.* Translated by Virginia Cox. Chicago: The University of Chicago Press, 1997.

Franco, Niccolò. *Le pistole vulgari.* Venice, 1539 and 1542.

Franco, Veronica. *Poems and Selected Letters.* Edited and translated by Ann Rosalind Jones and Margaret F. Rosenthal. Chicago: The University of Chicago Press, 1998.

_____. "Sonnet I to Henry III of France." In *Women Poets of the Italian Renaissance: Courtly Ladies and Courtesans.* Edited by Laura Anna Stortoni, 178–9. New York: Italica Press, 1977.

Garzoni, Tommaso. *La piazza universale di tutte le professioni del mondo, e nobili e ignobili.* Edited by Paolo Cherchi and Beatrice Collona. 2 vols. Turin: Einaudi, 1996.

Glissenti, Fabio. *Discorsi morali contra il dispiacer del morire.* Venice, 1609.

Grecchi, Z. G. *Le formalità del processo criminale nel dominio veneto.* Padua, 1790.

Groff, Silvano, ed. *Statuti della Val di Ledro del 1435.* Rome: Jouvence, 1989.

Guazzo, Stefano. *La civil conversazione.* Edited by Amedeo Quondam. 2 vols. Modena: Panini, 1993.

Guicciardini, Lodovico. *Detti, et fatti, piacevoli, et gravi, di diversi principi, filosofi, et cortigiani, raccolti dal Guicciardini, et ridotti a moralità.* Venice, 1571.

_____. *L'ore di ricreazione.* Edited by Anne-Marie van Passen. Rome: Bulzoni, 1990.

Isonaini, F., ed. "Breve Pisani Communis 1286." In *Statuti inediti della città di Pisa dal XII al XIV secolo.* 2 vols. Florence: 1854.

Kohl, B. G., and R. E. Witt, eds. and trans. *The Earthly Republic: Italian Humanists on Goverment and Society.* Philadelphia: University of Pennsylvania Press, 1978.

Lando, Ortensio. *Commentario delle piu notabili, et mostruose cose d'Italia, e altri luoghi, di lingua aramea in italiana tradotto, nel qual s'impara, e prendesi istremo piacere.* Venice, 1550.

_____. *Sette libri de cataloghi.* Venice, 1552.

Latini, Brunetto. *L'ethica d'Aristotile.* Lyon, 1568.

Lind, L. R. *Studies in Pre-Vesalian Anatomy: Biography, Translations, Documents.* Philadelphia: The American Philosophical Society, 1975.

Lorenzi, Giovanni Battista de, ed. *Leggi e memorie venete sulla prostituzione.* Venice, 1870–2.

Malespini, Cesare. *Ducento novelle.* Venice, 1609.

Marinella, Lucrezia. *Le nobilità et eccellenze delle donne, et i diffetti e mancamenti degli huomini.* Venice, 1600.

Masini, Eliseo. *Sacro arsenale overo prattica criminale dell'officio della Santa Inquisitione.* Rome, 1705.

Memmo, Giovanni Maria. *Dialogo nel quale dopo alcune filosofiche dispute, si forma un perfetto principe, et una perfetta repubblica.* Venice, 1563.

Milani, Marissa, ed. *Contro le puttane: Rime venete del XVI secolo.* Bassano del Grappa: Ghedina e Tassotti, 1994.

————. *Due processi per stregoneria: Venezia 1574*. Padua: Letteratura delle Tradizioni Popolari, 1994.

————. *Streghe e diavoli nei processi del S. Uffizio, Venezia 1554–1587*. Bassano del Grappa: Ghedina and Tassotti Editori, 1994.

Montaigne, Michel de. *The Complete Essays of Montaigne*. Translated by Donald M. Frame. Stanford: Stanford University Press, 1965.

————. *Journal de voyage en Italie*. Edited by Maurice Rat. Paris: Editions Garnier, 1955.

Orlando, Ermanno, ed. *Statuti di Riva del Garda del 1451*. Venice: Il Cardo, 1994.

Ortalli, Gherardo, Monica Pasqualetto, and Alessandra Rizzi, eds. *Statuti della laguna veneta dei secoli XIV–XVI*. Rome: Jouvence, 1989.

Oscuro, Giorgio, and Marco Pozza, eds. *Statuti di Pordenone del 1438*. Rome: Jouvence, 1986.

Ottaviani, Maria Grazia Nico, ed. *Lo statuto di Gualdo Cattaneo del 1483*. Spoleto: Centro Italiano di Studi Sull'Alto Medioevo, 1991.

Pagan, Mattio. *Pronostico alla villota sopra le puttane*. Venice, 1558.

Parabosco, Girolamo. *Quattro libri delle lettere amorose*. Venice, 1611.

Parcianello, Federica, ed. *Statuti di Rovereto del 1425*. Venice: Il Cardo, 1991.

Pasqualigo, Benedetto. *Della giurisprudenza criminale teorica e pratica*. Venice, 1731.

Passi, Giuseppe. *I donneschi difetti*. Venezia, 1605.

Piccolomini, Alessandro. *Gli costumi lodevoli che a nobili gentildonne si convengono*. Venice, 1622.

Pontano, Giovanni. *De sermone*. Edited by Alessandra Mantovani. Rome: Carocci, 2002.

Pozza, Marco, ed. *Statuti di Lendinara del 1321*. Rome: Jouvence, 1984.

————. *Statuti di Pordenone del 1438*. Rome: Jouvence, 1986.

Priori, Lorenzo. *Prattica criminale secondo il rito delle leggi della serenissima repubblica di Venetia*. Venice, 1622.

Priuli, Girolamo. *I diarii*. In *Rerum italicarum scriptores*, Tome 24, part 3. Bologna: Nicola Zanichelli, 1940.

Ragionamento del Zoppino. Edited by Mario Cicognani. Milan: Longanesi, 1969.

Riva, Bonvesin de la. *Le cinquanta cortesie da tavola*. Edited by Mario Cantella and Donatella Magrassi. Milan: La Spiga, 1985.

Roberti, Melchiorre. *Le magistrature giudiziarie veneziane e i loro capitolari fino al 1300*. Vol. 3. Padua, 1906–1911.

Romei, Annibale. *Ferrara e la corte estense nella seconda metà del secolo decimosesto. I discorsi*. Citta di Castello: Lapi, 1981.

Romoli, Domenico. *La singolare dottrina*. Venice, 1550.

Ruzante, Bilora. In *Teatro italiano: Le origini e il Rinascimento*, Edited and translated by Silvio D'Amico, 477–501. Milan: Nuova Accademia, 1955.

Sansovino, Francesco. *L'arte oratoria secondo i modi della lingua volgare*. Venice, 1546.

————. *L'edificio del corpo humano*. Venice, 1550.

———. *Le osservationi della lingua volgare.* Venice, 1562.

———. *Ragionamento, nel quale brevemente s'insegna a giovani huomini la bella arte d'amore.* Venice, 1545.

———. *Venetia città nobilissima et singolare, con aggiunta da Giustiniano Martinioni.* Venice: Filippi, 1968.

Sanudo, Marin. *I diarii di Marino Sanudo.* Edited by Rinaldo Fulin and others. 58 vols. Venice: Fratelli Visentini, 1879–1903.

Sarpi, Paolo. *Discorso dell'origine forma, leggi, ed uso dell'ufficio dell'inquisitione nella citta, e dominio di Venetia.* Venice, 1638.

Scentoni, Gina, ed. *Statuto di Canale.* Spoleto: Centro Italiano di studi sull'alto medioevo, 1994.

Siena, Bernardino da. *Prediche vulgari sul campo di Siena, 1427.* Edited by Carlo Delcorno. 2 vols. Milan: Rusconi, 1989.

Tasso, Torquato. *Discorso della virtù feminile e donnesca.* Venice, 1582.

Tiraboscho, Marc'Antonio. *Ristretto di prattica criminale che serve per la formatione de processi ad offesa.* Venice, 1636.

Valverde, Giovan. *La anatomia del corpo umano.* Venice, 1586.

Vecellio, Cesare. *Habiti antichi e moderni.* Venice, 1598.

Vesalius, Andreas. *On the Fabric of the Human Body – A Translation of De Humani Corporis Fabrica Libri Septem. Book II.* Edited and translated by William Frank Richardson and John Burd Carman. San Francisco: Norman Publishing, 1998.

Zettele, Balissera. *Istrutione, et prattica criminale utilissima si alli avocati come alli cancellieri, et altri.* Venice, 1648.

Zorzanello, Pietro, and Giulio Zorzanello. *Inventari dei manoscritte delle biblioteche d'Italia.* Florence: Olschki, 1956.

SECONDARY SOURCES

Anderson, Perry. *Lineages of the Absolutist State.* London: N.L.B., 1974.

Appuhn, Karl. "Inventing Nature; Forests, Forestry, and State Power in Renaissance Venice." *The Journal of Modern History* 72 (2000): 861–89.

Arnaldi, Girolamo and Manlio Pastore Stocchi, eds. *Storia della cultura veneta: Dal primo quattrocento al Concilio di Trento.* 3 vols. Vicenza: Neri Pozzi, 1980.

Bailey, F. G. *Gifts and Poison: The Politics of Reputation.* Oxford: Basil Blackwell, 1971.

Bakhtin, Mikhail. *Rabelais and His World.* Cambridge: MIT Press, 1968.

Bardsley, Sandy. *Venomous Tongues: Speech and Gender in Late Medieval England.* Philadelphia: University of Pennsylvania Press, 2006.

Bareggi, Claudia di Filippo. *Il mestiere di scrivere: Lavoro intelletuale e mercato librario a Venezia nel Cinquecento.* Rome: Bulzoni, 1988.

Barry, J. "Literacy and Literature in Popular Culture." In *Popular Culture in England, 1500–1850,* edited by Tim Harris, 69–94. New York: MacMillan, 1995.

Bassanese, Fiora A. "Private Lives and Public Lies: Texts by Courtesans of the Italian Renaissance." *Texas Studies in Literature and Language* 30 (1988): 295–319.

Barzaghi, Antonio. *Donne o cortigiane? La prostituzione a Venezia. Documenti di costumi dal XVI al XVIII secolo.* Verona: Bertani, 1980.

Bell, Rudolph M. *How to Do It: Guides to Good Living for Renaissance Italians.* Chicago and London: The University of Chicago Press, 1999.

Beltrami, Daniele. *Storia della popolazione di Venezia dalla fine del secolo XVI alla caduta della repubblica.* Padua: CEDAM, 1954.

Benzoni, G. "Antonino Collurafi." In *Dizionario biografico degli italiani.* Vol. 27, 91–94. Rome: Istituto della Enciclopedia Italiana, 1982.

Bettoni, Antonella. "Voci malevole: Fama, notizia del cimine, e azione del giudice nel processo criminale (secc. xvi–xvii)." *Quaderni storici* 121 (2006): 13–38.

Bianchi, G. *Proverbi e modi proverbiali veneti.* Milan: Tipofgrafia Bernardoni di C. Rebeschini, 1901.

Boerio, Giuseppe. *Dizionario del dialetto veneziano,* 2d ed. Venice: Premiata Tipografia di Giovanni Cecchini, 1856.

Bok, Sissela. *Secrets.* New York: Pantheon, 1982.

Bourdieu, Pierre. *Language and Symbolic Power.* Edited by John B. Thompson. Cambridge, MA: Harvard University Press, 1991.

Briggs, Robin. *Witches and Neighbors: The Social and Cultural Context of European Witchcraft.* New York: Penguin, 1996.

Brucker, Gene. "Civic Traditions in Premodern Italy," *Journal of Interdisciplinary History* 29 (1999): 357–77.

Buganza, Gianni. "Il potere della parola: La forza e le responsabilità della deposizione tertimoniale nel processo penale veneziano (secoli XVI–XVII)." In *La parola all' accusato,* edited by Jean-Louis Biget, Jean-Claude Maire Vigueur, and Agostino Paravicini Bagliani, 124–38. Palermo: Sellerio, 1991.

———. "Il Teste e la testimonianza tra magistratura secolare e magistratura ecclesiastica." *Atti dell'istituto veneto di scienze, lettere ed arti* 145 (1986–87): 257–80.

Burckhardt, Jacob. *The Civilization of the Renaissance in Italy.* 2 vols. New York: Harper and Row, 1958.

Burke, Peter. *The Art of Conversation.* Cambridge: Polity Press, 1993.

———. "The Art of Insult in Early Modern Italy." *Culture and History* 2 (1987): 68–79.

———. "The Courtier Abroad: Or, the Uses of Italy." In *Die Renaissance im Blick der Nationen Europas,* edited by Georg Kauffman, 1–14. Wiesbaden: Otto Harrassowitz, 1991.

———. *The Fortunes of the Courtier.* Cambridge: Polity Press, 1995.

———. *The Historical Anthropology of Early Modern Italy: Essays on Perception and Communication.* New York: Cambridge University Press, 1987.

———. "Language and Anti-Language in Early Modern Italy." *History Workshop* 11 (1981): 24–32.

———. *Language and Communities in Early Modern Europe.* Cambridge: Cambridge University Press, 2004.

_____. *Popular Culture in Early Modern Europe.* New York: Harper and Row, 1978.

_____. "The Renaissance Dialogue." *Renaissance Studies* 4 (1989): 1–12.

Burke, Peter, and Roy Porter, eds. *The Social History of Language.* New York: Cambridge University Press, 1987.

Bynum, Caroline. "Why all the Fuss about the Body? A Medievalist's Perspective." *Critical Inquiry* 22 (1995): 52–79.

Cabantous, Alain. *Histoire du blasphème en occident: Fin XVIe-milieu XIXe siécle.* Paris: Editions Albin Michel, 1998.

Cairns, Christopher. *Pietro Aretino and the Republic of Venice: Researches on Aretino and His Circle in Venice, 1527–1556.* Florence: Leo S. Olschki, 1985.

Calitti, Floriana, ed. *L'arte della conversazione nelle corti del Rinascimento.* Rome: Istituto Poligrafico, 2003.

Camporesi, Piero. *Il pane selvaggio.* Bologna: Mulino, 1980.

Capp, Bernard. *When Gossips Meet: Women, Family and Neighbourhood in Early Modern England.* Oxford: Oxford University Press, 2003.

Caretti, Lanfranco. *Antichi e moderni: Studi di letteratura italiana.* Turin: Einaudi, 1976.

Carroll, Linda L. "A Nontheistic Paradise in Renaissance Padua." *The Sixteenth Century Journal* 24 (1993): 881–98.

_____. "Ruzante's Early Adaptations from More and Erasmus." *Italica* 66 (1989): 29–34.

Casagrande, Carla. *I peccati della lingua: Disciplina ed etica della parola nella cultura medievale.* Rome: Istituto della Enciclopedia Italiana, 1987.

Cavallo, Sandra, and Simona Ceruti. "Female Honor and the Social Control of Reproduction." In *Sex and Gender in Historical Perspective*, edited by Edward Muir and Guido Ruggiero, 73–109. Baltimore: The Johns Hopkins University Press, 1990.

Cavanagh, Dermot and Tim Kirk. *Subversion and Scurrility: Popular Discourse in Europe from 1500 to the Present.* Aldershot: Ashgate, 2000.

Chakrabarty, Dipesh. *Provincializing Europe.* Princeton: Princeton University Press, 2000.

Chittolini, Giorgio and Anthony Molho. *Origini dello stato: Processi di formazione statale in Italia fra medioevo e età moderna.* Bologna: Mulino, 1994.

Chojnacka, Monica. *Working Women of Early Modern Venice.* Baltimore and London: The Johns Hopkins University Press, 2001.

Chojnacki, Stanley. "Social Identity in Renaissance Venice: The Second Serrata." *Renaissance Studies* 8 (1994): 341–58.

_____, ed. *Women and Men in Renaissance Venice: Twelve Essays on Patrician Society.* Baltimore and London: The Johns Hopkins University Press, 2000.

Cibotto, Antonio. *Proverbi del veneto.* Florence: Giunti, 1995.

Clark, Stuart. *Thinking with Demons: The Idea of Witchcraft in Early Modern Europe.* Oxford: Oxford University Press, 1997.

Cochrane, Eric. "The Renaissance Academies in their Italian and European Setting." In *The Fairest Flower: The Emergence of Linguistic National Consciousness in Renaissance Europe*, 21–39. Florence: Presso l'accademia [della Crusca], 1985.

Cohen, Beth, ed. *The Distaff Side: Representing the Female in Homer's Odyssey.* New York: Oxford University Press, 1995.

Cohen, Elizabeth S. "'Courtesans' and 'Whores': Words and Behavior in Roman Streets." *Women's Studies* 19 (1991): 201–8.

―――. "Honor and Gender in Early Modern Rome." *Journal of Interdisciplinary History* 4 (1992): 597–626.

Cohen, Elizabeth S. and Thomas V. "Camilla the Go-Between: The Politics of Gender in a Roman Household." *Continuity and Change* 4 (1989): 53–77.

Col, Andrea Del. "I processi dell'Inquisizione come fonte: Considerazioni dipomatiche e storiche." *Annuario dell'istituto storico italiano per l'età moderna e contemporranea* 35–36 (1983–84): 31–49.

Collins, Gail. *Scorpion Tongues: Gossip, Celebrity, and American Politics.* New York: Morrow, 1998.

Coudert, Allison. "Some Theories of a Natural Language from the Renaissance to the Seventeenth Century." In *Magia Naturalis und Die Entstehung der Modernen Naturwissenschaften: Studiea Leibnitiana 7*, 56–118. Wiesbaden: Franz Steiner Verlag GMBH, 1978.

Couliano, Ioan P. *Eros and Magic in the Renaissance.* Chicago: The University of Chicago Press, 1987.

Cox, Virginia. *The Renaissance Dialogue: Literary Dialogue in its Social and Political Contexts, Castiglione to Galileo.* Cambridge: Harvard University Press, 1992.

―――. "Rhetoric and Humanism in Quattrocento Venice." *Renaissance Quarterly* 56 (2003): 652–94.

Cozzi, Gaetano. *Religione, moralità e giustizia a Venezia: Vicende della magistratura degli esecutori contro la bestemmia.* Padua: Cooperativa Libraria Editrice degli Studenti dell'Università di Padova, 1967–68.

―――, ed. *Stato, società, e giustizia nella repubblica veneta, sec. XV–XVIII.* Rome: Società Editoriale Jouvence, 1980.

Craun, Edwin D. " 'Inordinata Locutio': Blasphemy in Pastoral Literature, 1200–1500." *Traditio* 39 (1983): 135–62.

―――. *Lies, Slander and Obscenity in Medieval English Literature: Pastoral Rhetoric and the Deviant Speaker.* Cambridge: Cambridge University Press, 1997.

Craveri, Benedetta. *The Age of Conversation*, translated by Teresa Waugh. New York: New York Review Books, 2005.

Crouzet-Pavan, Elizabeth. "Potere politico e spazio sociale: Il controllo della notte a Venezia nei secoli XIII–XV." In *La notte: Ordine, sicurezza, e disciplinamento in età moderna*, edited by Mario Sbriccoli, 46–66. Florence: Ponte alle Grazie, 1991.

_____. "Les mots de Venise: Sur le contrôle du langage dans une cité-etat italienne." In *La circulation des nouvelles au moyen âge: XXIVe congrès des historiens médiévistes de l'enseignement supérier public*, 205–18. Paris: Publications de la Sorbonne, 1994.

_____. *Sopra le acque salse: Espaces, pouvoir, et sociéte à Venise à la fin du moyen âge*. Rome: Istituto Palazzo Borromini, 1992.

da Mosto, Andrea. *L'archivio di stato di Venezia: Indice generale, storico, descrittivo ed analitico*. Vol. 1. Rome, 1937.

Dean, Trevor. "Gender and Insult in an Italian City: Bologna in the Later Middle Ages." *Social History* 29 (2004): 217–31.

Delumeau, Jean, ed. *Injures et blasphèmes*. Paris: Editions Imago, 1989.

de'Paratesi, Nora Galli. *Le brutte parole: Semantica dell' eufemismo*. Turin: Mondadori, 1973.

Dersofi, Nancy. "Translating Ruzante's Obscenities." In *Studies for Dante: Essays in Honor of Dante Della Terza*, edited by Franco Fido, Rena A. Syska-Lamparska, Pamela D. Stewart, and Dante Della Terza, 103–10. Fiesole: Cadmo, 1998.

Dionisotti, Carlo. *Geographia e storia della letteratura italiana*. Turin: Einaudi, 1967.

Dizionario biografico italiano. Rome: Istituto della Enciclopedia Italiana, 1960–2006.

Donati, Claudio. *L'idea di nobiltà in Italia, secoli XIV–XVIII*. Rome: Laterza, 1988.

Duden, Barbara. *The Woman Beneath the Skin: A Doctor's Patients in Eighteenth-Century Germany*. Cambridge: Harvard University Press, 1991.

Dunbar, Robin. *Grooming, Gossip and the Evolution of Language*. Cambridge, MA: Harvard University Press, 1996.

Eamon, William. "The Canker Friar: Piety and Intrigue in an Era of New Diseases." In *Piety and Plague in Europe: From Antiquity to the Early Modern Period*, edited by Franco Mormando and Thomas W. Worcester, Sixteenth Century Essays and Studies, 156–76. Kirksville, MO: Truman State University Press, 2007.

Egmond, Florike and Robert Zwijnenberg, eds. *Bodily Extremities: Preoccupations with the Human Body in Early Modern European Culture*. Aldershot: Ashgate, 2003.

Elias, Norbert. *The Civilizing Process: The Development of Manners: Changes in the Code of Conduct and Feeling in Early Modern Times*. Translated by E. Jephcott. New York: Urizon Books, 1978.

Ertman, Thomas. *The Birth of the Leviathan: Building States and Regimes in Medieval and Early Modern Europe*. Cambridge: Cambridge University Press, 1997.

Faccioli, Emilio, ed. *Arte della cucina*. Milan: Edizioni il Polifilo, 1996.

Farge, Arlette. *Subversive Words: Public Opinion in Eighteenth-Century France*. Cambridge: Polity Press, 1994.

Farge, Arlette and Jacques Revel. *The Vanishing Children of Paris: Rumor and Politics Before the French Revolution*. Cambridge, MA: Harvard University Press, 1991.

Fedi, Roberto. "La Fondazione dei Modelli: Bembo, Castiglione, Della Casa." In *Storia della letteratura italiana*, Vol. 4, *Il primo Cinquecento*, edited by Enrico Malato, 507–594. Rome: Salerno Editrice, 1996.

Feldman, Martha and Bonnie Gordon, eds. *The Courtesan's Arts: Cross-Cultural Perspectives*. Oxford: Oxford University Press, 2006.

Fenlon, Dermot. *Heresy and Obedience in Tridentine Italy*. Cambridge: Harvard University Press, 1972.

Fenster, Thelma S. and Daniel Lord Smail, eds. *Fama: The Politics of Talk and Reputation in Medieval Europe*. Ithaca: Cornell University Press, 2003.

Ferguson, Margaret. "A Room Not Their Own: Renaissance Women as Readers and Writers." In *The Comparative Perspective on Literature: Approaches to Theory and Practice*, edited by Clayton Koelb and Susan Noakes, 93–116. Ithaca: Cornell University Press, 1988.

Ferguson, Margaret, Maureen Quilligan, and Nancy J. Vickers, eds. *Rewriting the Renaissance: The Discourses of Sexual Difference in Early Modern Europe*. Chicago: The University of Chicago Press, 1986.

Ferguson, Ronnie. *A Linguistic History of Venice*. Florence: Leo S. Olschki, 2007.

Ferraro, Joanne. "The Power to Decide: Battered Wives in Early Modern Venice." *Renaissance Quarterly* 48 (1995): 492–512.

––––––. *Marriage Wars in Late Renaissance Venice*. Oxford: Oxford University Press, 2001.

Ferroni, Giulio. "Il teatro della Nanna." In *Le voci dell'istrione: Pietro Aretino e la dissoluzione del teatro*, edited by Giulio Ferroni, 136–202. Naples: Liguori, 1977.

Filippi, Franco. *Anche questa è Venezia*. Venice: Filippi Editore, 2005.

Finlay, Robert. *Politics in Renaissance Venice*. New Brunswick, NJ: Rutgers University Press, 1980.

Finucci, Valeria. "In the Name of the Brother: Male Rivalry and Social Order in Baldassarre Castiglione's *Il libro del cortegiano*." *Exemplaria* 9 (1997): 91–116.

––––––. *The Lady Vanishes: Subjectivity and Representation in Castiglione and Ariosto*. Stanford: Stanford University Press, 1992.

Flynn, Maureen. "Blasphemy and the Play of Anger in Sixteenth-Century Spain." *Past and Present* 149 (1995): 29–55.

Foucault, Michel. *The History of Sexuality: Volume One, An Introduction*. New York: Vintage Books, 1990.

Fox, Adam. *Oral and Literate Culture in England, 1500–1700*. Oxford: Oxford University Press, 2000.

Fox, Adam and Daniel Woolf, eds. *The Spoken Word: Oral Culture in Britain 1500–1800*. Manchester: Manchester University Press, 2002.

Frayer, Richard M. "Conviction According to Conscience: The Medieval Jurists' Debate Concerning Judicial Discretion and the Law of Proof." *Law and History Review* 7 (1989): 23–88.

Fudge, E., R. Gilbert, and S. Wiseman, eds. *At The Borders of the Human . . . Beasts, Bodies, and National Philosophy in the Early Modern Period*. London: Macmillan, 1999.

Gavitt, Philip. "Charity and State Building in Cinquecento Florence: Vincenzo Borghini as Administrator of the Ospedale degli Innocenti." *Journal of Modern History* 69 (1997): 230–70.

Gent, L. and N. Llewellyn, eds. *Renaissance Bodies: The Human Figure in English Culture, c. 1540–1660*. London: Reaktion Books, 1990.

Girardi, Raffaele. *La società del dialogo. Retorica e ideologia nella letteratura conviviale del Cinquecento*. Bari: Adriatica, 1989.

Gleason, Elizabeth. *Gasparo Contarini: Venice, Rome and Reform*. Berkeley: University of California Press, 1993.

Godsall-Myers, Jean E., ed. *Speaking the Medieval World*. Leiden and Boston: Brill, 2003.

Goldberg, Jonathan. *Sodometries: Renaissance Texts, Modern Sexualities*. Stanford: Stanford University Press, 1992.

Goldthwaite, Richard A. *Wealth and the Demand for Art in Italy, 1000–1600*. Baltimore and London: The Johns Hopkins University Press, 1993.

Gowing, Laura. *Domestic Dangers: Women, Words, and Sex in Early Modern London*. Oxford: Clarendon Press, 1996.

Gowland, Angus. "The Problem of Early Modern Melancholy." *Past and Present* 191 (2006): 77–120.

Graf, Arturo. *Attraverso il Cinquecento*. Turin: Ermanno Loescher, 1888.

Graham, Lisa Jane. *If the King Only Knew: Seditious Speech in the Reign of Louis XV*. Charlottesville: University Press of Virginia, 2000.

Gramsci, Antonio. *Quaderni del carcere*. Edited by Valentino Gerratana. Vol. 3. Turin: Einaudi, 1977.

Greenblatt, Stephen. *Renaissance Self-Fashioning: From More to Shakespeare*. Chicago and London: The University of Chicago Press, 1980.

Grendler, Paul. *Critics of the Italian World, 1530–1560: Anton Francesco Doni, Nicolò Franco, and Ortensio Lando*. Madison: University of Wisconsin Press, 1969.

———. *The Roman Inquisition and the Venetian Press, 1540–1605*. Princeton: Princeton University Press, 1977.

———. *Schooling in Renaissance Italy, Literacy and Learning 1300–1600*. Baltimore: The Johns Hopkins University Press, 1989.

Gumperz, J. J. and Dell Hymes, eds. *Directions in Sociolinguistics: The Ethnography of Communication*. New York: Holt, Rinehart, and Winston, 1972.

Hale, J. R., ed. *Renaissance Venice*. London: Faber and Faber, 1973.

Haliczer, Stephen. *Inquisition and Society in the Kingdom of Valencia, 1478–1834*. Berkeley: University of California Press, 1990.

Harrison, John L. "The Convention of the 'Heart and Tongue' and the Meaning of *Measure for Measure.*" *Shakespeare Quarterly* 5 (1954): 1–10.

Heitsch, Dorothea and Jean-François Vallée, eds. *Printed Voices: The Renaissance Culture of Dialogue.* Toronto: University of Toronto Press, 2004.

Heller, Wendy. *Emblems of Eloquence: Opera and Women's Voices in Seventeenth-Century Venice.* Berkeley: University of California Press, 2003.

Helmholz, R. H. "Blasphemy." In *Dictionary of the Middle Ages*, edited by Joseph R. Strayer. Vol. 2, 271–72. New York: Charles Scribner's Sons, 1982.

Hillman, David and Carla Mazzio, eds. *The Body in Parts: Fantasies of Corporeality in Early Modern Europe.* New York: Routledge, 1996.

Hindle, S. "The Shaming of Margaret Knowsley: Gossip, Gender and the Experience of Authority in Early Modern England." *Continuity and Change* 9 (1994): 391–419.

Howard, Deborah. *Jacopo Sansovino: Architecture and Patronage in Renaissance Venice.* New Haven: Yale University Press, 1975.

Howells, William Dean. *Venetian Life.* Boston: Houghton Mifflin, 1896.

Hughes, G. *Swearing: A Social History of Profanity, Oaths, and Foul Language in English.* Oxford: Blackwell, 1991.

Huizinga, J. *The Waning of the Middle Ages.* Garden City, NY: Doubleday and Company, Inc., 1954.

Lynn Hunt, ed. *The Invention of Pornography: Obscenity and the Origins of Modernity, 1500–1800.* New York: Zone Books, 1993.

Hutson, Lorna, ed. *Feminism and Renaissance Studies.* Oxford: Oxford University Press, 1999.

Hymes, Dell H. *Language in Culture and Society.* New York: Harper and Row, 1964.

Imhaus, Brunehilde. *Le minoranze orientali a venezia, 1300–1510.* Rome: Il Veltro, 1997.

Infelise, Mario. "The War, the News, and the Curious: Military Gazettes in Italy." In *The Politics of Information in Early Modern Europe*, edited by Brendan Dooley and Sabrina A. Baron, 216–32. London and New York: Routledge, 2001.

Ingram, Martin. "Law, Litigants and the Construction of 'Honour': Slander Suits in Early Modern England." In *The Moral World of the Law*, edited by Peter Coss, 134–60. Cambridge: Cambridge University Press, 2000.

Jardine, Lisa. *Worldy Goods: A New History of the Renaissance.* New York: Doubleday, 1996.

Jeanneret, Michel. *A Feast of Words: Banquets and Table-Talk in the Renaissance.* Cambridge: Polity Press, 1991.

Johnson, Eugene J. "The Short, Lascivious Lives of Two Venetian Theaters, 1580–85." *Renaissance Quarterly* 105 (2002): 936–68.

Jones, Ann Rosalind. "Surprising Fame: Renaissance Gender Ideologies and Women's Lyric." In *The Poetics of Gender*, edited by Nancy K. Miller, 74–95. New York: Columbia University Press, 1986.

Kamensky, Jane. *Governing the Tongue: The Politics of Speech in Early New England.* New York: Oxford University Press, 1998.

———. *Governing the Tongue: Speech and Society in Early New England*, Ph.D. diss., Yale University, 1992.

Kapferer, Jean-Noel. *Rumeurs, le plus vieux media du monde.* Paris: Editions du Seuil, 1990.

Kasson, J. F. *Rudeness and Civility: Manners in Nineteenth-Century Urban America.* New York: Hill and Wang, 1990.

Kelly, Joan. "Did Women Have a Renaissance?" In *Women, History and Theory: The Essays of Joan Kelly*, 30–47. Chicago: The University of Chicago Press, 1984.

Kent, D. V and F. W. Kent. *Neighbours and Neighbourhood in Renaissance Florence.* Locust Valley, NY: J. J. Augustin, 1982.

King, Margaret and Al Rabil, eds. *Her Immaculate Hand: Selected Works by and about the Women Humanists of Quattrocento Italy.* Binghamton, NY: Center for Medieval and Early Renaissance Studies, 1983.

Kirshner, Julius, ed. *The Origins of the State in Italy, 1300–1600.* Chicago: The University of Chicago Press, 1995.

Kolsky, Stephen. *Courts and Courtiers in Renaissance Northern Italy.* Aldershot: Ashgate, 2003.

———. "Graceful Performances: The Social and Political Context of Music and Dance in the *Cortegiano.*" *Italian Studies* 53 (1998): 1–19.

———. "Making and Breaking the Rules: Castiglione's *Cortegiano.*" *Renaissance Studies* 11 (1997): 358–80.

Kuehn, Thomas. *Law, Family and Women: Toward a Legal Anthropology of Renaissance Italy.* Chicago: The University of Chicago Press, 1991.

Lakoff, R. *Language and Women's Place.* New York: Harper and Row, 1975.

Lane, Frederic C. *Venice, A Maritime Republic.* Baltimore: The Johns Hopkins University Press, 1973.

Lane, Frederic C. and Reinhold Mueller. *Money and Banking in Medieval and Renaissance Venice, Volume I: Coins and Moneys of Account.* Baltimore: The Johns Hopkins University Press, 1985.

Larivaille, Paul. *La vie quotidienne des courtesans en Italie au temps de la renaissance.* Paris: Hachette, 1975.

———. *Pietro Aretino: Fra Rinascimento e manierismo.* Translated by Mariella Di Maio and Maria Luisa Rispoli. Rome: Bulzoni, 1980.

Larner, John. "Europe of the Courts." *The Journal of Modern History* 55 (1983): 669–81.

Laughran, Michelle. "The Body, Public Health, and Social Control in Sixteenth-Century Venice." Ph.D. diss., The University of Connecticut, 1998.

Laven, Mary. *Virgins of Venice: Broken Vows and Cloistered Lives in the Renaissance Convent.* London: Penguin Books, 2002.

Lawner, Lynn. "Gaspara Stampa and the Rhetoric of Submission." In *Renaissance Studies in Honor of Craig Hugh Smyth*, edited by Andrew Morrogh, Fiorella

Superbi Gioffredi, Piero Morselli and Eve Borsook. Vol. 1, 345–62. Florence: Giunti Barbèra, 1985.

Lawton, David. *Blasphemy*. Philadelphia: University of Pennsylvania Press, 1993.

Lesnick, Daniel. "Insults and Threats in Medieval Todi." *Journal of Medieval History* 17 (1991): 71–89.

———. *Preaching in Medieval Florence*. Ithaca: Cornell University Press, 1978.

Leveleux, Corinne. *La parole interdite: Le blasphème dans la France médiévale (XIIIe–XVIe siècles): Du péché au crime*. Paris: De Boccard, 2001.

Levy, Leonard W. *Treason Against God: A History of the Offense of Blasphemy*. New York: Schocken Books, 1981.

Lievsay, John Leon. *Stefano Guazzo and the English Renaissance*. Chapel Hill: The University of North Carolina Press, 1961.

Little, Lester K. *Religious Poverty and the Profit Economy in Medieval Europe*. Ithaca: Cornell University Press, 1978.

Lowe, K. J. P. *Nuns' Chronicles and Convent Culture in Renaissance and Counter-Reformation Italy*. Cambridge: Cambridge University Press, 2003.

Luzio, Alessandro. *Pietro Aretino nei primi suoi anni a Venezia*. Turin: Ermanno Loescher, 1888.

Luzzato, Gino. *Storia economica di Venezia dall xi al xvi secolo*. Venice: Centro Internazionale delle Arti e del Costume, 1961.

Maclean, Ian. *The Renaissance Notion of Woman*. Cambridge: Cambridge University Press, 1980.

Maggi, Armando. *Satan's Rhetoric: A Study of Renaissance Demonology*. Chicago: The University of Chicago Press, 2001.

Manfredini, A. *La diffamazione verbale nel diritto romano*. Milan: A. Giuffrè, 1979.

Maranini, Giuseppe. *La costituzione di Venezia*. 2 vols. Florence: La Nuova Italia, 1974.

Marin, L. *Food for Thought*. Baltimore: The Johns Hopkins University Press, 1989.

Marsh, David. *The Quattrocento Dialogue: Classical Tradition and Humanist Innovation*. Cambridge, MA: Harvard University Press, 1980.

Martin, John. "The Imaginary Piazza: Tommaso Garzoni and the Late Italian Renaissance." In *Portraits of Medieval and Renaissance Living: Essays in Memory of David Herlihy*, edited by Samuel K. Cohn Jr. and Steven Epstein, 439–54. Ann Arbor, MI: The University of Michigan Press, 1996.

———. "Inventing Sincerity, Refashioning Prudence: The Discovery of the Individual in Renaissance Europe." *The American Historical Review* 102 (1997): 1309–42.

———. *Myths of Renaissance Individualism*. London: Palgrave, 2004.

———. *Venice's Hidden Enemies: Italian Heretics in a Renaissance City*. Berkeley: University of California Press, 1993.

Martin, John and Dennis Romano, eds. *Venice Reconsidered: The History and Civilization of an Italian City State, 1297–1797*. Baltimore: The Johns Hopkins University Press, 2000.

Martin, Ruth. *Witchcraft and the Inquisition in Venice, 1550–1650*. Oxford: Basil Blackwell, 1989.

Martines, Lauro. *Power and Imagination: City-States in Renaissance Italy*. New York: Alfred A. Knopf, 1979.

_____. "The Renaissance and the Birth of Consumer Society." *Renaissance Quarterly* 51 (1998): 193–203.

_____. *Strong Words: Writing and Social Strain in the Italian Renaissance*. Baltimore and London: The Johns Hopkins University Press, 2001.

Masson, Georgina. *Courtesans of the Italian Renaissance*. London: Secker and Warburg, 1975.

Matthew, Louisa C. "The Painter's Presence: Signatures in Venetian Renaissance Pictures." *Art Bulletin* 53 (1998): 616–48.

Mazzacurati, Giancarlo. *La crisi della retorica umanistica nel Cinquecento (Antonio Riccobono)*. Naples: Libreria Scientifica Editirice, 1961.

McNeill, William H. *The Pursuit of Power: Technology, Armed Force, and Society Since A.D. 1000*. Chicago: The University of Chicago Press, 1982.

McKendrick, N, J. Brewer, and J. H. Plumb. *The Birth of a Consumer Society: The Commercialization of Eighteenth-Century England*. Bloomington: Indiana University Press, 1982.

Menetto, L. and G. Zennaro. *Storia del malcostume nei secoli XVI e XVII*. Abano Terme: Piovan Editore, 1987.

Menon, Madhavi. *Wanton Words: Rhetoric and Sexuality in English Renaissance Drama*. Toronto: The University of Toronto Press, 2004.

Migiel, Marilyn. *A Rhetoric of the Decameron*. Toronto: University of Toronto Press, 2003.

Migliorini, Bruno. *Storia della lingua italiana*. Florence: Sansoni, 1961.

Milani, Marisa. "Cortigiane e inquisizione a Venezia nel secondo '500." In *Stregoneria e streghe nell'Europa moderna*, edited by Giovanna Bosco and Patrizia Castelli, 307–16. Pisa: Ministero per i Beni Culturali, 1996.

_____. "L'≪incanto≫ di Veronica Franco." *Giornale storico della letteratura italiana* 162 (1985): 250–63.

_____. *Piccole storie di stregoneria nella Venezia del '500*. Verona: Essedue Edizioni, 1989

Molho, Anthony. "Cosimo de Medici: *Pater Patriae or Padrino?*" *Stanford Italian Review* 1 (1979): 5–33.

_____. "Patronage and the State in Early Modern Italy." In *Klientelsysteme im Europa der fruhen Neuzeit*, edited by Antoni Maczak, 91–115. Munich: Verlag, 1988.

Molmenti, Pompeo. "La corruzione dei costumi veneziani nel Rinascimento," *Archivio storico italiano* Tome 31 (1903): 281–307.

————. *La storia di Venezia nella vita private: Dalle origini alla caduta della repubblica.* 3 vols. Trieste: Edizioni Lint, 1973.

Montague, A. *The Anatomy of Swearing.* Philadelphia: University of Pennsylvania Press, 1991.

Moogk, Peter N. "'Thieving Buggers' and 'Stupid Sluts': Insults and Popular Culture in New France." *William and Mary Quarterly* 36 (1979): 524–47.

Mueller, Reinhold C. *Money and Banking in Medieval and Renaissance Venice. Volume II, The Venetian Money Market, Banks, Panics and the Public Debt, 1200–1500.* Baltimore: The Johns Hopkins University Press, 1997.

Muir, Edward. *Civic Ritual in Renaissance Venice.* Princeton: Princeton University Press, 1981.

————. "The Sources of Civil Society in Italy." *Journal of Interdisciplinary History* 29 (1999): 379–406.

————. "Why Venice? Venetian Society and the Success of Early Opera." *Journal of Interdisciplinary History* 36 (2006): 331–53.

Mutini, C. "Baldesar Castiglione." In *Dizionario biografico italiano,* 53–68. Rome: Istituto della Enciclopedia Italiana, 1979.

Nash, David. *Blasphemy in Modern Britain: 1789 to the Present.* Aldershot: Ashgate, 1999.

Niccoli, Ottavia. *Prophecy and People in Renaissance Italy.* Translated by Lydia G. Cochrane. Princeton: Princeton University Press, 1990.

Nicholls, Jonathan. *The Matter of Courtesy: Medieval Courtesy Books and the Gawain Poet.* Woodbridge, Suffolk: D. S. Brewer, 1985.

Niero, Antonio. "Statuto della confraternità di Santa Maria della Misericordia di Chirignago (Venezia)." *Rivista di storia della chiesa in Italia* 20 (1966): 389–409.

Nolhac, P. and A. Solerti. *Il viaggio in Italia di Enrico III, re di Francia.* Turin, 1890.

Nokes, G. D. *A History of the Crime of Blasphemy.* London: Sweet and Maxwell, 1928.

Norton, Mary Beth. "Gender and Defamation in Seventeenth-Century Maryland." *William and Mary Quarterly* 44 (1987): 3–39.

O'Neill, Ynez Violé. *Speech and Speech Disorders in Western Thought Before 1600.* Westport, CT: Greenwood Press, 1980.

Ong, Walter. "Orality, Literacy, and Medieval Textualization." *New Literary History* 26 (1994): 1–12.

————. *Presence of the Word: Some Prolegomena for Cultural and Religious History.* New Haven: Yale University Press, 1967.

Ordine, Nuccio. "Grandi modelli, rovesciamenti dei codici, precettistica del quotidiano." In *Manuale di letteratura italiana: Storia per generi e problemi,* edited by Franco Brioschi and Costanzodi Girolamo, 505–22. Turin: Bollati Boringhieri, 1994.

Ossola, C., ed. *La corte e il "Cortegiano."* Vol. 1, *La scena del testo.* Rome: Bulzoni, 1980.

Parker, Patricia. *Literary Fat Ladies: Rhetoric, Gender, Property.* New York: Methuen, 1987.

_____. "On the Tongue: Cross Gendering, Effeminacy, and the Art of Words." *Style* 23 (1989): 445–465.

Pateman, Carole. *The Sexual Contract.* Stanford: Stanford University Press, 1988.

Patrizi, Giorgio. "*Galateo* di Giovanni Della Casa." In *Letteratura italiana: Le opere, vol. II, Dal Cinquecento al Settecento,* 453–477. Turin: Einaudi, 1993.

_____, ed. *Stefano Guazzo e la 'Civil conversazione.'* Rome: 1990.

Patrone, Anna Maria. *Il messaggio dell'ingiuria nel piemonte del tardo medioevo.* Cavallermaggiore: Gribaudo, 1993.

Pecchiai, Pio. *Imperia.* Padua: CEDAM, 1958.

Phillips, Susan E. *Transforming Talk: The Problem with Gossip in Late Medieval England.* University Park, PA: The Pennsylvania State University Press, 2007.

Poli, Doretta Davanzo and Irene Ariano, eds. *Il gioco dell'amore. Le cortigiane di Venezia dal Trecento al Settecento.* Milan: Berenice, 1990.

Poos, L. R. "Sex, Lies, and the Church Courts of Pre-Reformation England." *Journal of Interdisciplinary History* 25 (1995): 585–607.

Povoledo, Elizabeth. "Venice Bristles at the Savannah Treatment," *The New York Times,* 15 February 2006.

Prodi, Paolo. *Il sacramento del potere.* Bologna: Mulino, 1992.

Prosperi, A. *La corte e il "Cortegiano."* Vol. 2, *Un modello europeo.* Rome: Bulzoni, 1980.

I proverbi de me nono: Modi de dire e de sentenziare del veneto da na volta. Padua: n.p., 1988.

Pullan, Brian. ed. *Crisis and Change in the Sixteenth and Seventeenth Centuries.* London: Methuen, 1968.

_____. *Rich and Poor in Renaissance Venice: The Social Institutions of a Catholic State to 1620.* Oxford: Oxford University Press, 1971.

Queller, Donald. *The Venetian Patriciate: Reality versus Myth.* Urbana and Chicago: University of Illinois Press, 1986.

Quilley, Stephen, and Steven Loyal, "Towards a 'Central Theory': The Scope and Relevance of the Sociology of Nobert Elias." In *The Sociology of Norbert Elias,* edited by Steven Loyal and Stephen Quilley, 1–24. Cambridge: Cambridge University Press, 2004.

Raines, D. "Office Seeking, Broglio and the Pocket Political Guide-books in Cinquecento and Seicento Venice," *Studi veneziani* 22 (1991): 137–94.

Rebhorn, Wayne. *Courtly Performances: Masking and Festivity in Castiglione's Book of the Courtier.* Detroit: Wayne State University Press, 1978.

_____. *The Emperor of Men's Minds: Literature and the Renaissance Discourse of Rhetoric.* Ithaca: Cornell University Press, 1995.

_____, ed. and trans. *Renaissance Debates on Rhetoric.* Ithaca and London: Cornell University Press, 2000.

Ries, Nancy. *Russian Talk: Culture and Conversation During Perestroika.* Ithaca and London: Cornell University Press, 1997.

Roche, D. *A History of Everyday Things: The Birth of Consumption in France, 1600–1800*. Cambridge and New York: Cambridge University Press, 2000.

Rocke, Michael. *Forbidden Friendships: Homosexuality and Male Culture in Renaissance Florence*. New York: Oxford University Press, 1996.

Romagnoli, Daniela and Elena Brambila, eds. *La città e la corte: Buone e cattive maniere tra medioevo ed età moderna*. Milan: Guerini, 1991.

Romaine, Suzanne. *Language in Society: An Introduction to Sociolinguistics*. Oxford: Oxford University Press, 1994.

Romano, Dennis. "Gender and the Urban Geography of Renaissance Venice." *Journal of Social History* 23 (1989): 339–53.

_____. *Housecraft and Statecraft: Domestic Service in Renaissance Venice, 1400–1600*. Baltimore: The Johns Hopkins University Press, 1996.

_____. *Patricians and Popolani: The Social Foundations of the Venetian Renaissance State*. Baltimore and London: The Johns Hopkins University Press, 1987.

Roper, Lyndal. *Oedipus and the Devil: Witchcraft, Sexuality, and Religion in Early Modern Europe*. London: Routledge, 1994.

Roppo, Sabino. *Lapidario veneziano*. Venice: Editoria Universitaria, 1996.

Rosand, David and Robert Hanning, eds. *Castiglione: The Ideal and the Real in Renaissance Culture*. New Haven: Yale University Press, 1983.

Rosenthal, Margaret F. *The Honest Courtesan: Veronica Franco, Citizen and Writer in Sixteenth-Century Venice*. Chicago: The University of Chicago Press, 1992.

Ruggiero, Guido. *Binding Passions: Tales of Magic, Marriage, and Power at the End of the Renaissance*. Oxford: Oxford University Press, 1993.

_____. *The Boundaries of Eros: Sex Crime and Sexuality in Renaissance Venice*. New York: Oxford University Press, 1985.

_____. *Violence in Early Renaissance Venice*. New Brunswick, NJ: Rutgers University Press, 1980.

Sabean, David. *Power in the Blood: Popular Culture and Village Discourse in Early Modern Germany*. Cambridge: Cambridge University Press, 1984.

Santosuosso, Antonio. *Vita di Giovanni Della Casa*. Rome: Bulzoni, 1979.

Schroeder, H. J. *Canons and Decrees of the Council of Trent*. London: B. Herder, 1941.

Schutte, Ann Jacobson. "Introduction." In *Cecilia Ferrazzi, Autobiography of an Aspiring Saint*, edited and translated by Anne Jacobson Schutte, 3–18. Chicago: The University of Chicago Press, 1996.

Scott, James C. *Domination and the Arts of Resistance: Hidden Transcripts*. New Haven: Yale University Press, 1990.

_____. *Seeing Like a State: How Certain Schemes to Improve the Human Condition Have Failed*. New Haven and London: Yale University Press, 1998.

Sharpe, J. A. "Defamation and Sexual Slander in Early Modern England." *Borthwick Papers* 58 (1980): 1–36.

Shaw, James. *The Justice of Venice: Authorities and Liberties in the Urban Economy, 1550–1700*. Oxford: Oxford University Press for the British Academy, 2006.

Simmons, J. L. "The Tongue and Its Office in The Revenger's Tragedy." *PMLA* 92 (1977): 56–68.

Smarr, Janet Levarie. *Joining the Conversation: Dialogues by Renaissance Women.* Ann Arbor: The University of Michigan Press, 2005.

Smith, S. A. "The Social Meanings of Swearing: Workers and Bad Language in Late Imperial and Early Soviet Russia." *Past and Present* 160 (1998): 167–202.

Snyder, Jon. *Writing the Scene of Speaking: Theories of Dialogue in the Late Italian Renaissance.* Stanford: Stanford University Press, 1989.

Spacks, Patricia Meyer. *Gossip.* Chicago: The University of Chicago Press, 1986.

Stagg, Kevin. "The Body." In *Writing Early Modern History*, edited by Garthine Walker, 205–26. London: Hodder Arnold, 2005.

Stallybrass, Peter. "Reading the Body and the Jacobean Theater of Consumption." In *Staging the Renaissance-Reinterpretations of Elizabethan and Jacobean Drama*, edited by David Scott Kastan and Peter Stallybrass, 210–20. New York: Routledge, 1991.

Stallybrass, Peter, and Allon White. *The Politics and Poetics of Transgression.* Ithaca: Cornell University Press, 1986.

Tafuri, Manfredo. *Venezia e il Rinascimento: Religione, scienza, architettura.* Turin: Einaudi, 1985.

Talvacchia, Bette. *Taking Positions: On the Erotic in Renaissance Culture.* Princeton: Princeton University Press, 1999.

Tannen, Deborah. *You Just Don't Understand: Women and Men in Conversation.* New York: Morrow, 1990.

Tassini, Giuseppe. *Alcune delle più clamorose condanne capitali eseguite in Venezia.* Venice: Tipografia di G. Cecchini, 1866.

Taunton, Nina and Darryll Grantley. "Introduction." In *The Body in Late Medieval and Early Modern Culture*, edited by Darryll Grantley and Nina Taunton, 1–10. Aldershot: Ashgate, 2000.

Tebbutt, Melanie. *Women's Talk? A Social History of 'Gossip' in Working-Class Neighborhoods, 1880–1960.* Aldershot: Scolar Press, 1995.

Thomas, Keith. *Religion and the Decline of Magic: Studies in Popular Beliefs in Sixteenth- and Seventeenth-Century England.* London: Weidenfeld and Nicolson, 1971.

Tilly, Charles. *Coercion, Capital and European States, AD 990–1990.* Cambridge, MA: Basil Blackwell, 1990.

Toffanin, Giuseppe. *Storia letteraria d'Italia.* 7th ed. Milan: Casa Editrice Dr. Francesco Vallardi, 1965.

Trexler, Richard C. "Correre La Terra: Collective Insults in the Late Middle Ages." *Mélanges de l'école francaise de Rome, moyen âge temps modernes* 96 (1984): 845–902.

Unsworth, Clive. "Blasphemy, Cultural Divergence and Legal Relativism." *The Modern Law Review* 58 (1995): 670.

Valmaggi, L. "Per le fonti del *Cortegiano*." *Giornale storico della letteratura italiana* 14 (1889): 72–93.

Viaro, Roberta. *"La Magistratura degli esecutori contro la bestemmia nel XVI secolo."* Ph.D. thesis, University of Padua, 1969–70.

Villari, Rosario. *Elogio della dissimulazione: La lotta political nel Seicento.* Rome: Laterza, 1987.

Villaviera, Rita Casagrande di. *Le cortigiane veneziane del Cinquecento.* Milan: Longanese, 1968.

Vitale, Maurizio. *La questione della lingua.* Palermo: Palumbo, 1978.

Vivo, Filippo de. *Information and Communication in Venice: Rethinking Early Modern Politics.* Oxford: Oxford University Press, 2007.

Walker, Jonathan. *"Bravi* and Venetian Nobles, c. 1550–1650." *Studi veneziani* 36 (1999): 85–113.

———. "Gambling and Venetian Noblemen c. 1500–1700." *Past and Present* 162 (1999): 28–69.

———. *"Honour and the Culture of Male Venetian Nobles, c. 1500–1650."* Ph.D. diss., The University of Cambridge, 1998.

Weber, Max. *Economy and Society.* Berkeley: University of California Press, 1978.

Weinstein, Donald. "Fighting or Flyting? Verbal Dueling in Mid-Sixteenth-Century Italy." In *Crime, Society and the Law in Renaissance Italy,* edited by Trevor Dean and K. J. P. Lowe, 204–220. Cambridge: Cambridge University Press, 1994.

Welch, Evelyn. *Shopping in the Renaissance: Consumer Cultures in Italy, 1400–1600.* New Haven: Yale University Press, 2005.

Wickham, Chris. "Gossip and Resistance Among the Medieval Peasantry." *Past and Present* 160 (1998): 3–24.

Whigham, Frank. *Ambition and Privilege: The Social Tropes of Elizabethan Courtesy Theory.* Berkeley: University of California Press, 1984.

Woodward, William Harrison. *Vittorino da Feltre and Other Humanist Educators.* New York: Bureau of Publications, Teachers' College, Columbia University, 1963.

Wootton, David. *Paolo Sarpi between the Renaissance and Enlightenment.* Cambridge: Cambridge University Press, 1983.

Zagorin, Perez. *Ways of Lying: Dissimulation, Persecution, and Conformity in Early Modern Europe.* Cambridge, MA: Harvard University Press, 1990.

Zemon Davis, Natalie. *Society and Culture in Early Modern France.* Stanford: Stanford University Press, 1975.

Zorzi, Alvise. *Venice 697–1797: A City, A Republic, An Empire.* Woodstock, NY: The Overlook Press, 1999.

Index